P9-DVC-932

# To View Your Data

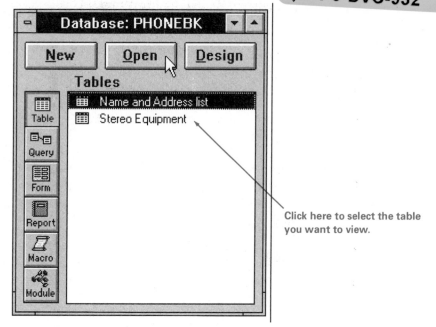

Click here to select the table you want to view.

1. From the Database window, click on Table.

2. Click on the name of the table you want to view.

3. Click on Open.

## Computer users are not all alike. Neither are SYBEX books.

We know our customers have a variety of needs. They've told us so. And because we've listened, we've developed several distinct types of books to meet the needs of each of our customers. What are you looking for in computer help?

If you're looking for the basics, try the **ABC's** series. You'll find short, unintimidating tutorials and helpful illustrations. For a more visual approach, select **Teach Yourself**, featuring screen-by-screen illustrations of how to use your latest software purchase.

**Mastering** and **Understanding** titles offer you a step-by-step introduction, plus an in-depth examination of intermediate-level features, to use as you progress.

Our **Up & Running** series is designed for computer-literate consumers who want a no-nonsense overview of new programs. Just 20 basic lessons, and you're on your way.

We also publish two types of reference books. Our **Instant References** provide quick access to each of a program's commands and functions. SYBEX **Encyclopedias** and **Desktop References** provide a *comprehensive reference* and explanation of all of the commands, features, and functions of the subject software.

Sometimes a subject requires a special treatment that our standard series don't provide. So you'll find we have titles like **Advanced Techniques**, **Handbooks**, **Tips & Tricks**, and others that are specifically tailored to satisfy a unique need.

We carefully select our authors for their in-depth understanding of the software they're writing about, as well as their ability to write clearly and communicate effectively. Each manuscript is thoroughly reviewed by our technical staff to ensure its complete accuracy. Our production department makes sure it's easy to use. All of this adds up to the highest quality books available, consistently appearing on best-seller charts worldwide.

You'll find SYBEX publishes a variety of books on every popular software package. Looking for computer help? Help Yourself to SYBEX.

### For a complete catalog of our publications:

SYBEX Inc.
2021 Challenger Drive, Alameda, CA 94501
Tel: (510) 523-8233/(800) 227-2346 Telex: 336311
Fax: (510) 523-2373

SYBEX is committed to using natural resources wisely to preserve and improve our environment. As a leader in the computer book publishing industry, we are aware that over 40% of America's solid waste is paper. This is why we have been printing the text of books like this one on recycled paper since 1982.

This year our use of recycled paper will result in the saving of more than 15,300 trees. We will lower air pollution effluents by 54,000 pounds, save 6,300,000 gallons of water, and reduce landfill by 2,700 cubic yards.

In choosing a SYBEX book you are not only making a choice for the best in skills and information, you are also choosing to enhance the quality of life for all of us.

# The ABC's of Microsoft Access

MILLS C      E
L

# The ABC's of
# Microsoft® Access

ROBERT COWART

SYBEX ®

*San Francisco*
*Paris*
*Düsseldorf*
*Soest*

ACQUISITIONS EDITOR: Dianne King
DEVELOPMENTAL EDITOR: David Peal
EDITOR: Brendan Fletcher
PROJECT EDITOR: Abby Azrael
TECHNICAL EDITOR: John Maurer
SCREEN GRAPHICS AND TECHNICAL ART: Cuong Le
PAGE LAYOUT AND TYPESETTER: Stephanie Hollier
CHAPTER ART: Helen Bruno
PRODUCTION ASSISTANT: Lisa Haden
INDEXER: Matthew Spence
COVER DESIGNER: Archer Design
COVER PHOTO DESIGNER: Ingalls + Associates
COVER PHOTOGRAPHER: Michael Lamott
Book design based on a design by Amparo del Rio
Screen reproductions produced with Collage Plus.

Collage Plus is a trademark of Inner Media Inc.

SYBEX is a registered trademark of SYBEX Inc.

TRADEMARKS: SYBEX has attempted throughout this book to distinguish proprietary trademarks from descriptive terms by following the capitalization style used by the manufacturer.

SYBEX is not affiliated with any manufacturer.

Every effort has been made to supply complete and accurate information. However, SYBEX assumes no responsibility for its use, nor for any infringement of the intellectual property rights of third parties which would result from such use.

Copyright ©1993 SYBEX Inc., 2021 Challenger Drive, Alameda, CA 94501. World rights reserved. No part of this publication may be stored in a retrieval system, transmitted, or reproduced in any way, including but not limited to photocopy, photograph, magnetic or other record, without the prior agreement and written permission of the publisher.

Library of Congress Card Number: 92-63121
ISBN: 0-7821-1189-0

Manufactured in the United States of America

10 9 8 7 6 5 4 3 2 1

005.7565
A169c
1993

*To Helen and Meredith*

Mills College Library
Withdrawn

MILLS COLLEGE
LIBRARY

Mills College Library
Withdrawn

# ACKNOWLEDGMENTS

I want to extend my thanks to all those who participated in the process of creating *The ABC's of Microsoft Access*. The production of this book has been possible because of the well-oiled machinery of the SYBEX editorial and production crew. In particular, many heartfelt thanks to my Editor, Brendan Fletcher, for his astute discrimination and judgment, and to Developmental Editor David Peal.

When compiling a book containing many step-by-step instructions, there's no overestimating the value of sharp technical editing, and for this, thanks go to John Maurer. Additionally, thanks are in order to the following editorial and production personnel, who are often overworked and unseen: Abby Azrael, Project Editor; Cuong Le, Graphic Artist; Helen Bruno, Chapter Artist; Stephanie Hollier, Typesetter; Lisa Haden, Production Assistant.

Sincere thanks to my Acquisitions Editor, Dianne King, and to SYBEX's Editor-in-Chief, Dr. Rudolph Langer, for their continued support over the years; and thanks also to my agent, Bill Gladstone, for his guidance, efficiency, and enthusiasm.

Finally, thanks to the members of the SYBEX sales and marketing teams, without whom my books (and those of others) wouldn't appear in the stores. SYBEX maintains a top-notch independent sales force that pounds the pavements of America, promoting SYBEX books exclusively. These people work hard and know their product line. Thanks also to members of the international marketing department, who oversee things overseas, and to the people in the academic sales force, who keep tabs on the university and trade school markets.

# Contents at a Glance

Introduction . . . . . . . . . . . . . . . . . . . . . . . . . *xix*

## CHAPTERS

*1*   What Is a Database?                                          1

*2*   Getting Oriented                                            14

*3*   Creating Your First Table                                   29

*4*   Modifying the Database Structure                            51

*5*   Entering Data                                               63

*6*   Retrieving the Data                                         72

*7*   Changing Your Screen Display                                87

*8*   Using Queries                                              104

*9*   Combining Search Criteria                                  121

*10*  Sorting Records for Faster Access                          136

*11*  Updating Your Records                                      160

*12*  Creating Reports                                           183

*13*  Printing Mailing Labels                                    220

*14*  Working with Numbers, Dates, and
      Yes/No Fields                                              231

*15*  Working with Multiple Tables                               260

## APPENDIX

Installing Microsoft Access                                      278

*Index* . . . . . . . . . . . . . . . . . . . . . . . . . 285

# Table of Contents

**Introduction** · · · · · · · · · · · · · · · · · · · · · · · · · · · **xix**

CHAPTERS

## Chapter 1

**WHAT IS A DATABASE?**                                                    **1**

What Is a Database? · · · · · · · · · · · · · · · · · 2
Why Use a Computer? · · · · · · · · · · · · · · · · 3
What Is Microsoft Access? · · · · · · · · · · · · · · 6
Computer Basics · · · · · · · · · · · · · · · · · · · 7
  The Keyboard · · · · · · · · · · · · · · · · · · · 7
  The Mouse · · · · · · · · · · · · · · · · · · · · 12
  Saving Your Work · · · · · · · · · · · · · · · · 13

## Chapter 2

**GETTING ORIENTED**                                                      **14**

Starting Microsoft Access · · · · · · · · · · · · · · 14
A Windows Refresher · · · · · · · · · · · · · · · · 18
  Using Menus · · · · · · · · · · · · · · · · · · · 19
  Using Windows · · · · · · · · · · · · · · · · · · 21
Using Function Keys · · · · · · · · · · · · · · · · · 22
Getting Help When You Need It · · · · · · · · · · · 23
  Keeping Help at Hand · · · · · · · · · · · · · · 26
  Getting Help about Help and Quitting Help · · · · · 27
Taking a Break · · · · · · · · · · · · · · · · · · · 28

## Chapter 3

**CREATING YOUR FIRST TABLE**                                             **29**

Naming Files · · · · · · · · · · · · · · · · · · · · 30
How to Create a New Database · · · · · · · · · · · 31

How to Create Your First Table's Structure . . . . . . . . 35
    Defining Fields . . . . . . . . . . . . . . 36
    Creating the Structure . . . . . . . . . . . . . 38
    Setting the Field Properties . . . . . . . . . . . . 42
    Saving the Table . . . . . . . . . . . . . . . 44
    Returning to the Database Window . . . . . . . . 46
How to Back Up Your Data . . . . . . . . . . . . . . 47
    Making a Backup From Windows . . . . . . . . . 47
    Making a Backup From DOS . . . . . . . . . . 49
    Making Copies of Large Databases . . . . . . . . 50

# Chapter 4

**MODIFYING THE DATABASE STRUCTURE**      **51**
Modifying the Structure . . . . . . . . . . . . . . . 52
    Adding New Fields . . . . . . . . . . . . . . . 54
    Rearranging and Deleting Fields . . . . . . . . . . 58
    Creating a Primary Key . . . . . . . . . . . . . 60
    Modifying the Structure When the Database
    Contains Data . . . . . . . . . . . . . . . . 61

# Chapter 5

**ENTERING DATA**      **63**
How to Enter Your First Record . . . . . . . . . . . 64
How to Fix Typos . . . . . . . . . . . . . . . . . 66
How to Complete the Sample Database . . . . . . . . 68
A Reminder about Backups . . . . . . . . . . . . . 71

# Chapter 6

**RETRIEVING THE DATA**      **72**
Viewing Multiple Records Using the Datasheet . . . . . 74
How to Jump to Specific Records . . . . . . . . . . 77
    Searching by Record Number . . . . . . . . . . 77
    Searching a Field for Specific Information . . . . . . . 79

Matching Uppercase and Lowercase Letters . . . . . 82
How to Use Wildcards as Search Criteria . . . . . . . . 84

## Chapter 7

CHANGING YOUR SCREEN DISPLAY                                    87
Hiding Fields on a Datasheet . . . . . . . . . . . . . 88
Resizing Your Columns . . . . . . . . . . . . . 89
Moving Columns . . . . . . . . . . . . . . . . 92
Saving Your Datasheet Design Changes . . . . . . . . 95
Oops! I Don't Want To Save My Changes! . . . . . . 95
Creating a Simple Data Form . . . . . . . . . . . 96
Saving Your Form . . . . . . . . . . . . . . . . . . 101
Viewing a Datasheet
and a Form at the Same Time . . . . . . . . . . . . 101
Using a Form When Conducting a Search . . . . . . 102

## Chapter 8

USING QUERIES                                                  104
Queries in Access . . . . . . . . . . . . . . . . . . 105
Filters in Access . . . . . . . . . . . . . . . . . . 106
How to Start a New Query . . . . . . . . . . . . . 107
Parts of the Screen . . . . . . . . . . . . . . . . . 108
Adding the Fields . . . . . . . . . . . . . . . . . . 110
Rearranging the Order of Fields . . . . . . . . . . . 110
How to List Records
That Meet a Specified Condition . . . . . . . . . . 112
Adding More Fields . . . . . . . . . . . . . . . . . 113
Entering Some Criteria . . . . . . . . . . . . . . . 113
If Access Can't Find Any Records . . . . . . . . . . 116
Using Like and Wildcards in a Query . . . . . . . . 116
If You Make a Mistake Entering Criteria . . . . . . . 119
How to Save a Query . . . . . . . . . . . . . . . . 119

## Chapter 9

**COMBINING SEARCH CRITERIA**                                          **121**
How to Combine Search Criteria . . . . . . . . . . . .  122
   Using Logical Operators to Combine Relational
   Expressions  . . . . . . . . . . . . . . . . . . . . . .  123
   Complex Queries  . . . . . . . . . . . . . . . . . . .  129
Listing Only Records Whose Fields Are Filled In  . . .  132
Listing Only Records Whose Fields Are Unique . . . .  133

## Chapter 10

**SORTING RECORDS FOR FASTER ACCESS**                                 **136**
Making a New Table for Sorting Experiments . . . . .  138
Sorting Records by Assigning a Primary Key . . . . . .  142
Sorting Records with a Query  . . . . . . . . . . . . .  145
   Ascending versus Descending Order  . . . . . . . .  146
   How Access Sorts  . . . . . . . . . . . . . . . . . .  148
   Sorting on a Text Field . . . . . . . . . . . . . . . .  149
   Creating a Multilevel Sort  . . . . . . . . . . . . . .  150
   Saving and Reusing Your Sorted Views  . . . . . . .  152
How to Sort Tables Using a Filter  . . . . . . . . . . .  154
About Indexes  . . . . . . . . . . . . . . . . . . . . .  156
   Creating Multifield Indexes . . . . . . . . . . . . .  158
   Closing Up the Database . . . . . . . . . . . . . . .  159

## Chapter 11

**UPDATING YOUR RECORDS**                                             **160**
How to Edit Data  in a Form Window . . . . . . . . .  161
   Jumping to the Desired Record  . . . . . . . . . . .  164
   Using the Memo Editor  . . . . . . . . . . . . . . .  167
   Saving Your Edits  . . . . . . . . . . . . . . . . . .  170
   Undoing Edits  . . . . . . . . . . . . . . . . . . . .  171
How to Modify Data on a Datasheet . . . . . . . . . .  172
   Moving and Editing on a Datasheet . . . . . . . . .  172

Freezing and Unfreezing Columns . . . . . . . . . 174
How to Add New Records . . . . . . . . . . . . . 175
Copying, Cutting, and Pasting Data . . . . . . . . . . 176
Copying a Record in a Datasheet . . . . . . . . . 177
Copying Multiple Records in a Datasheet . . . . . . 178
Cutting , Copying, and
Pasting Records in Forms . . . . . . . . . . . . 179
How to Remove Records from a Table . . . . . . . . . 181
Deleting Single Records . . . . . . . . . . . . 181
Using a Query to Delete Multiple Records . . . . . . 182

## Chapter 12

**CREATING REPORTS**        **183**

Simple Printing from Forms and Datasheets . . . . . . 184
Squeezing More Data onto a Printed Page . . . . . 187
Printing in Form View . . . . . . . . . . . . . 189
Printing Fancier Reports . . . . . . . . . . . . . . 191
How to Create a Quick Report with Wizards . . . . . 194
Making Wizard Reports with Subgrouping . . . . . 197
How to Create Custom Reports . . . . . . . . . . . 203
Understanding the Sections of a Report . . . . . . . 204
Making Some Room for Additional Fields . . . . . 207
Adding the Calculated Fields . . . . . . . . . . 210
Adding the Subtotal Fields . . . . . . . . . . 212
Final Preparations . . . . . . . . . . . . . . 213
If You Got an Error Message While Running
A Report . . . . . . . . . . . . . . . . . . 218

## Chapter 13

**PRINTING MAILING LABELS**        **220**

How to Design a Label . . . . . . . . . . . . . . 221
Choosing the Fields . . . . . . . . . . . . . . 223
Choosing the Label Size . . . . . . . . . . . . 226
Modifying the Labels . . . . . . . . . . . . . . . 227

Modifying the Labels . . . . . . . . . . . . . . . . . 227
Tips about Label Printing . . . . . . . . . . . . . . . 229

## Chapter 14

**WORKING WITH NUMBERS, DATES, AND YES/NO FIELDS**          **231**

How to Use Arithmetic and Comparison Operators . . 232
    Arithmetic Operators . . . . . . . . . . . . . . . 232
    Using Calculated Fields in a Query . . . . . . . . 233
    Using Comparison Operators
    with Numeric Data . . . . . . . . . . . . . . . . . 236
How to Use Aggregate Functions . . . . . . . . . . . 239
    Using Sum to Total Data from Different Records . . 240
    Using Avg to Calculate Averages . . . . . . . . . 243
    Counting Records That Meet Certain Criteria . . . . 245
    Finding Minimum and Maximum Values . . . . . . 248
How to Use Date/Time Fields . . . . . . . . . . . 249
    Adding a Date/Time Field . . . . . . . . . . . . . 250
    Using the Date Field with Queries . . . . . . . . . 251
Using Yes/No Fields . . . . . . . . . . . . . . . . . 253
    Adding a Yes/No Field to a Table's Structure . . . . 254
    Using Logical Fields to Find Data . . . . . . . . . 255
    Basing Update Queries on Yes/No Fields . . . . . 255
    Combining Logical Fields with Other Search
    Criteria . . . . . . . . . . . . . . . . . . . . . . . 258
A Tip about Expressions . . . . . . . . . . . . . . . 258

## Chapter 15

**WORKING WITH MULTIPLE TABLES**          **260**

How to Append Data from Another Database . . . . . 261
    Merging the Tables . . . . . . . . . . . . . . . . . 262
    Rules for Merging Tables with Append . . . . . . . 265
How to View Fields from Two
or More Tables at Once . . . . . . . . . . . . . . . . 268
    Preparing the Join . . . . . . . . . . . . . . . . . 269

Creating the Join . . . . . . . . . . . . . . . . . . 271
Choosing Which Fields to Display . . . . . . . . . 273
Working with Multitable Dynasets . . . . . . . . . . . 275
Using Criteria in a Multitable Query . . . . . . . . 276
Saving a Multitable Query for Later Use . . . . . . . 276


INSTALLING MICROSOFT ACCESS                                278
How to Set Up Access . . . . . . . . . . . . . . . . 279
Hardware and Software Requirements . . . . . . . . 279
Performing the Installation . . . . . . . . . . . . . 280


Index . . . . . . . . . . . . . . . . . . . . . . . . . . . . 285

# INTRODUCTION

I f you've never used Microsoft Access before and you want to learn how, this book is for you. If you already know Access and someone else has asked you to teach it to them, this book is for them—it will save *you* precious hours.

Here's why. This book is a compact, direct, and practical introduction to Microsoft Access. All the essentials of Access are covered here, with step-by-step instructions and a down-to- earth style that will make learning Access a breeze. I've designed the fifteen chapters to guide you through the steps of such real-life applications as creating databases for a mailing list and an inventory system. And everything is presented in bite-sized chunks, with lots of practical examples that make it clear how to use the resources of Access in the work you do.

I've based this book on my popular *ABC's of dBASE III PLUS* and *ABC's of dBASE IV*—time-tested books that have sold a couple hundred thousand copies around the world, as of this writing. In this book, I've adapted the essential database concepts to the Windows environment, so you can get up to speed quickly with Access.

## What Can Microsoft Access Do?

Microsoft Access marks a quantum leap forward in software designed for manipulating large amounts of data. Though there are some good database programs around for PCs, most of them run under DOS, which has certain limitations when it comes to sharing data with other programs, printing, and displaying data on the screen. And though many Windows users employ programs like Excel or 1-2-3 as ad hoc database managers, they're not really the right tools for the job.

The graphical nature of Windows, along with its ability to share information with other programs using OLE (Object Linking and Embedding) and the Windows Clipboard, make Microsoft Access a qualitatively different animal from its predecessors. Because of its graphical capabilities, it's much easier to set up impressive-looking reports, create custom screen forms, and print mailing labels accurately with Access than it is with other database programs.

Microsoft Access also lets you use tables created in other database programs, such as dBASE, Paradox, Btrieve, and SQL, while leaving those tables compatible with the source application. This way you can use Access, but you don't have to lock yourself out of those other programs. If your existing accounting system or inventory list is set up in another database program, you can still use Access to create fancy reports, update your data, or perform queries. You can even link files from different programs—all without corrupting any of your data.

## Why This Book?

You probably wouldn't be reading this if you thought a book wasn't a good idea. But just in case, sure, Access is supposed to be a database program that's really easy to learn—all you have to be able to do is "point and click." The promise was that all Windows programs would be easy to learn.

Unfortunately, we'll all be waiting more than a few more years before computers are intelligent enough to allow us to say "Hey, set up a report that compares sales from each office and update the sales reps' salaries on the basis of the results." Despite the advances that Windows and graphical interfaces have brought us, learning the basics of a program as complex as Access still takes some time and effort.

That's where *The ABC's of Microsoft Access* comes in. I've designed this book to get you working productively with Access right from the start. As you follow the exercises step by step, you'll be told exactly which keys to press and which commands to use. And since each chapter's exercises build upon the skills you've learned in previous chapters, your confidence and familiarity with Access will grow as you progress to more advanced uses. In the process, you'll build some databases you may even end up using later.

# How to Use This Book

If you're one of those folks who just bought Access, looked at the manuals, and headed out for the bookstore in hopes of rescue, chances are you haven't even installed Access on your computer. So for starters, you should begin with the appendix, which covers installation. If you have already installed the program according to the instructions in the manual supplied by Microsoft, just move ahead to the first chapter.

From the first chapter to the last, each chapter in this book will take you further in the direction of becoming a proficient user of Microsoft Access. The more advanced chapters assume you have read earlier chapters, so it's best to work through them in order. Once you have finished all the chapters and built all the databases, you'll have a pretty thorough understanding of the concepts involved, and when and where to use them. Then you will find this book a valuable resource for reminding yourself how to do a particular task. Since I've broken up the book into discrete chapters, you can use the Table of Contents to look up the topic you're interested in with ease.

## HOW THIS BOOK IS ORGANIZED

Beginning with Chapter 1, you'll start learning about databases—what they are, how they work, and what you can use them for. Then, the next several chapters will take you through the steps of creating your first database. Chapters 6–10 show you how to reorder and select particular records from your data using queries, sorts, and other techniques.

In Chapter 11, you'll learn how to edit your data to keep it up-to-date. Chapter 12 shows you how to create professional-looking printed reports in a variety of styles. Chapter 13 takes you through the steps of printing mailing labels, and Chapter 14 shows you how to use numbers, dates, and "logical" (yes/no) information in your databases for calculations and other purposes. Chapter 15 shows you a number of ways to link several databases into a single application. The appendix, as mentioned, covers installation.

# CONVENTIONS USED IN THIS BOOK

To pack all this concisely into a book of this size, we've had to devise some rules for differentiating between the things you type, the things Access itself displays, and the instructions you're being given by me. The rules are as follows:

- Explanatory notes or discussion are presented in standard paragraphs.

- When I want you to actually do something specific on your computer, I will tell you in a series of numbered steps:

  **1.**

  **2.**

  **3.**

  etc.

- When Access shows something on the screen in response to something you have done, I will generally use a picture or say something like, "Access responds with," and then show you the response printed in a different color, like this:

  **Access response**

- When I ask you to type something in from the keyboard, I will show you what to type in boldface letters, as in "Type **THIS** and press ↵." If what you are to type is on a separate line, it will look like this:

  **What you type**

FEATURING

Database
Systems

The Keyboard

Saving Your
Work

▼

# What Is a Database?

Databases are nothing new, but as often occurs in the computer world, a cryptic pseudonym has replaced a common term. Databases probably made their first appearance as pictures on the walls of Cro-Magnon caves to assist people in remembering (and avoiding) the migration routes of mastodons, or maybe they were used for keeping track of all of those collected berries. Nowadays most of us probably use databases more frequently than the Cro-Magnons did, but like those ancient people, we don't think of them as databases.

Encyclopedias, dictionaries, phone books, and even shopping catalogs are all examples of common databases you probably use on a regular basis. What qualifies these documents as databases? Why isn't a novel or a magazine a database too?

## What Is a Database?

Basically, a database is an organized list of data (information) that provides a way of finding information quickly and easily based on a chosen reference point, such as a last name or a social security number. Since the entries in an encyclopedia are arranged in alphabetical order, an encyclopedia qualifies as a database. On the other hand, some collections of information, such as novels, are not organized around a simple reference point, so they do not allow systematic access. Thus novels don't qualify as databases.

The most common databases are really nothing but a series of rows and columns filled in with information and laid out in such a way that any specific piece of information is easily available. Typically, each column has a heading that describes the type of information in it, and each row contains the information itself. In database terminology, the columns are called *fields* and the rows are called *records*. To be technically accurate, such a database is really called a *data table*, or just a *table*.

Consider one common household data table: a checkbook register. Yours is probably laid out something like this:

| CHECK NO. | DESCRIPTION | CHARGES | CREDITS | BALANCE |
|---|---|---|---|---|
| 100 | | | | |
| 101 | | | | |
| 102 | | | | |

You can think of each of these familiar columns as a field in the table, with each check entry constituting one record. Should you need to look up the details of a particular check, you can do so easily by referring to the check number, since checks are listed in numerical order.

Here's another example. Suppose you want to look up the phone number of your friend, Karen Lucic, in the telephone book. Your reference point (sometimes called a *key* in database terminology) is, in this case, Karen's last name. From this one piece of information you should be able to find Karen's phone number and her address (if it is listed). Conceptually, such a record in the table looks something like this:

| NAME | ADDRESS | CITY | PHONE NO. |
|------|---------|------|-----------|
| Lucic, Karen | 8071 Claremont | Berkeley | 555-1212 |

## Why Use a Computer?

The next question you may ask is "So, who needs a computer? I can make lists like this more easily and cheaply on paper!" This is a good point. In some cases, it would be foolish to use a computer. Let's consider the telephone book example. So long as you want to look up Karen's phone number on the basis of her name, you are better off using a book rather than a computer. However, what if you already knew Karen's phone number but had forgotten her last name? Or suppose you needed a list of everyone whose phone number started with 555? With its inexhaustible capacity for drudgery, a computer is the perfect tool for answering these types of questions.

But the computer doesn't only help you to find the desired information easily. It also lets you add more records to a table and keep listings up-to-date as information, such as phone numbers and addresses, changes. Another advantage to using a computer is the ease with which it can combine several existing tables into one larger *database system*. Large business databases often consist of numerous tables, such as receivables, payables, inventory, and general ledger, all linked together, as in Figure 1.1.

Sometimes people confuse the words *database* and *table*. Often, the term *database* is mistakenly given to a simple table of information such as the check register or the phone book we've been discussing. Only when tables are linked together as in Figure 1.1 is the entire collection of data called a *database*.

Of course, keeping track of all this information could be (and sometimes still is) done by hand, particularly the actual collection of data. But as we all know, collecting exorbitant amounts of information is a cinch. Most of us have more facts, figures, dates, prices, and memos than we know what to do with. The real questions are: Once you have this data, what can you do with it? Where do you keep it?

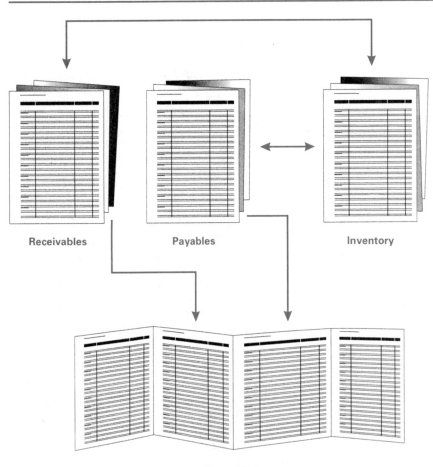

**FIGURE 1.1:**

Databases often consist of numerous tables.

Receivables        Payables        Inventory

General ledger

How do you find particular items of information later? What does the data mean? Does the data indicate some trends or patterns that have escaped your eye? Answering questions like these is where computers can help the most.

In a world burdened with information overload, computers offer a means of efficiently and constructively managing the masses of data we have created, discovered, or collected, leaving us time to pursue more creative and interesting endeavors. The computer tools designed for this information management task are called *database management systems* (DBMSs). A good computerized database system not only helps you store data, it also allows you to extract data that meets specific criteria. That is, a DBMS lets you search even huge databases relatively quickly— it lets you look for a needle in a haystack, with success.

Microsoft Access goes one step beyond a plain-vanilla DBMS. Access is technically called an RDBMS, or *Relational Database Management System*. More jargon. But it's an important concept, so bear with me for a second. To help you understand what this means, think of the illustration above for a minute—the one with receivables, payables, inventory, and general ledger. There's something in common between these tables that links them and makes them sort of related to each other. Here's an example: If you ship something out of inventory, you're likely to bill someone for it, and so you'll want to make an entry to that effect in your receivables table and your general ledger. Or, if you pay a client, the transaction should be posted to your payables and the general ledger. An action that affects one table or list will often have consequences on one or more other tables.

Now, the connection between two such tables is called a *relation*. Thus, a program that can maintain the relationship between two tables, such as automatically updating the general ledger when you pay a client, is called a relational database management system. Make sense? You'll learn how to set up relations later. For the moment, just remember the concept.

## What Is Microsoft Access?

Sophisticated database management systems have been available on large (that is, expensive) computers for a couple decades. And for close to a decade, some pretty good ones, such as dBASE, FoxPro, and Paradox, have been available on PCs. Unfortunately, you had to be a rocket scientist to get anything really fancy out of them. That's one reason why databases have remained in the land of the arcane, whereas millions of people know how to use word processors and spreadsheet programs.

This is precisely where Microsoft Access comes in. With Microsoft Access, you can easily

- Create a wide variety of both stand-alone tables and databases that link many tables together.

- Add to and edit your databases by simply filling in the blanks on your computer's screen.

- Search for and display information in an almost endless variety of ways, then print out the results.

- Generate printed reports and mailing labels in a variety of sizes and formats.

- Automatically perform mathematical calculations on numerical data in your database. Microsoft Access can incorporate the results of calculations in printed reports, and it can actually store the results in a database for future use in applications such as balance sheets, sales transactions, and accounts-receivable reports.

- include graphs, charts, and pictures in reports.

Many of these capabilities result from the flexible design of Microsoft Access. For instance, suppose you create a telephone directory database. At first you may want to search for people's phone numbers on the basis of only their names, but later you may want to use another reference point for the search (perhaps the city or state). Access lets you make such changes in your approach to the data. With some less flexible database management systems, everything must be prearranged, and no afterthoughts are allowed.

## Computer Basics

Before you begin to delve into Microsoft Access, there are a few topics you need to know about to follow the examples and exercises in this book.

Although the majority of the instructions throughout this book assume that you'll be using a mouse to perform the required steps, your computer's keyboard is also a necessary and important piece of equipment when using Access. There are times when the mouse can't do what an operation requires, or when keystrokes will make your task easier and save you time. The following sections detail the use of both the keyboard and the mouse so you will be comfortable with both. Then you can decide which you prefer to use in a given situation.

## THE KEYBOARD

This book uses the enhanced IBM XT/AT/PS2 keyboard layout in text and figures (see Figure 1.2). Chances are that your computer's keyboard is very similar, if not identical, to this standard. If you have another kind of keyboard, such as those supplied with older IBM PCs and XT compatibles, your key placement will differ. You can refer to the operations manual for your computer if you have trouble locating specific keys.

Regardless of which kind of keyboard you use, its layout is probably very similar to that of a typewriter. All the letter and number keys are in exactly the same locations as you'd expect, though a few punctuation marks may be rearranged. The only real difference between a typewriter and a computer keyboard is the *addition* of extra keys, each of which has its own purpose.

PC/AT

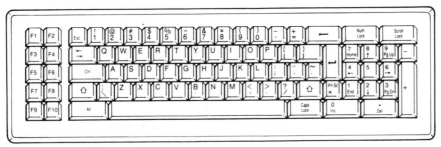

PC/XT

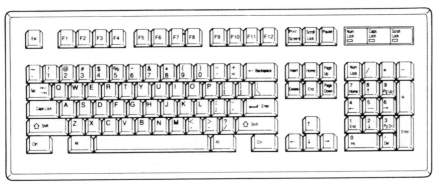

PS/2

## The Function Keys

Across the top or at the far left side of the keyboard are 12 keys labeled F1 to F12. (Some keyboards have only 10 such keys.) These are called *function keys*. The effect of pressing a given function key varies, depending on the program you are running (Word, Excel, or whatever). One key, however, is common to Windows programs, including Microsoft Access: Pressing the F1 key always displays a Help screen of useful information about whatever you're working on at the time. Once you learn to use the Help key, you'll probably be using it a lot with Access.

## The Escape Key

In the upper left corner of most keyboards is the key labeled Esc, or Escape. Pressing this key generally lets you back out of, or escape from, a choice you have made in Access. For example, when the screen displays a submenu or prompt, pressing Esc returns you to the previous step. We'll discuss menus later, but for the time being, you can think of the Esc key as a means of making an escape.

## The Control Key

The Ctrl, or Control, key is located just below the Shift key (or sometimes to the left of the *A* key). The Ctrl key is similar in operation to the Shift key on a typewriter in that it is always used in conjunction with another key. To display a capital letter, you hold down the Shift key and then press the letter you want capitalized. You use the Ctrl key the same way, only with different results. With Access, the Ctrl key is used mostly for editing (changing) data in your database. The important point to remember is that for the Ctrl key to work, you must press it first, before you press the key it modifies, and keep it down. Then you press the second key. Also, be careful not to press the Ctrl key when you mean to press the Shift key. They are close to each other and easily confused.

## The Alt Key

The Alt key is somewhere in the lower left of your keyboard. It works similarly to the Ctrl key, only the Alt key is used as a shortcut to select commands from menus and dialog boxes. When you see an underlined letter on a menu, in a dialog box, or on a menu bar, this means that pressing and holding Alt and then pressing that letter will quickly activate the command. In general you'd use the Alt key in lieu of clicking somewhere with the mouse.

## The Shift Keys

The Shift keys work much as they do on a typewriter. They are located at the right and left of the bottom row of letter keys, and they are labeled with upward-pointing arrow outlines.

## The Enter Key

The Enter key, represented in this book by ↵, has several effects, depending on what you are doing. In general, pressing ↵ tells the computer to accept or act on what you have typed and then respond accordingly. You can think of ↵ as the go-ahead key.

If a menu is displayed, pressing ↵ confirms that you want to select the menu option you have highlighted. If you are entering data into a field, pressing ↵ moves you down to the next field. In some operations, pressing ↵ may move you to the next record. In a few operations, ↵ acts like an on/off switch. Pressing it once selects an option, and pressing it again deselects the option.

Your Enter key may be labeled ENTER, RETURN, or CR (carriage return), if it is not labeled ↵.

## The Cursor Keys

At the right side of many keyboards is a block of number keys. Notice that the 2, 4, 6, and 8 keys have arrows on them. These keys control the movement of the cursor, letting you move around on your computer's screen to highlight menu options, type commands, or enter data into databases. The enhanced IBM keyboard also has a separate set of four arrow keys below and to the left of the numeric keypad that do the same thing. You may use either of the two sets of arrow keys when following the exercises in this book.

However, to use the arrows in the numbered keypad portion of the keyboard, you must make sure these keys are not in the Num-Lock mode. If NumLock is on, these keys will type only numbers and will not control the cursor. Most keyboards have a light in the upper right corner that indicates whether NumLock mode is active. This book uses the same arrows that appear on the keys($\rightarrow$, $\leftarrow$, $\uparrow$, and $\downarrow$) to represent the cursor-movement (or arrow) keys on your keyboard.

## The Backspace Key

The Backspace key is located at the upper right of the main keyboard. This key often has a mark on it similar to that on the $\leftarrow$ key, or it may have a larger arrow on it, though still pointing to the left. This key, however, does more than just move the cursor to the left. It also erases the letters you backspace over. It makes your computer work like a self-correcting typewriter. Be careful with this key, because it can erase valuable information in your database if you use it unintentionally.

## The End, Home, Page Up, and Page Down Keys

Notice that the 1, 7, 9, and 3 keys on the numeric keypad say End, Home, PgUp, and PgDn, respectively (on some keyboards these are located between the numeric pad and the letter keys). Like the ↵ key, the effect of these keys depends on what you're doing in Microsoft Access. In general, these keys move the cursor in larger jumps than the arrow keys do, meaning that instead of moving one letter at a time, they may move a whole word or a whole screen at a time.

One final note about the keyboard. Almost all the keys on the keyboard are *repeating* keys. If you hold down a key more than about one second, it will begin to repeat continually. Therefore, when entering data, be careful not to accidentally press down a key for too long; if you do, unpredictable results can occur, such as the name John Dooooooooe showing up in a database table.

# THE MOUSE

One of the most significant advantages of Microsoft Access over many other database programs is that it's a Windows program. Instead of typing in lots of commands from the keyboard, Windows programs let you perform many simple and even powerful operations by pointing with the mouse and clicking on menus, dialog boxes, and other graphical objects.

Depending on what you're trying to accomplish, sometimes the mouse is a welcome improvement, but in other places it's not such a big advantage. If your computer has a mouse and you need help with this, try the Mouse tutorial that came with Windows. Get to the Program Manager window, open the File menu, and choose Run. Then type in **WINTUTOR** and press Enter. Press **M** to run the Mouse tutorial lesson.

In case you don't have the tutorial on your disk, or you don't want to run it, here's a review of basic mouse procedure.

Once your mouse is running in Access, you'll see an arrow on the screen that moves when you move the mouse on your desk. This is the *mouse pointer*. To perform an operation using the mouse, first position the pointer over a screen item you want to activate. (A screen item may be a menu option, a file name, a choice displayed in a list, or some text.) To activate the item, click, double-click, or drag it, as described below:

- *Click:* Press the mouse button once and release it.

- *Double-click:* Press and release the mouse button twice in quick succession. If it doesn't work as it should, try adjusting the speed of your two clicks.

- *Drag:* Press the mouse button and hold it down while you move the mouse pointer to highlight some text or move an object on the screen. To end the drag, simply release the mouse button.

If your mouse has more than one button, you'll only use the left one. In addition to the conventions listed above, there are some conventions of mouse usage specific to Microsoft Access that will become apparent as you work through this book. Since they vary from area to area, rather than list them all here, I'll include instructions with each of the steps that you'll perform as you learn how to use Access.

## SAVING YOUR WORK

As is the case with most computer programs, your work in Microsoft Access at any given point is actually being done inside the computer's memory chips, called *RAM* (for random-access memory). Using RAM allows the computer to work with your data more quickly than if it worked only with your disk drives. The disadvantage is that when you turn your computer off, data stored in RAM is lost. It's a bit like a classroom blackboard: Once the lecture is over, someone is bound to come in and erase the whole board, so you'd better take some notes first.

Your computer can use your floppy disk drive or hard disk drive to store the information that would otherwise be lost when the computer's power is shut off. But the computer doesn't store information automatically. It's up to you to remember to save your work on a disk before you turn off your computer.

Microsoft Access provides several ways to save your work, but the surest one is to select the Save option from the File menu. The first time you do this you have to give the file a name. You'll learn more about this later. Also, Access is pretty good about prompting you to save your work and has some automatic data-saving schemes built in that can prevent some disasters.

Incidentally, you should always quit Access and Windows and return to DOS before turning off your computer. If you are using a floppy disk drive to store your data, you must make sure not to switch disks between the time you begin work with Microsoft Access and the time you quit.

FEATURING

**Bringing Up Microsoft Access**

**Windows Concepts Reviewed**

**Using Help**

**Exiting Access and Windows**

▼

# Getting Oriented

With the background information provided in Chapter 1, you're ready to do some useful work. In this chapter, you'll learn how to start Access, how to move around the screen, and how to use Access's extensive online Help system.

## Starting Microsoft Access

Your first step is to start Windows, then run the Access program.

1. Make sure your computer is on. If your system is already running and you're in Windows, skip to step 3. If your system isn't running Windows, exit any program you're running and get to the DOS prompt (e.g., **C>**). If you just installed Access, reset

the computer by pressing the Ctrl, Alt, and Del keys simultaneously (see Figure 2.1).

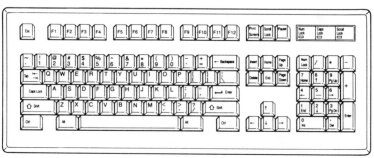

**FIGURE 2.1:**

Ctrl, Alt, and Del keys

PS/2

2. When the **C>** prompt appears (your **C>** prompt may look slightly different), the next step is to run Windows. You *must* run Windows in order to run Access. Just type

    **win** ⏎

3. The Windows sign-on screen appears, and in a few seconds, the Program Manager window will appear somewhere on your screen. If it does, go ahead and skip to step 5. If the Program Manager doesn't appear, it is probably *iconized* (as a little picture) at the bottom of your screen, or maybe another window is obscuring it. Switch to the Program Manager by pressing Ctrl+Esc (Ctrl and Esc at the same time). The Task List will come up, as you see in Figure 2.2.

4. Click on Program Manager, then click on OK.

5. Once the Program Manager window is visible, you have to open the Microsoft Access *group* (the window that holds the Access program). If the Access group window is already open, simply click anywhere inside the window's periphery to activate it. If the group window isn't open, find the Microsoft Access *group icon*. (It will be somewhere near the

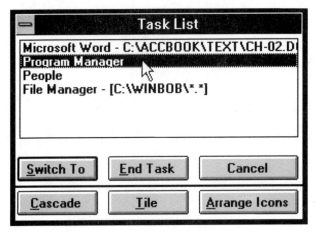

**FIGURE 2.2:**

If the Program Manager window isn't visible, try pressing Ctrl+Esc to bring up the Task List. Then click on Program Manager and click OK.

bottom of your Program Manager window, as you see in Figure 2.3.)

**6.** Double-click on the icon (click the left mouse button twice quickly). The Microsoft Access group now opens, as you see below.

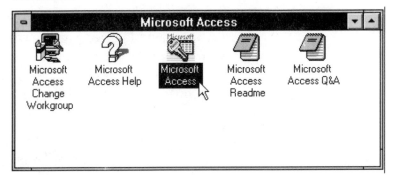

**7.** Now double-click on the Microsoft Access program icon (the one the pointer's on in the picture above). Don't worry about the other icons in the group (Readme, Q&A, etc.). You don't need them now.

The pointer will change to a little hour glass, indicating that Access is loading. In a few seconds the Microsoft Access sign-on screen

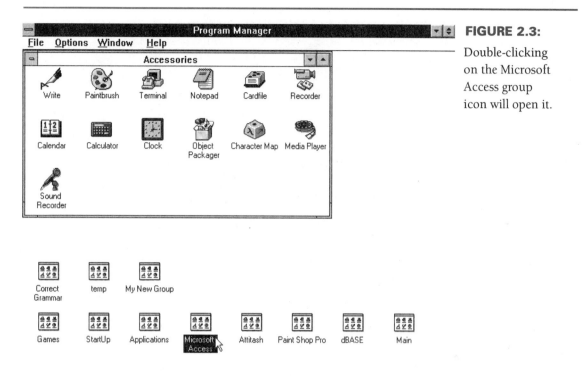

Double-clicking on the Microsoft Access group icon will open it.

will come up, showing your name and company name in a small box. Then you see the "Welcome to Microsoft Access" screen, shown in Figure 2.4.

This Welcome window is a part of the Microsoft Access Help system, and will come up each time you run Access unless you click on the check box at the bottom of the window that reads "Don't display this startup screen again." Most of the Welcome window is taken up with descriptions of the online tutorials provided with Access. If you want, you can experiment with these tutorials by clicking on the little arrow buttons next to the descriptions. Now close the window by clicking on Close. You're left with the main Microsoft Access screen.

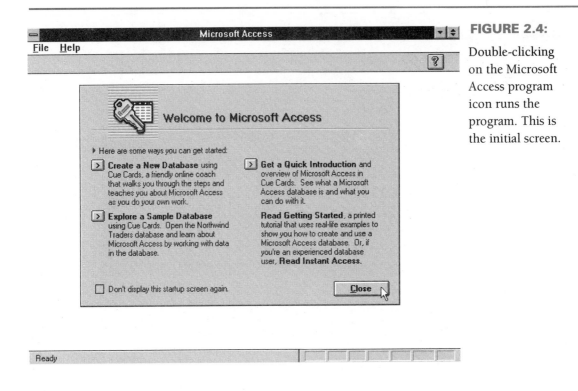

**FIGURE 2.4:**

**FIGURE 2.4:**

Double-clicking on the Microsoft Access program icon runs the program. This is the initial screen.

# A Windows Refresher

Access's main screen is like the main screens of many other Windows programs. As you probably know, all Windows programs use a similar set of graphical doo-dads, just like Apple Macintosh programs do. If you've used Windows at all, you probably already know how to use the basic graphical elements like menus, check boxes, and dialog boxes. In case you're not among the initiated, or if you feel you need a refresher, here's a quick course.

*Note:* If you want to learn more about Windows, I have written two other books you might want to read. One, for beginners, is called *Windows Quick and Easy*. This book offers a new, visual approach to learning Windows, and it's packed with four-color illustrations and easy-to-follow instructions. The other is a more extensive volume (1000 pages) covering everything you could ever want to know about

Windows (and maybe more). It's called *Mastering Windows 3.1 Special Edition*. Both books are from SYBEX and are "available from better bookstores everywhere," as they say.

## USING MENUS

Much of your work with Microsoft Access involves using *commands*, and many of the commands you're going to use are on *menus*. A menu is a list of options, shown on the screen, that you can choose from. Using a menu is a little like ordering a meal from a restaurant menu, which explains the name. When you first start up Access, you'll see two menu names at the top of the screen:

**File   Help**

These are the names of the menus currently available for you to work with, and the line where they are listed is called the *menu bar*. The choices on each menu aren't displayed until you open up the desired menu. Let's try that now.

1. Click on the word *Help* (or press Alt+H) to open the Help menu. Your screen should look like Figure 2.5. Notice that this menu offers four choices. One is shown highlighted, and it may appear in a different color, depending on your screen type and Windows color settings. The highlight indicates that this choice is *selected*. Sometimes there will be darker or dimmed options; these are choices you can't take at this time because they are not applicable to the current task.

2. Press the ↓ key several times. Then press the ↑ key several times. Notice that each press of an arrow key moves the

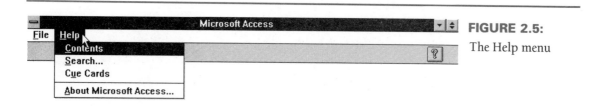

**FIGURE 2.5:**

The Help menu

highlight up or down to the next available menu option.
Press the ← key (not the Backspace key, the left arrow key)
and notice that the File menu opens. Press → and the Help
menu opens again.

3. To tell Microsoft Access to go ahead and perform a task
listed on a menu, you click on the command you want (or
press ↵ when the command is highlighted). If you want to
close the menu, just press the Esc key, or click anywhere
outside of the menu. Let's try this now. With the Help menu
open, click on About Microsoft Access. A dialog box similar
to the one below appears.

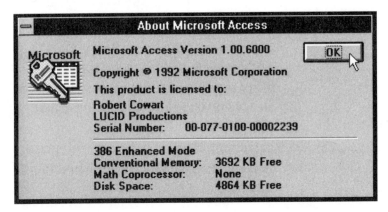

Your box may report other settings or numbers, based on
your computer system. Click on OK after you're done reading the box.

4. Now open the File menu and use the ↑ and ↓ keys to highlight
different menu choices. Notice as you move the highlight
through the choices that the bottom line on the Microsoft Access window, called the *status line*, displays a description of
each choice. This short line of text is often helpful when you
don't remember what a given command does.

5. Now notice that some commands on a menu have three dots after them. As in other Windows programs, this means that if you choose this command, a dialog box will appear, asking you for some more information.

6. As an example, open the Help menu and click on Search... (or highlight it with the arrows and press ↵). Up comes a dialog box asking what topic you want help on. Click on Cancel to close the box.

# USING WINDOWS

As you probably know, Windows puts each program and document in separate windows (or boxes) on the screen. Sometimes I'll ask you to move these windows around, or resize them so you can see more information at one time. If you're unfamiliar with the procedures involved, read this section.

## *Resizing a Window*

In case you don't know how to resize or move windows around, here's a brief review. To resize a window:

1. First make the window smaller than the whole screen, so it has a place to go. If the window is taking up the whole screen, click on the upper left corner of the window (on the Control Box) and choose Restore.

2. Position the pointer on the window's border. The pointer changes to a two-headed arrow.

3. Hold down the left mouse button and drag the window's border to the approximate size you want.

4. Release the button and the window resizes.

If you drag one of the lower *corners* of the window (rather than its side, top, or bottom, you can resize in both the horizontal and vertical dimensions at once.

## *Repositioning a Window*

To reposition a window without resizing it:

1. First the window has to be in a size that's smaller than the whole screen. See step 1 of the previous section for instructions.

2. Position the pointer on the window's *title bar*. The title bar is the top line of the window, the one that displays the program's name, such as Microsoft Access Help or Microsoft Access.

3. Now drag the window. As you do, an outline of the window will indicate where it will end up. Position the outline as you wish, and release the mouse button.

## Using Function Keys

Though you can do most everything in Access using the mouse, there are shortcut keys that can speed up your work. Many of the shortcuts use the *function keys*. As you know, pressing F1 always brings up a window containing some helpful information. The other function keys have their own effects. For example, when you're finished using a database, pressing Shift+F12 will close it and save your changes on your hard disk.

Sometimes you will have to press the Shift, the Ctrl, or the Alt key before pressing a function key, the same way that you press the Shift key to capitalize a letter. For example, I might ask you to press Ctrl+F11 to lock the contents of a field. That means press Ctrl and hold it, then press F11. Then release both keys. (If your keyboard has only ten function keys, you'll have to press Alt+F1 for F11, and Alt+F2 for F12—that is, hold down the Alt key and press F1 or F2.)

For most of this book, I'll describe the mouse commands rather than shortcut-key commands. But it's still a good idea to learn some of the keyboard commands, just to speed up your work, or in case your mouse goes dead, or you forget to bring it with you when using a portable computer.

The Help system has a list of Access's keyboard shortcuts. If you want to read them, press F1. When the Help screen comes up, click on Search and then conduct a search for Shortcut Keys, as explained in the following section.

## Getting Help When You Need It

The last thing I want to cover in a little more detail before we get going is the Help system. Let's experiment with it a bit so you get a sense of the way it works. That way you'll have another means of learning about Access as we go along, if you forget something or need some extra help along the way.

1.  Open the Help menu and choose Contents. Up comes the initial Help screen, as shown in Figure 2.6. Notice that the pointer will change to a little pointing hand when you position it over any of the underlined words. This means the pointer is on a "hot spot." Clicking while the pointer is a hand will cause some kind of action, such as a definition popping up or Help jumping you to another screenful of information.

2.  For example, click on Databases. A new screen displaying information about databases comes up.

3.  Now click on the Back button. This takes you back to the previous screen—the main Help screen.

4.  Position the pointer over the word *Glossary* at the bottom of the Help window, and click. Up comes a glossary of

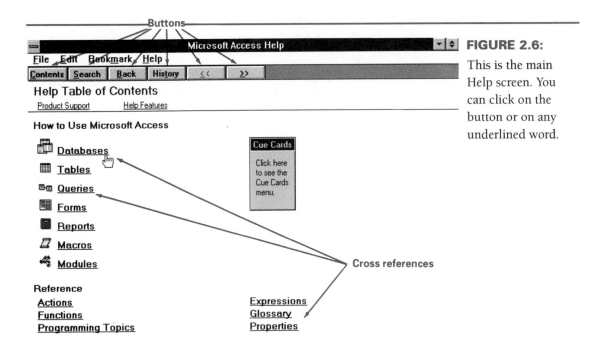

**FIGURE 2.6:**

This is the main Help screen. You can click on the button or on any underlined word.

terms. Click on the little square with the letter *D* in it. Now the glossary jumps to the *D* entries.

**5.** Look at the underlined word *database*. This word is one of the glossary's definitions. Definitions are always underlined words. Now click on *database*, and a definition pops up, as you see in Figure 2.7.

**6.** Click anywhere, and the definition box goes away.

**7.** As you can see, not all the definition words are showing on your screen at once. You can't even see all the D's. Press the PgDn and PgUp keys to scroll the screen up and down. Remember this when you want to read text that "runs off" the bottom or top of the screen.

**8.** Click on the Back button once, and then again. Now you're back on the Contents (main) page.

**database**
A collection of data related to a particular topic or purpose.  A database file can contain tables, queries, forms, reports, macros, and modules.

Aside from the general Help information, Microsoft Access has an extensive *context-sensitive* help facility built right into the program. This means that it keeps track of what menus and commands you're using, so that when you ask for help, it offers the appropriate information. When you're in the middle of some procedure and get stuck, press F1 and some relevant information will appear.

You can also use context-sensitive Help to explain portions of the screen. If you press Shift+F1, the pointer changes shape to include a question mark under it. Pointing at a screen element and clicking will bring up some information about that element.

There's another Help feature, called Cue Cards, that you can use for reference when you get stuck doing some procedure. Click on the Cue Cards square in the Help screen, and you'll see a list of items you can learn about should you want to take the time. The Cue Cards will actually walk you through procedures, and they will also stay visible on-screen as you work.

Finally, you can search for help on a given topic, such as keyboard shortcuts, as I mentioned above. You just:

1. Open the Access Help menu and choose Search (or click on the Search button if Help is already open).

2. Type in the word or concept you want to search for, or type the first letter of the topic and use the ↑ and ↓ keys to locate the desired topic.

3. Click on Show Topics.

4. In the lower portion of the window, click on the subtopic you want to read about and click on Go To.

As you can see, Help is pretty extensive. You can spend a whole day reading all the Help information and learn some pretty good stuff. By the same token, you can waste a lot of time. Sometimes the cross references run you around in circles and you get caught up in a loop with no new information. Unlike a book, where it's easy to get an overview of the amount of information on each subject, Windows-based help systems (called *hypertext systems*) can leave you wondering just how much information is in there, and how much you'll be missing if you click on the Cancel button.

## KEEPING HELP AT HAND

Once you've gotten to the page you want to read, how do you get back to Access? Just use the Task List by pressing Ctrl+Esc and choosing Access. A faster way is to press Alt+Tab. Alt+Tab always switches between the last two programs you were using. One press of Alt+Tab will switch back to Access. Press Alt+Tab again, and you're back to Help.

At times you might want to be able to see both your Access window and the Help window at the same time. How can you do this?

1. Open the Help window's Help menu.

2. Choose Always on Top. This causes any Help page you're reading to stay "on top of " any other windows that are open (visible).

3. Switch back to Access with Alt+Tab or via the Task List.

4. Size the Help window so you can see Access and Help as you need. You might want to make the Help window small and place it down in the right-hand corner if you need to. Figure 2.8 shows an example of a resized Help window.

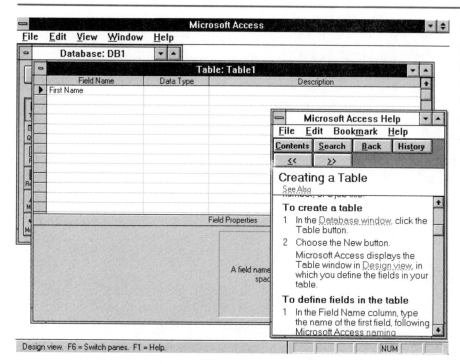

**FIGURE 2.8:**

If you refer to Help a lot, you can keep it visible. Open Help's Help menu and choose Always on Top.

# GETTING HELP ABOUT HELP AND QUITTING HELP

Remember that Help is a program in and of itself. If you use Help often, just leave it open during your Access sessions. If you don't use it much, you might as well quit Help because it uses up memory and can slow down your computer a bit.

If you want an in-depth discussion about using Help, open Help's Help menu and choose How to Use Help. Or, from Access's Contents page, click near the top of the window on Help Features.

To quit Help after looking something up,

1. Open the File menu.

2. Choose Exit.

## Taking a Break

If you want to take a break at this point, just follow these steps:

1. Switch to Access if it isn't the *active* window. (The active window is either the window that's taking up your whole screen or the window in front of other windows. The active window's title bar is in a color that's different from other windows' title bars.)

2. Open the File menu and choose Exit. As a shortcut you can double-click on the Control Box (the little square in the upper corner of the Microsoft Access window).

If Microsoft Access Help was open, it will be closed when you quit Access.

Depending on what other programs you were running, you may now see the Program Manager window, or some other program's window, such as the File Manager. When you want to quit totally and power down your computer, do this:

1. Switch to the Program Manager by using Alt+Tab or the Task List.

2. Open the Program Manager's File menu and choose Exit. You'll see this dialog box:

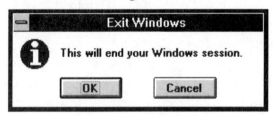

3. Click on OK. You'll be returned to the old familiar DOS prompt. If you forgot to save some of your work in Access or other Windows programs, you'll see a dialog box asking you about saving each file you were working on before Windows will exit. This is Windows' graceful way of reminding you to save your work on disk before quitting.

FEATURING

**Naming Your Database**

**The Table Design Screen**

**Adding Fields**

**Setting Field Properties**

**Saving Your Table on Disk**

**Making Backups**

▼

# Creating Your First Table

The telephone book example in Chapter 1 features a database everyone is familiar with and can use, so it's a good case study for our first database here. You might even want to save it to use later, after you've finished this book. Since this database includes addresses, you could also use it for creating mailing labels, which we'll do in Chapter 13.

Recall from Chapter 1 that you store your information in tables (matrices of columns and rows). Recall too that a database is a collection of such tables linked together, and that the information stored in the table is called the data.

Obviously, not all tables are of the same size or design. For example, one table may be a mailing list, another a payroll. One might be filled in with names, another with numbers or dates. Still another might have a combination of all these. To allow for this variability, you have to declare some of the basic layout of your table by designing it in advance.

A table's design is called its *structure*. Designing a table amounts to deciding how many fields it will have and what kind of information each field will hold. Microsoft Access needs to know this so that it can properly work with the data in each field, perform calculations, order records alphabetically, and so on. A table's structure is like an empty form that will later be filled in.

## Naming Files

With me so far? I hope so. OK, next point. Both the data and the table's structure are stored by your computer on a floppy disk or hard disk in a file, called a *relational database file*. A Microsoft Access relational database file can also include a bunch of other items, such as queries, forms, reports, and macros. In Microsoft's own lingo, these are all called *objects*. One neat thing about Access is that all these related objects are in one file—not in separate files as is the case with most other database programs (like dBASE). Having everything in one file eliminates the hassle of remembering which files work together, which files to copy when making backups, and so on.

In case you haven't already suspected, you have to give a file name to each database file you create. Without a name, your computer cannot find the file the next time you want to use it. During the course of this book, you'll create a couple of databases and give them names. You'll see how to do this when you create the phone book and address list. You'll assign a name to the database, and you'll define the database structure. Finally, you'll begin filling the file with data, just like you fill a filing cabinet with papers.

When embarking on a large project, you may want to keep your associated files in separate subdirectories. This makes the backup of important related files easier. For this book, all files will use the default directory C:\ACCESS.

File names for Microsoft Access databases have to comply with normal DOS file naming rules.

- They can't be longer than eight characters and must be at least one character long.

- No spaces are allowed.

- You can use letters and numbers as well as some punctuation marks and the following special characters: - & ! # ' ^ @ { } [ ] ( ) ~ % $ .

When you save a file, Microsoft Access adds an extension (a period and three letters) of .MDB (for Microsoft Data Base) to the file name you choose.

Some example of acceptable file names are

**revenues.mdb**
**store.mdb**
**nw-sales.mdb**
**newsale!.mdb**

## How to Create a New Database

Even if you're only going to create a single table with no other objects in it, you have to create an .MDB file. By having an .MDB file, you can later add more tables to it, set up queries to help you find data, and create reports to print out data. They'll all be lumped into the .MDB file. If you've used 1-2-3 for Windows, this is similar to the way a single 1-2-3 .WKS file can hold many separate worksheets that can be linked together.

Now let's create the new database file that will hold the phone book table. Follow these steps:

1. Start Microsoft Access, if it isn't already running.

2. Activate the Microsoft Access window.

3. Open the File menu.

4. Choose New Database. In a couple of seconds you're greeted by the New Database dialog box, as you see in Figure 3.1.

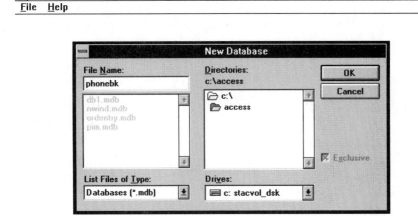

**FIGURE 3.1:**
To create a new database, open the File menu and choose New. Select the correct drive and directory (if necessary) and fill in the file's name.

This same box (or one like it) is used with all Windows programs when you save or open files stored on disk. Though you can do a lot of things with this box, basically Microsoft Access is just asking what you want to name the file, and which drive and directory it should be created in.

You enter a database name just like any other file name. You have only eight spaces to work with, so you should pick a name no longer than that. Access uses your chosen name and adds the file extension .MDB after the name to designate the file as a database.

5. Let's name our database PHONEBK, for phone book. When the box first opens, Access gives the new file a sort of arbitrary name such as *db1.mdb* and highlights it. That kind of name isn't very descriptive, so you can just type over it. If the text is highlighted, what you type will replace it. If the text isn't highlighted, click in the existing name (in the narrow white boxed area below File Name) and edit the text to read **phonebk**. (When you click in a text area this way, the blinking vertical bar—or text cursor—lands right where you click. Whatever you then type will be inserted at that position. To remove letters to the left of the cursor, press Backspace. To remove letters to the right, press Del. You can move the cursor left and right, letter by letter using, the → and ← keys before typing or deleting.)

6. Click on OK, and up comes a blank *Database window*. Your screen should now look like Figure 3.2.

Notice that the title bar (top line) of the database window shows the name of your new database,

**Database: PHONEBK**

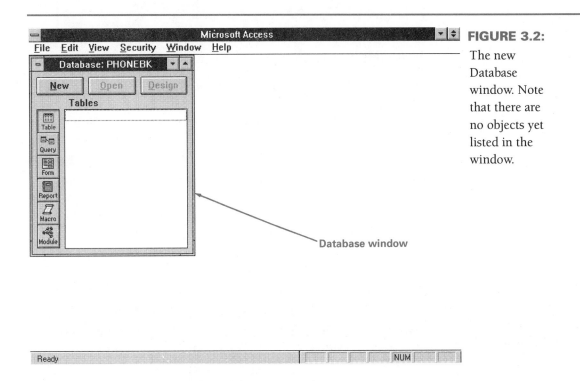

**FIGURE 3.2:**

The new Database window. Note that there are no objects yet listed in the window.

indicating that the new database we just created is open and ready for use. The Database window is central to everything you'll do in Access. It's sort of like the control center for all your activities with a given database. If you've used dBASE IV, you can equate the Database window with the dBASE Control Center.

Now look at the buttons down the left side of the Database window. Click on each one and notice how they "go in" as though you were pushing a button on an elevator. Notice how the word *Tables* above the list area changes to *Queries* when you click on Queries. Since you don't have any queries or other objects created yet, you don't see anything in the list box to the right of the buttons when you click one. But once you create queries, reports, and so on, they'll be listed.

## How to Create Your First Table's Structure

Next we'll need to create the table structure for our phone book. Here's how to do it. At the top of the Database window are three buttons: New, Open, and Design. Open and Design are grayed out and can't be selected, since you don't have anything to open or design yet. (Design should really be called "redesign" since it only works on existing objects.)

1. Click on the Table button, since you want to create a table.

2. Click on New. You'll see the Table Design window (Figure 3.3). It may look a little confusing at first, but don't worry. It's really not so complicated.

Essentially, Access is now asking you to define the database structure. Recall from Chapter 1 that *record* is the database term for one complete entry; a record is like a card in an index-card box or a

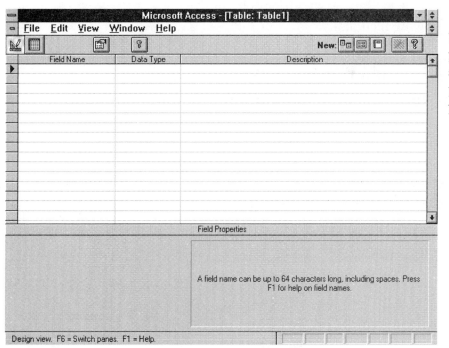

**FIGURE 3.3:**

This is where you declare the size and other properties of your table's fields.

listing in a phone book. Each record consists of fields, each of which stores one portion of the entry, such as the name, address, or phone number. You have to tell Access how many fields the records will have and what each field will contain.

Notice that the Table Design window is divided into three areas: Field Name, Data Type, and Description. Click in each area and notice how the text in the lower right of the box changes to guide you a bit.

Now you have to fill in the columns with these three pieces of information about each field in your phone book table. You do this for your first field on row one. Then you move down to row two and fill in the same specifications for the second field, and so on for all the fields you wish to include in your table's records.

Let's examine each of these field specifications and what your options are for each.

# DEFINING FIELDS

To create the table's structure, you need to define the fields you want to use in your records by specifying the options described in the following sections.

## Field Name

What do you want to name the field? The name can be up to 64 characters long (either uppercase or lowercase) and can contain letters, numbers, spaces, and special characters. The only characters not allowed are periods (.), exclamation points (!), and brackets ([ ]). Field names also mustn't start with a space. The fact that they can be 64 characters long allows you to give field names a description that makes sense to you, such as "Home telephone number," instead of the abbreviated names like HOME_PHONE that programs like dBASE limit you to.

## *Data Type*

What kind of information is this field going to hold? There are eight options, which you can select by clicking on the little arrow that appears when you are working in this column. Just click on the arrow and then on the desired type.

- Text: Text is the first option, since a majority of database fields are of the *text* type. Text fields can contain all the letters, punctuation marks, and special symbols, as well as any numerals that are merely going to be printed—not used in any mathematical calculations (zip codes and phone numbers, for example). A text field can be up to 255 characters long.

- Memo: Memo fields are a bit like text fields, but they can contain up to 32,000 characters. For example, for our phone book, we might use a Memo field to write a few notes about each person in the database.

- Number: Number fields can include any kind of numbers that will later require mathematical calculation. If they have a fixed number of decimal places (up to four) though, calculations can be faster and more accurate (fewer rounding-off errors) if you choose the Currency data type.

- Date/Time: These fields can contain date and time values for years from 100 to 9999.

- Currency: Use this choice for money fields. Calculations will be accurate to 15 digits on the left side of the decimal point and four digits to the right of the decimal.

- Counter: Use this type when you want the value of a field to be automatically incremented (increased by one) whenever you add a new record to a table.

- Yes/No: True or false, or yes or no entries. Good for things like "Is this person paid up?"

- OLE Object: This field is used when you want to have something like a graph, a drawing, or some part of a spreadsheet from another program such as Microsoft Excel added to your database. This is complicated stuff, so don't worry about it now.

If you want information about the field types, click in the Data Type column, press F1, and you'll see several Help screens.

## Description

You can optionally add a description for each field you create. This description will appear down at the bottom of the Access window when you or someone else clicks in the field in question. Make it descriptive, like

**Payment Method—(If credit card, include expiration date after card #)**

Your descriptions can be up to 255 characters long, including spaces.

# CREATING THE STRUCTURE

With the possible field types in mind, we can begin to plan our database structure. A little careful thinking at this stage will pay off in the long run, so let's revert to a bit of low technology for a minute by pulling out a piece of paper and a pencil. Imagining what your database would look like on paper simplifies the structuring process. Here's a list of what we probably want the phone book database to store.

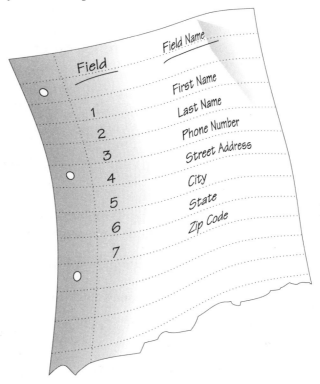

For the time being, we'll use this model for our structure. We'll modify it later as part of the tutorial. That way you can practice adding your own finishing touches to meet any specific needs you might have. In the meantime, perform the following steps. We will define the structure for each of the seven fields, one field at a time.

1. Click in the Field Name box for field number 1. Type **First Name**. If you make a mistake, simply press the Backspace key to back up and correct it.

**2.** Press ↵ or Tab to move to the next box, Data Type. The word *Text* appears in the box, and a little arrow shows up to the right of Text.  Access always assumes, by default, that you want your fields to be Text fields. Since you will not be doing mathematical calculations on any of the fields in your phone book (such as asking Access to find the average of, say, a group of numbers), you can accept the default assumption and categorize all the fields as Text. (Both you and Access will find it easier to use Text fields whenever possible, even though some of the fields, such as those for the phone number and zip code, actually will store numerals.)

**3.** To accept the Text setting and move to the next box, press ↵ or Tab again. The cursor moves to the Description area.

**4.** Type in a description for the First Name field:

**Enter person's First Name with first letter capitalized**

Your screen should now look like Figure 3.4.

Now fill in the rest of the fields, repeating the steps you just took, to make the screen look like Figure 3.5. And, as before, if you make a mistake while typing, use the Backspace key to back up and correct your error. You can also move between columns using the Tab key (to move right one column) or Shift+Tab (to move left one column). To edit a column you've moved out of, you have to click on it to land the cursor on it somewhere. (The problem with using the arrow keys and Tab key is that they highlight the whole column.) Once the text cursor is in a column, you can move the cursor one word at a time to the left with Ctrl+←, or one word to the right with Ctrl+→.

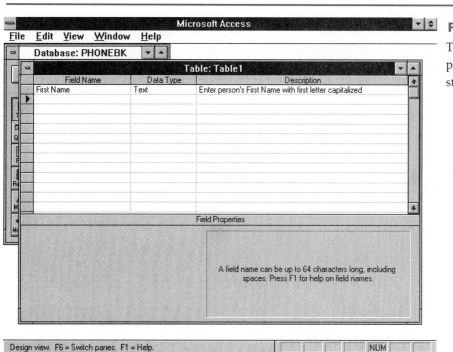

**FIGURE 3.4:**

The completed phone book structure

**FIGURE 3.5:**

This first field is now defined.

# SETTING THE FIELD PROPERTIES

As you were entering your fields, you may have noticed the Field Properties box down in the bottom part of the design window. It's the one that looks like this:

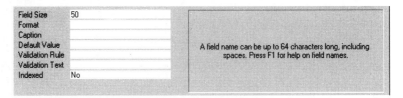

This box is where you enter details about the database fields, particularly how long you want the field to be. There are other settings you can make too, for things like preventing erroneous data entry into a table's field, causing the data to be formatted in a particular way, and so on. These details about your fields are called *properties*. For the moment we're only concerned with the issue of field length, so don't worry about the other properies.

What is the maximum number of letters, numbers, or other characters that you plan to put into the field? That is, how wide does the field need to be? Only Text fields need to have their size declared by you. All the other data types are automatically assigned a size by Access.

Why even bother setting the field length, you might ask? If you don't set the field length for your text fields, Access sets them for you. Doesn't sound like a big deal, does it? But you may have noticed that the setting Access used was 50. When we create other Access objects, such as forms, 50 will seem unreasonably long for a field length, so you'll want to shorten it. You can also speed up things like searching and sorting records if you're careful not to use longer fields than you need. However, if you make a field too short, you will have to abbreviate long names or numbers to fit them into your database.

So, it's research time. Pull out a phone book and get an idea of how long people's last names are. How long is the average street address? Count the letters in a few city names. You want your fields to be long enough for all relevant data, such as phone numbers and zip codes, but not so long that they end up being half-filled with blank spaces. You know your field length is correct when a name or address only occasionally won't fit in the field. You can usually abbreviate without ambiguity in these cases.

## *Setting the Field Lengths*

Now let's enter the field lengths in our phone book database.

1. Returning to the screen, click anywhere on the First Name field (field 1). The Properties box now says the field size is 50. You want to change it to 10. So, click after 50, hit Backspace twice and enter 10. (Here's a little trick. Double-click on 50 and just type 10.)

2. Move to the upper box and click anywhere on field 2, Last Name. Move down to the lower box. Edit the field size the same way, only to the correct size of 15.

3. Edit the remaining fields, using the sizes listed below.

| FIELD | FIELD NAME | FIELD SIZE |
|-------|------------|------------|
| 1 | First Name | 10 |
| 2 | Last Name | 15 |
| 3 | Phone Number | 12 |
| 4 | Street Address | 22 |
| 5 | City | 13 |
| 6 | State | 2 |
| 7 | Zip Code | 5 |

## The Indexed Box

You may have noticed that the Indexed box at the bottom of the Properties box says "No" for all the fields. This setting tells Access whether you want the database to be ordered according to the selected field. For example, you'll probably want to be able to display records in your phone book in alphabetical order according to people's last names, as well as in zip code order in case you want to do a bulk mailing. We'll discuss in Chapter 9 the various means for reorganizing the records in your database using this setting. For the time being, just leave them all set to No.

# SAVING THE TABLE

Now that you have defined all seven fields, you'll want to save the new table's structure on your hard disk and return to the database window. If you check out the title bar of the table's window, you'll see your table is currently called something totally meaningless, like *Table1*. So we'll also have to give it a description that will remind you later what it's for. As is the case with many of the objects you create in Access, you get to enter a fairly long description of your table file.

Here's how to save the table:

1. Open the File menu and choose Save. A little dialog box comes up, as you see in Figure 3.6.

2. Type the following text into the box:

    **Name and Address list**

    You can type file descriptions in lowercase or uppercase letters.

3. Click on OK.

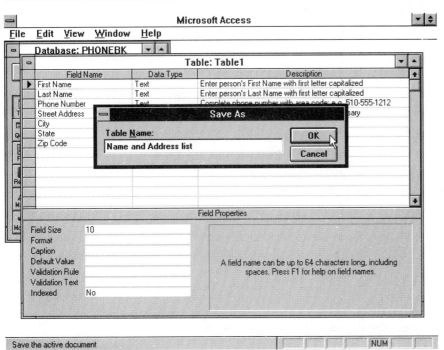

**FIGURE 3.6:**

To save a table you've created, open the file menu and choose Save. Then give it a descriptive name.

**4.** You'll see a dialog box about creating a *primary key*.

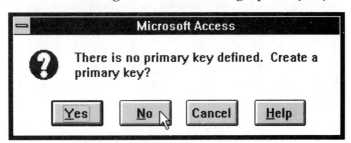

Don't worry about the primary key now. If you set a primary key, this will determine the order your records are displayed in. We want them to be displayed in the order they were entered, so just click on No. Now the new empty table of the seven fields is saved on your disk and added to the PHONEBK database.

# RETURNING TO
# THE DATABASE WINDOW

Let's close the design screen and get back to the Database window.

**1.** Click on the Control Box of the Table Design window. If you don't know where that is, look at Figure 3.7.

**2.** From the Control menu, choose Close.

**3.** Notice that *Name and Address list* has been added to the Database window as an available table.

**4.** Click on the large Query button. Since we created a table, not a query, Name and Address list disappears when Queries is pushed.

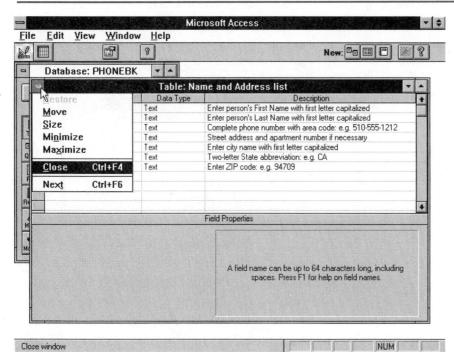

**FIGURE 3.7:**

To close the Table Design window, open its Control menu and choose close, or double-click on its Control Box.

5. Click on Tables. Now your new table shows up in the list again.

Congratulations! You have successfully created your first table, defined its structure, and saved it on your computer's hard disk. You may wish to take a break before going on to the next chapter, or you can go to the next section, "How to Back Up Your Data," and then move on to Chapter 4. However, if you do want to take a break now:

1. Open Access File menu.

2. Choose Exit.

You should now be returned to Windows. Exit Windows as explained in Chapter 2 if you want to turn off your computer.

## How to Back Up Your Data

Don't underestimate the value of making backup copies of your databases. Disks are delicate storage media, and it's not uncommon for a data file to be damaged in one way or another. The best protection against such an unhappy development is to regularly make backup copies of your important files. At this point, you've created only a database structure; if you lost it, you could easily reconstruct it (though you'd probably prefer not to). But once a database is filled with valuable information, losing your file could be a major disaster. To get into the habit of making backup copies of files, let's back up the PHONEBK database file now.

You can make backups in two ways: from Windows and from DOS.

## MAKING A BACKUP FROM WINDOWS

If you're the graphical type, you probably manage your files from File Manager or Norton Desktop for Windows. If you are a Norton Desktop user, you aren't the type who needs any instructions. If you're in Windows, don't have Norton Desktop, and are even a little familiar with File Manager, read on to see how to make a backup from Windows:

**1.** Exit Access, or close the PHONEBK database by opening Access's File menu and choosing Close Database. If you don't close the file first, Windows won't let you make a copy of it. You'll get an error message saying that the file may be in use. If you try copying it from a DOS-prompt window using the DOS COPY command or a program like XTree, you'll get a cryptic message about a "sharing violation."

**2.** Get to the Program Manager and open the Main group (click on the icon labeled Main).

**3.** Double-click on File Manager to run it.

**4.** Maximize the File Manager window.

**5.** Click on the disk-drive icon (near the top of the window) that contains your Access program (probably C).

**6.** Click on the Access directory in the directory (left-hand) pane of File Manager.

**7.** You should be able to spot the phonebk.mdb file among the files in the right side of the window. Your screen should look somewhat like Figure 3.8.

**8.** Insert a blank, formatted disk in your floppy drive, or a formatted disk with at least 100K bytes free. (For now the file is about 66K bytes, but we'll be adding data.)

**9.** Drag the phonebk.mdb file up to the destination drive icon (A or B) and release it. Your floppy disk drive light will come on and the database file will be copied onto the floppy.

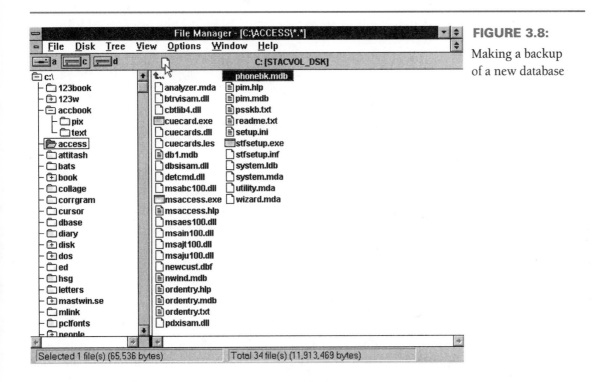

Making a backup of a new database

## MAKING A BACKUP FROM DOS

Prefer to make backups from DOS because you're used to the COPY command? OK. File Manager is great, but not everyone loves it.

1. Get to the DOS prompt either by quitting Windows or by switching to Program Manager, opening the Main group, and double-clicking on the MS-DOS Prompt icon.

2. Insert a floppy disk with some space on it. Let's say it's in drive A. Type

    **DIR A:** ↵

    At the bottom of your listing, you'll see how much room is left on your disk. The size of the database file with no records added yet requires 65,000 bytes for the backup.

It will increase in size as you add data, queries, and so on to the database.

3. Assuming you've been using the Access subdirectory on drive C for your data, type

**COPY C:\ACCESS\PHONEBK.MDB A:** ↵

The copy is made.

4. Now remove your backup disk from drive A, label it appropriately (using a felt-tip pen, not a ballpoint pen or pencil, if the label is already on a 5¼-inch disk), and store it in a safe place.

# MAKING COPIES OF LARGE DATABASES

When you're backing up large databases, you may run into trouble using either File Manager's or DOS's Copy commands. If the database's size exceeds that of the target floppy disk (which is not unheard of if you're storing lots of records or have a large number of fields for records), Copy won't work. The floppy will fill up before the whole database gets copied onto it, then the Copy command will bomb and you'll get some kind of error message to that effect. The only way to make a backup copy of a large hard disk file to a floppy disk is with a backup program like BACKUP, which comes with DOS and is probably on your hard disk in the DOS directory. Consult your PC-DOS or MS-DOS manual for instructions. There are lots of other backup programs around too, most of which do a better job than BACKUP, but you have to pay extra for them.

FEATURING

Adding Fields
Changing Fields
Deleting Fields
Rearranging Fields
Creating a Primary Key
Modifying the Structure
▼

# Modifying the Database Structure

n the last chapter, you learned how to create the structure of a Microsoft Access database. Using the Microsoft Access Table Design window, the process was relatively easy. You also learned how to set one of the field properties (size) for each field.

However, even the best-laid plans are sometimes shortsighted, and it's not uncommon to find that your database structure needs alteration, either to change the size of fields or to add or delete fields. In fact, you may already have thought of a few things we've left out of the phone book's structure.

For example, many people have a work phone number in addition to their home phone number, and we didn't include a place for this. Also, a slot for the name of the company for which each person works might be a good idea. A Memo field to hold notes about each person also might be useful. So now what? Is it too late to make changes? Do we have to start again from scratch?

No. Luckily, Microsoft Access accommodates 20/20 hindsight and allows you to modify an existing database structure. You can even change the structure after you have lots of data in the file, though at that stage there are some restrictions, which we'll discuss later.

## Modifying the Structure

If you quit Microsoft Access to take a break after the last chapter, start up Microsoft Access again. If you need to, refer to the instructions in Chapter 2. Now let's modify the table's structure.

1. Open the File menu. Assuming that you haven't been working with lots of other databases in the meantime, and that you have closed your database at least once since designing PHONEBK, you'll see something new in the File menu:

Notice that PHONEBK has been added to the menu. Access keeps track of the names of the last several databases you've been working on and adds them to this menu. It makes opening them easier.

2. Just type the number to the left of PHONEBK (it's probably 1) or click on the name in the menu.

3. Up comes the Database window, with the Tables button depressed and the Name and Address list showing, as in Figure 4.1.

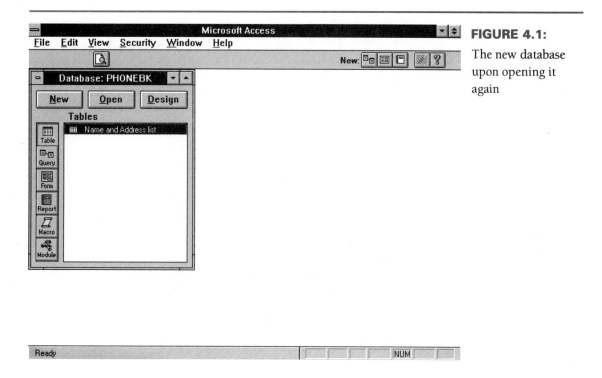

The new database upon opening it again

**4.** Next, you need to tell Microsoft Access what you want to do with the file. Since we want to experiment with altering the structure of the database, click on the Design button. Your screen now changes to look like Figure 4.2.

This screen should look familiar. It's the same Database Design screen we used to create the PHONEBK database structure in the last chapter. There really isn't any difference between the screens used to modify and create databases, except that now we'll use some additional keyboard commands to add new fields and to change a field name.

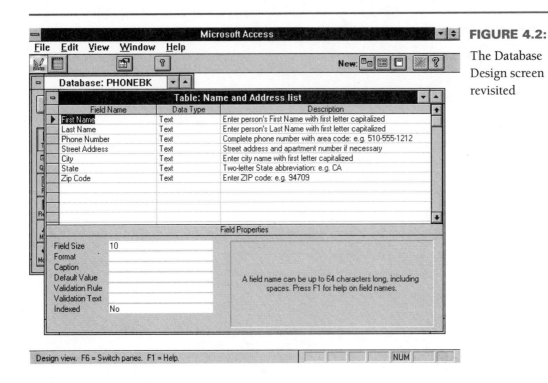

**FIGURE 4.2:**

The Database Design screen revisited

## ADDING NEW FIELDS

To add our first new field to the database structure, follow these steps:

**1.** The highlight is on the First Name field. Click on field 3, Phone Number, to highlight it.

**2.** We want to insert a new field between fields 2 and 3. This will be for the company name. To insert a field, you highlight the field that's just *below* where you want the new field. So press ↓ twice (or click on Phone Number).

**3.** Open the Edit menu and choose Insert Row. Phone Number now moves down one line, leaving a new, empty field 3 for you to define, as shown in Figure 4.3.

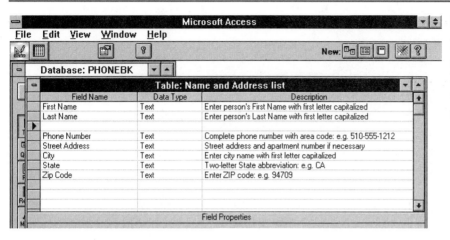

**FIGURE 4.3:**

Place the cursor and choose Insert Row from the Edit menu to add a new field.

4. Now fill in the new field, which will hold a company name for each person in the database. This will be a Text field named Company. Give it the description

**Enter name of company with proper capitalization**

5. Set the Field Size to 20.

The table now contains eight fields. Now let's add a field for the work phone number. Since this field is going to be almost identical to the other phone number field, why not just copy it from the field below? Here's how.

1. Click anywhere on what's now the fourth field, Phone Number, or highlight it using the ↓ key. Insert a row here by using the Edit menu's Insert Row command again. Now you have a new blank field.

2. Position the cursor carefully on the little tile to the left of the Phone Number field. The cursor should change shape to a little right-arrow. Now click. The whole field becomes highlighted:

Be careful not to drag the mouse when the cursor looks like an up/down arrow, because it will resize the row height, which we don't want to do at this point.

**3.** With all three columns of the Phone Number row highlighted, open the Edit menu and choose Copy. Nothing appears to happen, but you've just copied the Phone Number field, including its properties, to the Windows Clipboard so it can be pasted into another location. (The Clipboard is a sort of temporary holding tank for stuff you want to copy.)

**4.** Select the new empty field the same way you selected the previous one (with the little tile). It should become highlighted.

**5.** Open the Edit menu and choose Paste.

Now you have two fields that are identical. This could confuse data-entry people, and could even confuse Access, so we should edit them a bit to differentiate them. The easiest way to do this is to double-click on *Home* in the new line and type **Work**.

Your screen should look like Figure 4.4.

Finally, let's add a Memo field for jotting down notes about people. Recall that memo fields let you store up to 32,000 characters worth of information about a record. The neat thing about Memo fields is that each one doesn't necessarily take up 32K of disk space. They consume only as many characters as the memos you type in.

**1.** Click on the first blank row below the Zip Code row.

| Table: Name and Address list | | |
|---|---|---|
| **Field Name** | **Data Type** | **Description** |
| First Name | Text | Enter person's First Name with first letter capitalized |
| Last Name | Text | Enter person's Last Name with first letter capitalized |
| Company | Text | Enter name of company with proper capitalization |
| Work Phone Number | Text | Work phone number with area code: e.g. 510-555-1212 |
| Home Phone Number | Text | Home phone number with area code: e.g. 510-555-1212 |
| Street Address | Text | Street address and apartment number if necessary |
| City | Text | Enter city name with first letter capitalized |
| State | Text | Two-letter State abbreviation: e.g. CA |
| Zip Code | Text | Enter ZIP code: e.g. 94709 |

**Field Properties**

| | |
|---|---|
| Field Size | 12 |
| Format | |
| Caption | |
| Default Value | |
| Validation Rule | |
| Validation Text | |
| Indexed | No |

A field name can be up to 64 characters long, including spaces. Press F1 for help on field names.

**FIGURE 4.4:**

Name and Address table with Company and Work Phone Number fields added

**2.** Create a new field called Notes. Click in the Data Type box for the new field. Notice that there's a little button to the right of the box. Clicking on it causes a drop-down list to appear. Set the Data Type to Memo using this drop-down list, or with this shortcut: Just type the letter **M** in the Data Type column, then press ↵. (Except for the Currency and Counter data types, just typing the first letter of the data type will choose it. For currency and counter, you have to type the first two letters—*cu* or *co*.)

**3.** Enter the description

**A memo field for sundry information**

and press ↵ to move down to the next field.

Your screen should look like Figure 4.5.

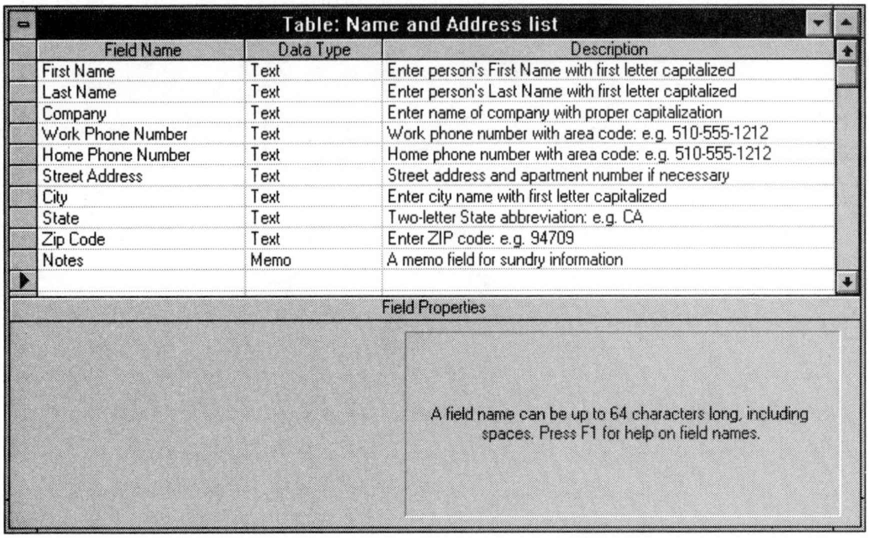

| Field Name | Data Type | Description |
|---|---|---|
| First Name | Text | Enter person's First Name with first letter capitalized |
| Last Name | Text | Enter person's Last Name with first letter capitalized |
| Company | Text | Enter name of company with proper capitalization |
| Work Phone Number | Text | Work phone number with area code: e.g. 510-555-1212 |
| Home Phone Number | Text | Home phone number with area code: e.g. 510-555-1212 |
| Street Address | Text | Street address and apartment number if necessary |
| City | Text | Enter city name with first letter capitalized |
| State | Text | Two-letter State abbreviation: e.g. CA |
| Zip Code | Text | Enter ZIP code: e.g. 94709 |
| Notes | Memo | A memo field for sundry information |

Table: Name and Address list

Field Properties

A field name can be up to 64 characters long, including spaces. Press F1 for help on field names.

**FIGURE 4.5:**

Name and Address list with all fields completed

# REARRANGING AND DELETING FIELDS

Two other tasks you might want to perform are deleting fields and rearranging fields. Let's say you decide after some time using this table that the Home Phone Number field doesn't really get used all that often. To save disk space you can delete it. Try this just to see how it works.

1. In the Table Design window, click on the row selector (the little tile) to the left of the Home Phone Number field. The whole row should now be selected.

2. Open the Edit menu and choose Delete. The field vanishes, and the others are pulled up to replace it.

3. Oops! Changed your mind? That's OK. Access remembers what you just did. *Before you do anything else* open the Edit menu and choose Undo Delete. The field row returns.

Sometimes you'll want to rearrange the order of rows. The order of the rows in the design screen dictates the order in which they will appear on other forms and screens. So, rearranging them here can save you some hassle in the long run. You'll see the effects of the field order later.

As an exercise, try reversing the positions of the Home and Work Phone fields. As you might expect, with the help of the mouse Access lets you do this easily.

**1.** Click on the row selector for Home Phone Number. This selects the field. The row selector shows a little triangle.

**2.** Position the mouse pointer on the triangle. Move the pointer slowly up and down a bit. Notice the various shapes the pointer takes:

 Row resizing pointer: Used for resizing the height of a row

 Row selector pointer: Used for selecting a whole row

 Regular Pointer: Used for dragging a row

**3.** Move the mouse around slowly over the little triangle until it looks like the third of these pointers. While it's in that shape, press the mouse button and hold it down. This grabs the field you're trying to move. Now drag the field upwards one row. As you do so, you'll see an outline of the row you're dragging.

**4.** Release the mouse button when the pointer is just over the Work Phone Number field. When you release, the fields are reversed.

**5.** Oops! Changed your mind? (Suppose we did.) How do you think you would reverse the move? Open the Edit menu and choose Undo Move. The fields return to their original order—Work Phone *above* Home Phone.

# CREATING A PRIMARY KEY

Good. All modifications to the structure are now complete. Let's save the changes. And while we're at it, we'll let Access create a *primary key* for the table, so it will stop bugging us about creating one, and so each record's number is visible in a field.

1. Open the File menu and choose Save. You'll be asked that question about the lack of a primary key again.

2. This time click on Yes. When you do so, Access creates a new field, called ID, which has the *Counter* data type. When you start entering data in your table, records will automatically be given ascending numbers in the ID field. You can use these record numbers later for finding and sorting and for linking your table to other tables. Your table design should now look like Figure 4.6. Notice the little key symbol to the left of the ID field.

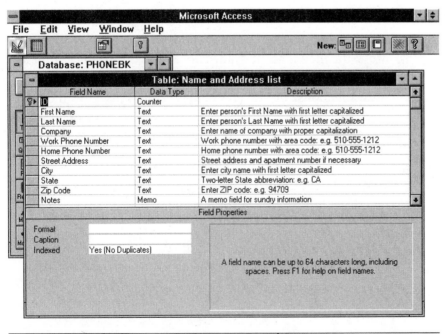

**FIGURE 4.6:**

The finished table with primary key field added

3. Now let's close the Table Design window. Open the File menu again and choose Close. The window closes and the Database window comes into view.

## MODIFYING THE STRUCTURE WHEN THE DATABASE CONTAINS DATA

So much for changing the structure of a database *before* it has any data in it. What if you want to change it to shorten a field or change its data type *after* it's got lots of valuable data in it?

If you're careful, you can get away with it. The process is the same as for modifying an empty database, except for a few restrictions. A warning is in order: If you *aren't* careful, you could lose some data. The "safety first" rule of thumb is: First back up your database file. Then, after every change, save the new structure. The specific rules are:

- If you change a field's name, do not change its position at the same time. Save the new structure first, with only the name change. Then change the position. (You can also first change the position and then the name.)

- If you change a field's length, do not change its name or position at the same time. Again, make the changes one at a time.

- Changing a field's type can cause data to be lost in that field.

- It's best to save the new database structure each time you change a field name. You do this with the Save This Database File Structure option on the Layout menu. Each time you save the structure, Access asks you in a dialog box for the file name. Choose ↵ if you don't want to change it; otherwise, type in the new name, then choose ↵. Another dialog box appears asking if you want data to be copied for all fields. Usually you'll want to use the data if you're just changing the name, so choose Yes, which is the default choice.

A third dialog box warns that you have made changes to the structure and asks if you want to save these changes; again choose Yes, the default answer.

- If you have linked tables, changing the name of a field that links two tables will break the link. You will have to relink them.

- If queries and forms use the field(s) whose name you're changing, those queries and forms will have to be updated to incorporate the new field names.

See the *Microsoft Access User's Guide*, Part I, for additional details.

# Entering Data

ow that you've created the table's basic structure, you're ready to put some names and addresses in your table. You will also learn how to fix simple data-entry errors and how to make backups of your work. If you took a break after the last chapter:

**1.** Start Microsoft Access again.

**2.** Open the PHONEBK database, this time using the File menu's Open command. (You'll have to use this technique sometimes when your database isn't listed on the File menu, so I'm breaking you in.)

**3.** When the dialog box comes up, double-click on PHONEBK.MDB to open the database.

If you didn't take a break, make sure you're back at the Database window and that the database that's open is PHONEBK, as shown in the title bar.

## How to Enter Your First Record

Now we're going to start entering data in the table, creating what is called a *datasheet*. To start entering records:

1. Click on the big Tables button.

2. Highlight the Name and Address list (if it isn't already).

3. Click on Open. This tells Access that you want to view, add, or edit records to the table. The Datasheet window opens, with one blank record, as in Figure 5.1.

As you can see, this window contains a series of empty fields, one for each field in your table—in essence, a blank form. The blinking cursor is to the left of the word *(Counter)*, which is in the first field of the table—the ID field. The other column heads in the datasheet are the names of the fields—the same names we typed into the structure in the last chapter. The status lines at the bottom of the

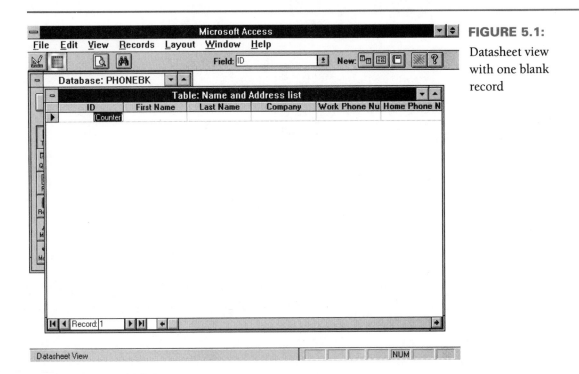

**FIGURE 5.1:**

Datasheet view with one blank record

windows say you're in Datasheet View mode, and that you're on Record 1.

4. The window is too short for all the fields (columns) to show. Some of the fields are off to the right. To see more fields, enlarge the Dataview window by clicking on the Maximize button (the little up-arrow in the upper right corner of the Datasheet window), as in the graphic below.

5. Go ahead and enter the first record, using the data listed below. Be sure to capitalize as indicated and don't forget to type the hyphens between the parts of the phone numbers. After you type each entry, press ↵ to jump to the next field. When you get to the Notes (Memo) field, just stop typing. We'll discuss later how to work with Memo fields.

|  |  |
| --- | --- |
| ID | (PRESS ↵) |
| First Name | Randolf |
| Last Name | Robbins |
| Company | Ralph Nicholby Inc. |
| Work Phone Number | 415-555-1212 |
| Home Phone Number | 415-555-1111 |
| Street | 374 Tipplemeyer Ave. |
| City | Cornmont |
| State | CA |
| Zip Code | 94709 |
| Notes | (leave blank) |

When you pressed ↵ to get out of the ID field, two things happened. The (Counter) dropped down to the next line, and a pencil showed up in the left margin.

The pencil icon means you have modified a record and that it hasn't yet been recorded on the hard disk. The counter drops down to the next row for no good reason (trust me). The asterisk indicates

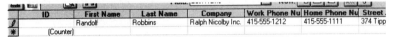

the end of the table (the last record).

Some of the columns were too narrow for the information you were entering into them. So, as you entered the text the information had to scroll to the left. This can be a little disconcerting at first, because you may think the beginning of what you've entered is being lost. But it isn't. We'll rearrange the screen columns later to make it easier to see everything you've entered.

## How to Fix Typos

There are several special keyboard commands for correcting mistakes as you type and for moving the cursor around within a record. You enter these commands with the *editing keys*. Table 5.1 lists these keys. You already know some of them. Many of the editing effects can be achieved in more than one way, using the mouse and menu commands. For example, you can jump the text cursor (blinking vertical line) to a new location by clicking there. Try experimenting with the editing keys just to get used to them. If you're used to the standard Windows editing keys, you're already familiar with these.

One special key you should experiment with is the Ins key. Press it several times and notice that the letters *OVR* appear and disappear at the far right of the status line. This indicates that you are turning Overwrite mode on and off. When it says OVR, Overwrite mode's on. In this mode, the text cursor gets bigger—it *covers* each letter instead of sitting *between* letters as it normally does. When you type in Overwrite mode, characters you type obliterate (type over) existing text. When OVR is off, you're in Insert mode, where what you type pushes existing text to the right.

| KEY | EFFECT |
|---|---|
| Tab | Moves cursor to the next field |
| ↵ | Moves cursor to the next field |
| → | If the field is empty or the cursor is at the end of the field, moves cursor to the next field |
| Shift+Tab | Moves cursor to the previous field |
| ← | If the field is empty or the cursor is at the beginning of the field, moves cursor to the previous field |
| → | Moves cursor one space forward |
| ← | Moves cursor one space backward |
| Ctrl+→ | Moves cursor to the next word |
| Ctrl+← | Moves cursor to the previous word |
| Home | Moves to the beginning of a field |
| End | Moves to the end of a field |
| Ctrl+Del | Deletes from the cursor to the end of a field |
| Del | Deletes the character to the right of the cursor or selected text |
| Backspace | Deletes the character to the left of the cursor |
| Ins | Turns Overwrite mode on and off |
| Shift | With arrow keys, selects text |
| Double-click | Selects the word under the cursor |
| Click-drag | Selects text under the cursor as mouse moves |
| Typing | Replaces any selected (highlighted) text |
| Ctrl+X | Cuts selected text onto the Clipboard for pasting |
| Ctrl+C | Copies selected text onto the Clipboard for pasting |
| Ctrl+V | Pastes what's on the Clipboard to where the cursor is now |

**TABLE 5.1:**

Editing Keys and
Their Effects

## How to Complete the Sample Database

The cursor should still be in the Notes field, the last field in the record. Don't enter anything into the Notes field just yet. For now, let's add the records for the rest of the people in our sample table. Later we'll add some memos.

1. Press ↵. Your disk-drive light may go on for a second. What happened? Access recorded the record on disk, and the little pencil disappeared. When the pencil is gone, this means your changes have been saved. This is a nice feature of Access. You don't have to worry too much about losing data. As soon as you switch off a record and on another one, any changes you made are saved. If you decide you want to reverse the changes you made, you can do this too. Access always remembers the record as it was. Just open the Edit menu and choose Undo Saved Record (or press Ctrl+Z). The record will be restored to its previous state.

2. The status line now indicates that you are on record 2. Enter the following names and addresses into the table, one after another, using initial caps as shown. Leave the memo fields blank.

> **Hank**
> **Davies**
> **Bass-O-Matic**
> **909-549-3787**
> **909-398-2563**
> **333 33rd St.**
> **West Goshen**
> **SD**
> **43312**
>
> **Adriator**
> **Wegwo**
> **Rug Flox, Inc.**
> **321-889-3674**
> **321-883-9821**

**158 Snorewell Blvd.**
**Sleepyhollow**
**CA**
**02587**

**Aretha**
**Phillipson**
**Soulariums-R-Us**
**908-776-5298**
**908-337-8194**
**999 Motor City Ave.**
**Detroit**
**MI**
**39482**

**Randy**
**Batterydown**
**Voltaics Inc.**
**809-675-4532**
**809-777-3300**
**495 Anode St.**
**Carbondale**
**IL**
**30129**

**Nimrod**
**Neverburger**
**Bab's Fish N Chips**
**822-991-2861**
**822-675-4500**
**77 Easy Street**
**Khozad**
**CA**
**89751**

**Marcel**
**Phillip**
**Feline Frenzy**
**310-563-0987**
**310-265-7560**

**456 Fresno St.**
**Paris**
**TX**
**55493**

**Valery**
**Kuletzski**
**Literary Allusions**
**529-221-9480**
**529-559-7300**
**451 Farenheit Ct.**
**Oakland**
**CA**
**95420**

**MARIAN**
**DAVIES**
**CITY OPERA CO.**
**211-334-9876**
**211-411-6111**
**344 MARKET ST**
**NEW YORK**
**NY**
**10021**

Type the last record in all uppercase letters, as shown. This is a deliberate data-entry error that we'll use for illustration later.

3. With the cursor on the Notes field of the last record, press ↵. Another blank record appears, and the last record is written to disk. This terminates the process of adding new records.

4. Open the File menu and choose Close. This closes the Datasheet window and returns you to the Database window. The Name and Address table now contains nine records.

# A Reminder About Backups

Recall from the end of Chapter 3 that you made a backup copy of the PHONEBK file. Now you have some data to back up, since you just entered nine records. You wouldn't want to have to type them all again if your table were somehow lost. Don't underestimate the power of Murphy's Law. Hard disks never die until you have something really important on them. Somehow they know. Database files are complex and it's not uncommon for one to be damaged in one way or another. The best protection against such an unhappy occurrence is to back up your important files regularly. To get into the habit of making backup copies, we'll go through the steps again here.

As you may remember from the end of Chapter 3, you can use the DOS COPY command or File Manager to make backup copies.

1. Close the PHONEBK database file using the File menu's Close Database command.

2. Insert a blank, formatted disk in drive A or B.

3. Use the DOS COPY command or File Manager to make the copy. If you're using DOS and you've been using the Access directory on drive C for your data, type the following at the DOS prompt:

**COPY C:\ACCESS\PHONEBK.MDB  A:**

Then press ⏎. (Type **B:** instead of **A:** if your disk is in drive B.) The files will be copied to your floppy disk, one by one.

Go ahead and make your backup copies, label the disks, and store them in a safe place. From now on, unless otherwise mentioned, it will be up to you to back up your work. In general, how frequently you back up your files should be determined by the value of your databases. Since most backup operations take only a few minutes, it's usually penny-wise and pound-foolish not to back up your data often.

# 6 CHAPTER

**FEATURING**

**Viewing the Data**

**Navigating in Datasheet View**

**The Record Pointer**

**Searching for Data with the Edit ➤ Find Command**

▼

# Retrieving the Data

Now that you have a number of records in the PHONEBK table, you can begin to experiment with the many useful ways in which Microsoft Access lets you retrieve and manipulate the data you've stored. As you already know, one of the best things about database systems is the quick, easy access they give to the information you've laboriously entered.

You can get information out of your table and onto your screen in three primary ways, short of creating a sophisticated report.

- You can visually scan the data table to find what you're looking for.

- You can tell Access to search for a specific record on the basis of information you enter, such as a customer number or last name.

- You can request to see only the records that meet specific conditions, such as records of customers who made purchases in the last year or who live in San Francisco—or both. This is called *querying*.

In this lesson, we'll experiment with the first two types of information retrieval. In Chapters 8 and 9, you'll learn about using queries.

*Note:* Beginning with this section, I'll use a shorthand method in the exercises for telling you to choose menu and submenu options. Here's how it works. Instead of explicitly spelling out how to choose each menu, option, and suboption in every example, exercises will display the names of the necessary options in a single abbreviated command line, and you will then be told to choose that series of options. For example, here's how an exercise would present the step telling you to exit Access and return to Windows:

Choose File ➤ Exit.

Within the line, a right arrow (➤) separates each level in the selection series. Most of the time, the first word after *choose* is a menu name, such as File, Edit, View, or Record. The subsequent words are the menu and submenu options, or possibly a file name, as in

Choose File ➤ Open Database ➤ PHONEBK.

This tells you to open the File menu, choose Open Database, and choose PHONEBK from the resulting file box.

## Viewing Multiple Records Using the Datasheet

The easiest technique for getting a bird's-eye view of the information in your table is simply to bring up the table in Datasheet view and look around. This view you're already familiar with, since it's how you entered your data. Try it again now:

**1.** If Access isn't running, run it, of course.

**2.** Open the PHONEBK database using the File menu.

**3.** In the Database window, click on the Tables button.

**4.** Highlight Name and Address list and click on Open. After maximizing the Dataview window, the table should look like Figure 6.1.

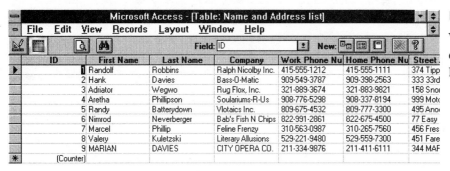

**FIGURE 6.1:**

Viewing all your data using Datasheet view

Unless you have a super-VGA screen (larger than normal) or some other type of higher-resolution screen, some of the fields (columns) are off the screen. On a standard VGA screen, only the first six fields are completely visible.

Luckily, you can browse (as well as perform many other Microsoft Access functions) in a selective manner, letting you tailor your listing to specific needs. For example, you can make only certain records visible. You can hide certain fields, and resize your text to squeeze more onto the screen or make it easier to read. You can also create screen "forms" that let you see one record's worth of data arranged in a vertical column rather than horizontally.

In many cases, displaying the data on a nonmodified datasheet is all you need to do to find the data you want. To do this though, you need to know how to move around on the screen. Here are a few exercises to try. Table 6.1 lists several other cursor-movement keys.

1. Press End. The cursor jumps to the far right of the current record, landing on the Notes field.

2. Press Home. This moves you to the first field in the current record.

3. Press Ctrl+Home. The cursor jumps to the first field in the whole table. Ctrl+End moves you to the last field.

4. Press Shift+Tab to move to the left one field at a time. Try the ← key. Same thing. Try Tab and →.

5. Move to a field using one of the arrow keys.

6. Press ↓ and ↑. These keys let you move between records.

7. Click on different records (rows). This is another way of moving between records.

8. Click anywhere on record number 3 (row 3). Look at the bottom row of the Datasheet window.

MILLS COLLEGE
LIBRARY

Notice that the current record number is shown. This number always tells you which record the cursor is on, and thus which record you're working with.

| KEY | EFFECT |
|---|---|
| Home | Moves to the first field in the current record |
| End | Moves to the last field in the current record |
| Tab, →, or Enter | Moves to the next field |
| Shift+Tab or ← | Moves to the previous field |
| ↓ | Moves to the current field in the next record |
| ↑ | Moves to the current field in the previous record |
| Ctrl+↓ | Moves to the current field in the last record |
| Ctrl+↑ | Moves to the current field in the first record |
| Ctrl+End | Moves to the last field in the last record |
| Ctrl+Home | Moves to the first field in the first record |
| PgDn | Moves down one screen |
| PgUp | Moves up one screen |
| Ctrl+PgDn | Moves right one screen |
| Ctrl+PgUp | Moves left one screen |

**TABLE 6.1:**

Navigating on the Dataview Screen

As you can see, your computer's screen is like a window through which you can see some, but not all, of the information in your table. Viewing the data is a bit like using a magnifying glass to read a newspaper, or like reading an ancient Egyptian scroll. In fact, moving right and left or up and down the screen is called *scrolling*. If you've used a word processing or spreadsheet program, you probably understand this concept already.

At this point, be sure all your data is entered correctly. If you need to make corrections, use the same procedure you used when you entered the data in the last Chapter. Just move to the field and type the correct information. ( If the whole ffield is highlighted, press F2 to get the text cursor to appear.) Use the Backspace key to erase any typing errors. We'll discuss the nitty-gritty of editing your data in Chapter 11.

# How to Jump to Specific Records

A powerful feature of Microsoft Access is that it allows you to search for and display selected records. You can specify the records you want Access to find in many different ways, as you'll learn in the following sections and in Chapter 8.

## SEARCHING BY RECORD NUMBER

In the same way that your eyes must focus on one line of text at a time when you read, Access is limited to focusing on just one table record at a time. The record that Access is aware of, or currently positioned on, is kept track of by the *record pointer.* The message on the status line indicates where the record pointer is located. For example, click anywhere on the first record, and you'll see the words *Record 1* on the status line.

This record number is used by Microsoft Access to keep track of your data in an orderly manner. Whenever you add a record to your table, it is automatically assigned a unique record number. In a large table, which may have thousands of records, record numbers can perform important functions. For example, Access allows you to link several tables together using record numbers to coordinate them.

You can also use record numbers to quickly find and display a record. You just type in the record number and have Access jump to it. Try the following exercise.

1. Double-click on the record number in the status line. Make sure to actually click on the number, not the word *Record*.

2. The current record number should be highlighted. Suppose we want to move the pointer to Randy Batterydown's record (number 5). Type in 5 and press ↵. The cursor lands on his record.

3. Now let's try another approach using the four small buttons surrounding the record number. These are like the buttons on a CD or cassette player.

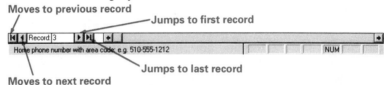

Try clicking on each one to see the immediate effect.

4. If you'd rather use menu commands instead of the little buttons, choose Records ➤ Go To. A drop-down menu appears:

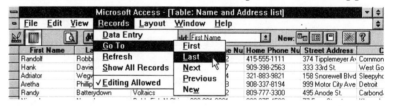

5. Click on Last. The highlight jumps to MARIAN DAVIES's record.

Now that you've started to use the menus quite a bit, you should know about a shortcut that makes opening menus easier at times. When you're moving around within a table, it may slow you down to take your hands off the keyboard to use the mouse. Using the shortcut, you can simply press the Alt key and the underlined letter of the menu you want to open. (This is standard Windows procedure, and if you're used to Windows, just skip this discussion.)

Here's an example. Pressing Alt+R opens the Records menu. You can then press the underlined letter of the command you want to use.

Pressing G, for example, opens the Go To submenu. Then pressing L jumps to the Last record. You don't have to press ↵. This method works with all menus.

## SEARCHING A FIELD FOR SPECIFIC INFORMATION

You may have noticed that the Edit menu has a choice called *Find*. If you suspected that this command can make short work of finding a specific record, you're right. When you only have a few records in a database, as we do, it's no big deal to find a specific record, and you can just move through them as we've been doing. But with lots of records, the Find command comes in real handy. With the Find command you can easily look up, say, John Doe's address if you need it, or search a table for that mysterious phone number you keep seeing on your telephone bill that you can't remember calling.

Find looks through the column the cursor is positioned on, beginning with the current record number, for whatever criteria you specify. A dialog box lets you set some other useful options, too.

Suppose you want to search for Nimrod's record so you can check his phone number:

**1.** Click on the First Name field of record 5.

**2.** Choose Edit ➤ Find (*or* click on the Binoculars button in the Toolbar *or* press F7).

**3.** A dialog box comes up:

| Find in field: 'First Name' | | |
|---|---|---|
| Find What: Nimrod | | Find First |
| Where: Match Whole Field | Direction | Find Next |
| Search In | ○ Up | |
| ◉ Current Field  ○ All Fields | ◉ Down | Close |
| ☐ Match Case    ☐ Search Fields as Formatted | | |

Notice that the current record's First Name, Randolf, is already entered. Since we want to search for Nimrod's record, just type **nimrod**. (You don't have to capitalize the *N*.)

**4.** Click on Find Next (or press ↵), and the highlight lands on Nimrod.

**5.** Click on the Find Next again, just for grins.

When Access reaches the end of the table, you'll get a message box about Access having reached the end of the *dynaset*. (I'll tell you more about dynasets later. For now just consider a dynaset the collection of records in your table.) The message box asks if you want to continue the search at the beginning of the table in order to check all the records. If you click on Yes, Access wraps around to the top of the table and works forward through the records until one meeting the search criteria is found, or until it reaches the record you started the search from.

If only one record matches, repeated searches will result in the message

**Microsoft Access reached the end of the dynaset.**

which, translated into English, means there aren't any more matching records.

## Upward and Downward Searching

Normally, Access searches from the current record down—that is, toward the end of the table. Sometimes you'll want to search from the current record toward the top of the table rather than in the normal direction, downward. Why? One example is that you may want to know if a record comes *before* or *after* the record you're currently on. Or you may be using a huge database and you know that the record you want is before the current record. Since the time it takes for a search is proportional to the number of records being searched, choosing the correct direction can speed things up.

To search upward from the current record, simply click on the Up button in the Direction section of the Find dialog box. A black dot appears next to Up. Then click on Find Next. Searching toward the top of the table works just like a downward search, only the search starts at the current record number and moves backward. When the top is reached you get a message box asking if you want to continue the search from the bottom of the table. If you click on Yes, the search continues until the starting record is reached.

## Searching All the Fields

If Access repeatedly fails to find a record, but you're pretty sure the record you're looking for is in the table, first make certain the cursor is in the correct field before you start the search, then try again.

If that doesn't solve your dilemma, maybe you're searching the wrong field. You could try each field separately, but that's a time-waster. When you don't know which field the data you're looking for is stored in, one of the options in the Find dialog box can come to the rescue. Though it will take longer (potentially *a lot* longer if you have many fields in your table), you can tell Access to scour all the fields of every record when looking for your data.

Here's an example. Suppose you remember something about a person whose name was Babs or worked at a place called Bab's—something having to do with Babs.

1. Move to the first record by pressing Ctrl+Home.

2. To start your search click on the Binoculars, press F7, or choose Edit ➤ Find—whichever you prefer.

3. Fill in the dialog box as you see in Figure 6.2. Notice I've clicked on the All Fields button, and that the Where box reads "Any Part of Field."

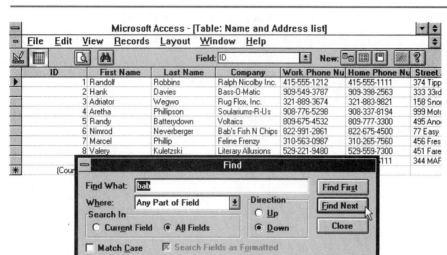

**FIGURE 6.2:**

Searching all
fields for an
occurrence of Bab

**4.** Click on OK. Bab is found in Bab's Fish N Chips, but you
may not be able to see it. You'll probably have to drag the
dialog box down a bit as I have in the figure. Grab it from
its title bar (the bar that reads "Find"). This is kind of a
goofy feature of Access. Your record may have been found
but you may not see it unless you move the dialog box
or look at the status line and see the message "Search
succeeded."

# MATCHING UPPERCASE
# AND LOWERCASE LETTERS

An otherwise correct search attempt may fail or produce duplicate
finds if you incorrectly specify capitalization requests in the Find
dialog box. Normally, Access considers uppercase and lowercase letters to be the same in search conditions: an *A* is the same as an *a*.

Thus, a search for *phillipson* will normally find *Phillipson*. An option in the Find dialog box can alter Access's behavior in this regard, however. Suppose you want to find Marian Davies, not Hank Davies. You can do this using the Match Case option.

1. Close the Find box by clicking on Close.

2. Move to the first record using the technique of your choice.

3. Move the cursor to the Last Name column.

4. Choose Edit ➤ Find. Fill in the box like this, making sure to turn on the Match Case option:

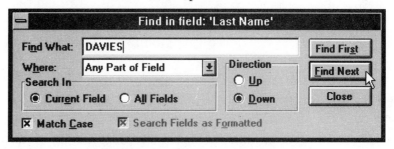

Notice that DAVIES is in all capitals.

5. OK the box and the cursor should move to Marian Davies's record, skipping Hank Davies's record. Why didn't the search find Hank? Because it was only looking for upper-case letters.

It's usually not too important to distinguish uppercase and lowercase letters in a search operation, since Access normally disregards case. But sometimes you can cut down on erroneous finds by using the Match Case option.

The contrary is true as well: if you can't find a record that you know is in your table, don't give up. Check the Match Case option. If it's on, turn it off and try again.

## How to Use Wildcards as Search Criteria

Sometimes you may not remember the complete spelling of a name you're searching for. Or you may want to broaden a search to look up, say, everyone whose phone number exchange is 777, regardless of the area code. This can be done using *wildcards*.

Wildcards are symbols that will match any text during a search. You use them in conjunction with normal search characters. For example, suppose you want to search for all Goldsteins, regardless of whether they are spelled with *i* before *e* or vice versa. You could just search for Gold and leave it at that, as long as the Where section of the dialog box was set to Any Part of Field. (When this option is set, Access doesn't care where in the field the searched data lives—it can be buried in the middle of it.) But this approach has a down side: you'll also find Goldblum, Goldman, and so on. To further narrow your search, you should use wildcards.

Access recognizes two wildcards: the question mark (?) and the asterisk (*). The ? represents one character, and the * represents any number of characters. You may be familiar with wildcard characters from using DOS, but there is one significant difference. When you use an asterisk in a string of characters in Access, the characters following the asterisk are not ignored. For example, **\*th** in Access will find Meredith, Smith, and Griffith. Or **\*Ave** will find all street addresses of people living on Avenues. With DOS, a command such as **DIR\*TH** would ignore the **th** and list all files.

Use the ? when you know the number of letters in the word you're looking for. Use the * when you're not sure of the number of letters. Searching for Goldst??n finds Goldstein, Goldstien, and even Goldstoon.

Suppose you want to see whose home phone number exchange (the first three numbers) starts with 777, regardless of area code. How would you do it?

**1.** Go to the first record.

**2.** Move to the Home Phone Number field.

**3.** Press F7 to start a search.

**4.** Fill in the box like this:

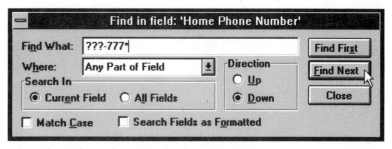

**5.** Click on Find Next. The status line should indicate the search was successful. Move the dialog box to see the result, record 5:

**809-777-3300**

**6.** Try the search again to see if any more records meet the criterion. Guess not, since you only get messages saying the end of the dynaset has been reached.

**7.** Close the Find box (tapping Esc is the fastest way).

**8.** Now move the cursor to the Company column in record 1 and do a search for the Literary Allusions company.

**9.** Press F7 again. Erase ???-777* and type **L*A***, like this:

Now press ↵. The cursor jumps to record 4, Soulariums-R-Us. Why? What's happened is that the *Where* option is set to look anywhere in a field, not necessarily starting at the beginning of the field. There's an *l* and an *a* in Sou*la*riums-R-Us, so it was found.

**10.** Continue the search by clicking again on Find Next (or pressing ↵). Now record 5, Voltaics, is found.

**11.** Search again, and record 8, Literary Allusions, is found.

Well, one out of three isn't bad, but in a large database this approach could have resulted in numerous erroneous finds, and lots of wasted time. Could we have done better? Sure. There are two fixes.

First off, you could turn on the Match Case option. Only capital L's and A's would be found. But let's try another approach using the Where options:

**1.** Close the box and move back to record 1.

**2.** Try the search again, but first click on the Where section in the dialog box (click right on the words *Any Part of Field*).

**3.** Three options appear from a drop-down list. Click on Start of Field to choose that option. This tells Access not to go looking for matches just anywhere in the field, but only from the start of the field onward.

**4.** Click on Find Next. This time Access jumps the highlight directly to record 8.

Remember to use Start of Field when you want to find something by specifying its first couple of characters—when you want to find *Lowenbrau*, *Lowenstein*, and *Lowe*, but not *Zilowski*. If you wanted to find only Lowe, an easier solution is just to choose Match Whole Field from the Where list. Choosing this option does an exact match, letter for letter. *Bob* will find Bob only—not Bobby.

FEATURING

**Hiding Columns**

**Sizing Columns**

**Moving Columns**

**Creating a Simple Data Form**

**Viewing a Form and Datasheet Simultaneously**

▼

# Changing Your Screen Display

Until now, you've been putting up with some inconveniences in the way the screen displays your data. You've had to deal with column headings and data being *truncated* (computer lingo for "cut off"), data that was off the screen, and fields displayed in the arbitrary order you added them to the structure.

Luckily, Microsoft Access lets you change the screen display so that it suits your needs. For example, you may want to rearrange the columns, hide certain fields from view, or decrease the width of some columns temporarily to see more of them at once. You might even want to create a form that lets you view all of the current record only, so you can add and edit records undistracted by other records or by having to scroll the screen left and right. In this chapter we'll experiment with how to do these things.

## Hiding Fields on a Datasheet

Sometimes you'll want to hide some fields from view because you don't want them printed out, because you don't want people to see what's in them (e.g., employee salaries), or just because they get in the way. If you are routinely working with just a few fields, you can hide all the others and not have to use the arrow keys as much. As you enter data, hidden fields will be left blank, but records will be added normally.

So far we really haven't used the ID field, and it's taking up a lot of room. Let's hide it for the time being.

1. Select the whole column by clicking on its *column selector bar* (the little tile at the top of the column) as shown in Figure 7.1. The whole column becomes selected.

| | Microsoft Access - [Table: Name and Address list] | | | | | | |
|---|---|---|---|---|---|---|---|
| _File_ _Edit_ _View_ _Records_ _Layout_ _Window_ _Help_ | | | | | | | |
| | | | Field: ID | | New: | | |
| ID | First Name | Last Name | Company | Work Phone Nu | Home Phone Nu | Street |
| 1 | Randolf | Robbins | Ralph Nicolby Inc. | 415-555-1212 | 415-555-1111 | 374 Tipp |
| 2 | Hank | Davies | Bass-O-Matic | 909-549-3787 | 909-398-2563 | 333 33rd |
| 3 | Adriator | Wegwo | Rug Flox, Inc. | 321-889-3674 | 321-883-9821 | 158 Snoi |
| 4 | Aretha | Phillipson | Soulariums-R-Us | 908-776-5298 | 908-337-8194 | 999 Moti |
| 5 | Randy | Batterydown | Voltaics | 809-675-4532 | 809-777-3300 | 495 Anoi |
| 6 | Nimrod | Neverberger | Bab's Fish N Chips | 822-991-2861 | 822-675-4500 | 77 Easy |
| 7 | Marcel | Phillip | Feline Frenzy | 310-563-0987 | 310-265-7560 | 456 Fres |
| 8 | Valery | Kuletzski | Literary Allusions | 529-221-9480 | 529-559-7300 | 451 Fare |
| 9 | MARIAN | DAVIES | CITY OPERA CO. | 211-334-9876 | 211-411-6111 | 344 MAF |
| (Counter) | | | | | | |

**FIGURE 7.1:**

To select a column click at its top.

**2.** Choose Layout ➤ Hide Columns. The column disappears!

**3.** Just to prove it's still there, choose Layout ➤ Show Columns.

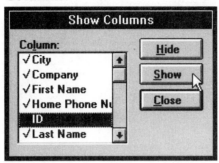

Notice that each field that's currently showing has a check next to it. The ID field doesn't since we've just hidden it.

**4.** Click on ID, then on Show, then on Close. The field column now returns to the display, just as it was before.

**5.** Now hide the ID field again.

As you might have guessed, you can use the Show Columns command to hide fields as well as show fields. Just use the box's Hide button. When you want to show or hide a bunch of fields in one fell swoop, use this command. Just click on each field, click on the appropriate button (Hide or Show), and click on Close. It's faster than hiding columns individually.

Now your screen looks like Figure 7.2. Notice that other field data has moved into view now.

# Resizing Your Columns

By default, Access made all the columns in your datasheet the same size, regardless of the field widths you declared when defining the table's structure. Occasionally you'll want to decrease the size of some columns on a datasheet to fit more fields on the screen. Note that

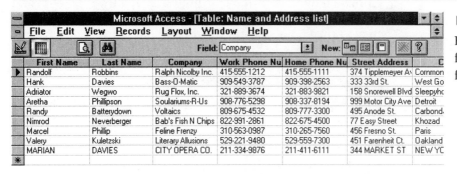

**FIGURE 7.2:**

Hiding the ID field makes room for other fields.

doing this doesn't change the size of the actual fields in the table—just its display. To change the actual size, you have to bring up the Table Design window and change the field properties as you did in Chapter 4. When a column's smaller than the data in it, you can still get to all the data, you just can't see it all at once. You have to use the arrow keys to scroll the data within the field.

Since Access is so graphically oriented, it's easy to change column width. You just use the mouse and drag the column's side. You can also do it from a menu if you don't like using the mouse, or don't have one. Let's experiment by shrinking the First Name and Last Name fields, since we've got some extra room to play with there.

**1.** Move the pointer up to the First Name column selector area, just as you did a minute ago.

2. Now move the pointer to the right edge of the selector bar (the column's edge) and notice that the pointer changes shape to a two-headed arrow.

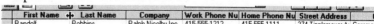

3. Press the mouse button and keep it down. Now drag the column dividing line to the left until it's approximately a space or two to the right of the longest name.

4. Now repeat the process for Last Name, Home Phone Number, and Work Phone Number.

5. Widen Street Address just a tad so that *Ave.* in record 1 fits in.

6. Decrease the size of the City and State columns. Depending on the size of your screen, resizing the State column may require getting the Zip Code field on-screen so you can grab the right column edge. Remember, the fast way to do this is by pressing End or using the scroll button in the lower right-hand corner of the Datasheet window.

7. Finally, decrease the Zip Code field. Leave the Notes field alone.

8. Now press Home to scroll the screen back to the left. It should look approximately like Figure 7.3. Don't lose sleep if it's not exact.

Of course, resizing has cut off some of the column names, but that's OK. There are enough left to see what each field is, and the advantage is that all your fields (except Notes) are now visible on a standard VGA screen without scrolling.

What if later you want to return one or all the fields to their original size? Just select a column, choose Layout ➤ Column Width, and in the dialog box set the Standard Width check box on.

**FIGURE 7.3:**

With fields resized, much more data fits on the screen.

Incidentally, there are limits to the widths of columns. If you try to make a column too wide or narrow for the type of data in the column, Access will alert you to the problem.

# Moving Columns

The last trick with columns I'll cover in this chapter is moving. Suppose you realize after creating a table that you'd like to group the columns differently. No problem. You can drag columns all over the place without having any effect on the structure of the table. Only the display is affected.

Let's take an example. Suppose in your particular line of work, you look up people by last name rather than by first. By reversing the order of the First Name and Last Name fields, you could more easily scan down the leftmost column for last names. Let's reverse the positions of these two columns.

1. Click on the selector bar at the top of the Last Name column. The pointer changes from a down arrow to a normal pointer, and the column becomes highlighted.

2. Position the pointer once again on the bar, and click and hold the mouse button down.

3. Drag the column to the left, on top of the First Name field. Notice that the pointer changes to a slightly different shape as you're doing this, as you see in Figure 7.4.

4. Release the mouse button. When you do, the column is repositioned, as you see in Figure 7.5.

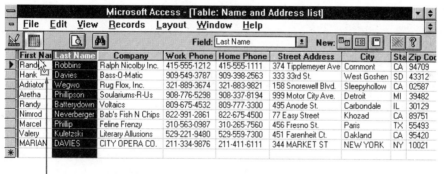

Drag the column name to the desired position.

**FIGURE 7.4:**

Dragging a column to a new location is simple. Select the column, click again, and drag it.

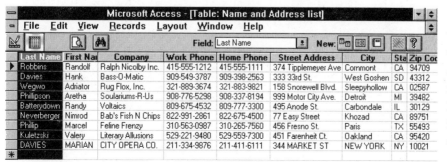

**FIGURE 7.5:**

Upon releasing the mouse, the columns are repositioned. Now Last Name is the first column.

If you prefer, you can move columns using the keyboard. Here are the steps:

1. Select the column.

2. Press Ctrl+F8. The letters *MOV* show up in the status bar at the bottom of the Datasheet window, indicating you're in MOVE mode.

3. Press → or ← to move the column. Each press moves the column immediately, jumping one column at a time. When you get it where you want it, stop using the arrow keys.

4. If you want to move an additional column, select it with the mouse and use → and ← as you just did. (MOVE mode stays active until you turn it off, so you don't have to press Ctrl+F8 again.) Continue moving columns to your heart's content.

5. Press Esc to get out of MOV mode, or else your keyboard won't work as it should. The MOV on the status line has to disappear for things to return to normal.

Now use either of the two moving techniques to return the Last Name field to its original position (column 2). We're going to need it there for later chapters.

1. Select the Last Name column.

2. Drag it to the right, or use the Ctrl+F8 key as outlined above to shove it back into position in the second column.

# Saving Your Datasheet Design

Whenever you make changes to the datasheet's layout, you should decide whether you want those changes to carry over to your next session. If you only want the changes in effect for the current session, then you don't have to do anything. But if you want them saved, you have to do the following:

1. Make the Datasheet window the active window. (Usually it already will be.)

2. Choose File ➤ Save Layout.

This saves the Datasheet's new properties, such as column locations and sizes (as well as some other properties that I'll talk about later, such as font size, grid lines, and row height) on the hard disk. The next time you view the table, the data will appear in the new format.

## OOPS! I DON'T WANT TO SAVE MY CHANGES!

Sometimes you'll futz around with a datasheet and then decide you don't want to save the changes you've made, either because you made some big mistake, or you only wanted to modify settings for a one-shot printout or session. No big deal. Here's what to do.

1. After you've made your changes, don't save the changes with the Save command on the File menu. Instead, choose File ➤ Close.

2. A dialog box will then appear, asking if you want to save changes to the form. Click No.

That's it.

## Creating a Simple Data Form

Depending on the size of your table, it can be a drag to enter and edit fields in the default columnar layout. If you've used other database programs, such as dBASE, Nutshell, Paradox, FileMaker, or others, you know that you can set up a form that displays one record at a time, with the fields placed vertically rather than horizontally. You can even dress up forms with instructions for data-entry people, with buttons for making multichoice entries (such as Mr., Mrs., and Ms.), for validation of data to prevent erroneous entries, and so on. I'll discuss these more advanced options later in the book. But in the meantime, I'll just show you how to set up a basic form. We'll use the Name and Address list.

1. The Name and Address list should still be open.

2. Choose File ➤ New ➤ Form.

3. You'll see the following dialog box:

4. Name and Address list should appear in the dialog box. Click the FormWizards button. Access has two "Wizards" built in—FormWizards and ReportWizards. Wizards is a name Microsoft dreamt up to describe fancy built-in commands that take the pain out of designing simple reports

and forms. Don't be thrown by the name, just click the Wizards button. You'll see:

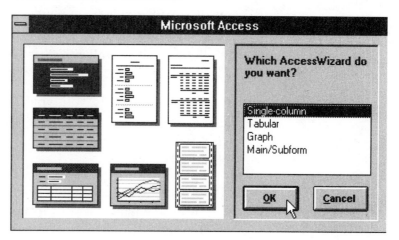

**5.** This dialog box is nice because it shows you the types of forms you can make. Unfortunately, they're not labeled. We want the one in the upper left corner, which is called a single-column form. With single-column form highlighted over the list box, click OK. The box shown in Figure 7.6 appears.

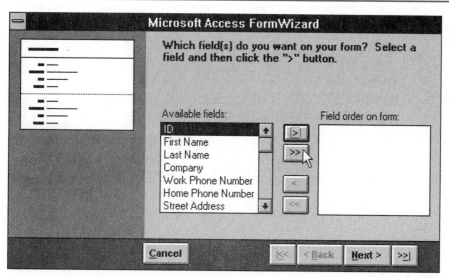

**FIGURE 7.6:**

In this box you choose which fields you want on your form. To add all the fields at once, click on the >> button. If you want to remove a few individual fields, just highlight each one and click on the < button.

**6.** Now you have to decide which fields you want on the form. You can pick and choose just as you can choose which fields to hide or show on your datasheet. You can add each field individually, but since we want to add all the fields, we'll just do it the quick way. Click on the >> button. Now all the field names jump to the right side of the box.

**7.** When using Wizards, you typically have to fill in several dialog boxes telling the Wizard what you want. You have to click on Next to move ahead to the next box of choices. Do this now.

**8.** The next box wants to know what groovy cosmetic effect you want the fields on your form to have. Click on each choice to see the effect displayed in the left side of the box. I'm going to choose Shadowed.

**9.** Click on Next. Now you're asked what name you want to give the new form, as shown in Figure 7.7. The name of the table is already typed in, and you can just use that if you want, but it won't be very descriptive. Add **single-column form** to the name.

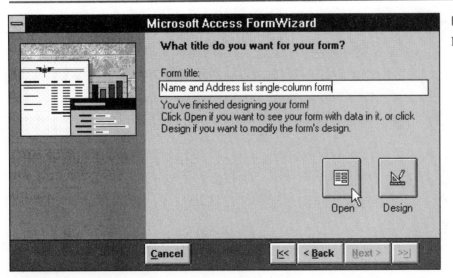

**FIGURE 7.7:**

Naming the form

**10.** Now you have two choices: Open and Design. Design lets you change the basic layout before Wizards creates the form. Open just creates the form. Click on Open. A little gauge will appear at the bottom of the Access window to indicate that things are being processed. Then a new window—the Form window—appears, as in Figure 7.8.

Notice that Access *cascaded* any open windows as a cleaning favor, which is why you see the Database window, the Datasheet window, and the Form window all lined up. Notice that the fields where the data is displayed are not all the same width as they were in the datasheet. Instead, they reflect the widths you chose back when you designed the table. Also observe that the name you just gave the form appears at the top of the window, and the message "Form View" appears on the message line at the bottom of the Form window.

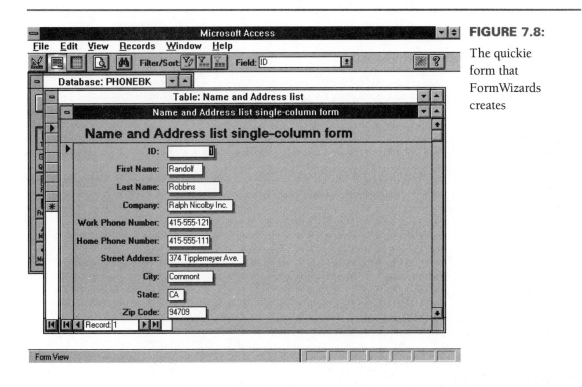

**FIGURE 7.8:**

The quickie form that FormWizards creates

Let's check out the new form a bit more:

1. Maximize the Form window. Now you can see the Notes field.

2. Press PgUp and PgDn. This moves you from record to record. The ID field at the top shows you what record you're on—a handy feature.

3. Try out the little arrow buttons at the bottom of the screen. They work just like the ones on the Datasheet window. You can jump to the first or last record, skip forward or backward a record, or enter a new number and press ↵ to jump to a specific record.

4. There's a new button in the Toolbar now, for Datasheet view.

This button makes it easy to jump to a datasheet-type view of whatever fields are in your form. Click it.

5. A datasheet appears. Click the button to the left of it (the one that looks like a form) and the form appears again.

Note that this Datasheet view isn't the same one you have seen before. Our Name and Address list is already displayed in another window, and it is still there. Clicking on the Datasheet button when you're using a form shows whatever fields your form includes, but in a tabular arrangement rather than as a form. Anything you stipulated when creating the form applies to this Datasheet view. For example, if you had chosen to add only a few fields to your form when you created it, switching to Datasheet view would have shown only those fields. In order to see the table's datasheet that we've been working with up to now, well, that's in a different window altogether. To see that, you have to open the Window menu and choose

**Table: Name and Address list**

which will bring up the whole table, unaffected by the form's design. This is one of those things that makes Access powerful and flexible, but a little confusing at first.

## SAVING YOUR FORM

We'll be using the Form view in a number of the subsequent chapters, so you'll have to save it.

**1.** Choose File ➤ Save Form.

**2.** In the resulting dialog box, type in the name as you see here:

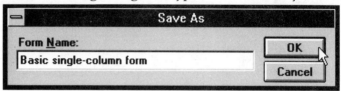

Then click OK.

**3.** Choose File ➤ Close. The window is closed, and you see the Database window, or the table's Datasheet window.

**4.** Just to check that your form was added to the database, choose Window ➤ Database. The name of the form you just created should now be listed on the right. If you click on Open, the form will open again, in a window.

So now you know how to create a simple form for viewing your data. This type of form comes in handy when you want to edit data too, as we'll discuss later.

## VIEWING A DATASHEET AND A FORM AT THE SAME TIME

Another neat feature of working with forms is that you can adjust your table's Datasheet and Form windows so that both are visible, giving you the best of both worlds. This lets you see records surrounding the record you're focusing on in Form view. Just minimize the Database window, then arrange the Form and Datasheet windows for best visibility.

Figure 7.9 shows an example. When you make changes, such as entering a new record or editing a record, in one window, the changes will be reflected in the other one. Sometimes you have to move off the altered record or you have to click on the changed field in the second window for the changes to take effect.

# USING A FORM WHEN CONDUCTING A SEARCH

You can also use forms to search for records. You already know how to conduct a search. We did it in the last chapter, using the Datasheet view. Try it now with the Form view.

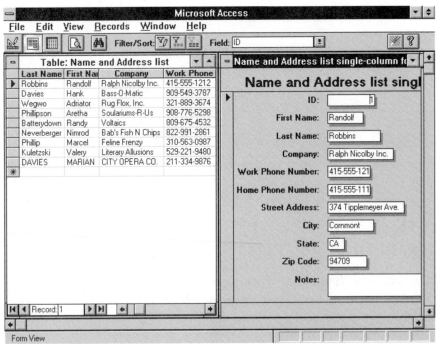

**FIGURE 7.9:**

You can display two views of the same data if you like. Altering records in either view updates the other.

1. Adjust the Form window so you can see all the fields.

2. Select the Form window by clicking on its title bar, or somewhere within the periphery of the window.

3. Choose Edit ➤ Find. Try conducting a search for someone, say, Randy Batterydown, using the rules you learned in Chapter 6. Figure 7.10 shows an example.

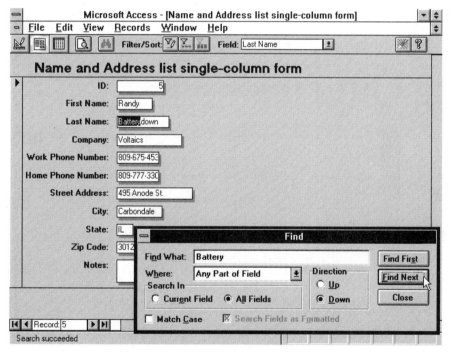

**FIGURE 7.10:**

You can search for data from a Form view just as you do from Datasheet view.

FEATURING

**The Query Design Screen**

**Running a Simple Query**

**Designing Conditional Queries**

**Using Wildcards to Broaden a Search**

**Saving a Query**
▼

# Using Queries

n earlier chapters, we've searched for records using only one criterion at a time, such as a person's last name. But without much difficulty, you can combine various criteria in the search conditions to achieve more complex and useful data extractions. In fact, you can select certain records in the database and create what appears to be a new temporary database of only those records that meet the criteria. This is unlike the searching we did in Chapter 6, which served only to move the cursor to a particular record.

For example, you can select the records of all people who live within a certain zip code range, or all customers with overdue payments, or all items in your inventory that cost over $100 and of which you have fewer than ten units in stock. Obviously, such searches are more complicated than searches for just a single record, like those we conducted in the last chapter. This type of search can involve combining several criteria from separate fields and using mathematical comparisons.

This process of selecting specific records can be done in Microsoft Access in two ways: *querying* or *filtering*.

## Queries in Access

Querying is the more powerful of these two options. Querying is achieved using Microsoft Access's Query Design screen. After you've created a query, you run it, applying it to the data in the source table. Since only certain records will meet the criteria of the query, the result is a subset of the table, called a *dynaset*. (This term was introduced in Chapter 6.) You can then view the dynaset's records, edit them, print them, and so on.

The dynaset isn't actually a table, though it looks like one. The records in the dynaset are lost when you close the query. But this is OK, since the tables the query was based on remain intact. When you run the query next time, even if data in your tables has been updated, the query's results will be accurate.

Using a query is like looking at the database from a certain angle. "Show me everyone who hasn't paid," "Show me everyone who lives in Massachusetts," and "List all new, unfilled orders" are examples of simple queries. More complex ones combine criteria, such as "Show me the people in Massachusetts who haven't paid."

Aside from culling out all unwanted records, the query can also remove unwanted fields from view, so the resulting dynaset doesn't distract you with data irrelevant to the task at hand.

The neat thing about queries is that they can be saved and run at any time, easily. And once you save a query, you can use it as the foundation for other Access objects. For example, you can run a report, print mailing labels, or use a form, using only the records the query extracts from a table.

A database can have any number of queries, giving the illusion of many separate tables, when actually there may be only one under- lying table of data. The query, then, is like a lens that sifts the data and displays only the records and fields that you need. In addition, as we'll see in later chapters, a query can include fields from several dif- ferent tables at once.

In this chapter, you'll be introduced to just the basics of query- ing—how to build up a query, how to run it, and how to save it.

## Filters in Access

Filters are similar to queries, but slightly different. Here's how. Some- times you just want to look quickly at a subset of records on a sort of ad hoc basis. You don't want to go through the hassle of creating a query and saving it, since you're not likely to use it again anyway. In situations like this, you'd use a filter. Filters can only be created from a form, but they're pretty easy to do, and good for spontaneous data searching. Queries, on the other hand, can be saved, and can be used as the foundation for other Access objects, which filters can't.

When deciding whether to use a filter or a query, ask yourself these questions:

- Will I need to generate this particular list of records again?

- Will I want to print mailing labels or a report using the records in the resulting list?

If the answer to either of these is Yes, then use a query. Other- wise, use a filter.

# How to Start a New Query

There are two basic sets of decisions you have to make when creating a query:

- Which fields you want to include

- What conditions you want to apply

Let's start by creating a query that displays all the records, but only certain fields. We won't use conditions to hide any particular records.

Suppose you want to see only the first name, last name, and company name for each record.

1. If you took a break after the last chapter, open the PHONEBK database using the File menu. If you're continuing from the last chapter and are already using the PHONEBK file, skip to step 2.

2. In the Database window, click on Query. Since you don't have any queries in this database yet, none appear in the list box to the right.

3. Click on the New button. This brings up the Query Design screen. Your screen should look something like Figure 8.1.

Notice that the window's title bar says

**Select Query: Query1**

This is the temporary name Access gave the query you're creating. We'll name it something else later when we save it. It says Select because that's the type of query we're making. There are three types of queries you can create:

- *Select queries* select certain records for your use.

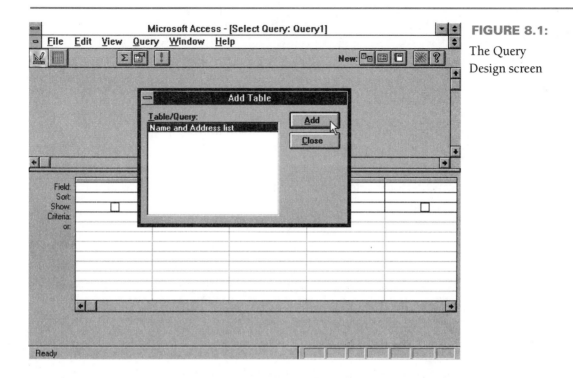

**FIGURE 8.1:**

The Query Design screen

- *Action queries* quickly make changes to multiple records in an automated fashion, such as decreasing all prices by 10%.

- *Crosstab queries* compile and convert data into a spreadsheet format.

Select queries are by far the most popular type, so we're going to focus on them. Later in the book I'll talk about action queries.

## PARTS OF THE SCREEN

The Query Design screen is a little confusing at first, so let's take a moment to examine it.

The first thing you have to tell Access is what table(s) you're going to be using in the query. That's why the dialog box in Figure 8.1 is there. All the tables in the current (open) database are listed in the box. Since we only have one table, you don't have to be a rocket scientist to make the right choice.

**1.** Click on Add. A little box listing our Name and Address fields pops onto the screen.

**2.** Click Close to get rid of the dialog box. You can see the whole Query Design screen.

Now take a look at the screen. The Query Design screen has two basic parts. The top part lists the fields in the table you're using: in this case, the Name and Address table. If you were adding more tables to the query, they'd show up to the right of the Name and Address list box.

The bottom part of the screen is where you specify the criteria that define the specific data you're looking for. For example, here you can ask Access to list all records for everyone who lives in a specific city, who has a salary of over $40,000, or whose last name is Smith. To search for everyone who lives in Seattle, for instance, you'd simply type the word **Seattle** in the City field. You just type an example of what you want Access to find for you, which is why this technique is called *query by example,* or QBE. QBE makes query creation easier, especially for complicated searches that combine several fields, such as listing the records of all people whose last names are between S and Z, who live in Seattle, and who have donated to the city zoo in the last five years.

## ADDING THE FIELDS

Now to create a query that lists just First Name, Last Name, and Company, the next thing to do is pick the fields we want displayed. As with almost everything in Access, there are about four ways to do this. We'll use the easiest.

1. In the first list, double-click on First Name. In a second, First Name appears in the lower section, in column 1 of the QBE grid.

2. Now double-click on Last Name in the field list. This adds Last Name to column 2. Access is smart enough to dump it into the second column.

3. Double-click on Company, and your screen should look like Figure 8.2. You've created the basis for the query.

4. Click on the Datasheet View button in the Toolbar (second one from the left). Access will process your query, and after a few seconds, deliver you a datasheet with the requested info, as in Figure 8.3. Notice that only three fields now appear on the screen.

## REARRANGING THE ORDER OF FIELDS

Now let's modify the field list using the same fields, but this time with the fields in this order: Company, First Name, Last Name. You could create a new query, but it's easier to modify the existing one. You can move the fields by dragging them around on the Query Design screen.

1. Click the Design button (farthest to the left) to return to the Query Design screen.

2. Position the mouse pointer just above the Company field, on the little bar. The cursor will change to a down arrow. Then click. This selects the field and the normal pointer returns.

**FIGURE 8.2:**

Three fields added to the query grid

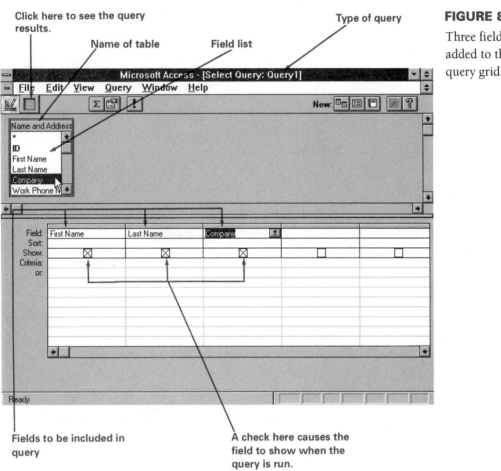

Click here to see the query results.

Name of table

Field list

Type of query

Fields to be included in query

A check here causes the field to show when the query is run.

**3.** Drag the field all the way to the left, and release. This puts Company in first position and kicks the other two fields to the right.

**4.** Run the query by clicking on the Datasheet button. The resulting dynaset looks like Figure 8.4.

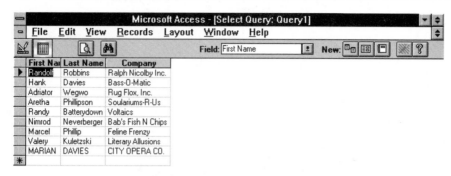

**FIGURE 8.3:**

The query results, showing only three fields

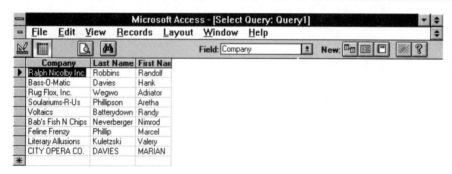

**FIGURE 8.4:**

Dynaset with Company as the first field

You might now want to experiment with various arrangements of listings on your own. Try choosing different fields and listing them in a variety of orders.

# How to List Records That Meet a Specified Condition

Right now you may feel as though you paid several hundred dollars for a program that simply lists data in pretty much the form you entered it, giving you information you could have obtained from manually written records. True, you've been able to select which fields are displayed, but what if you want to impose more particular conditions on your listing: to select only people who live in California or who work for a certain company or who have a specific name? To do this kind of a search, you

have to enter criteria into the Criteria line of the QBE grid.
Let's look at some examples.

## ADDING MORE FIELDS

Let's start by altering the fields a bit.

**1.** Return to the Query Design screen and move the Company
field back to position 3. You have to drop it to the *right* of
the Last Name field in the QBE grid.

Select the field and drag from  here to here.

The other fields move left to take up the space.

**2.** Move up to the field list and double-click on City to enter
that as field 4.

**3.** Repeat for the State and Zip Code fields, making them
fields 5 and 6. (You can't see the Zip field unless you scroll
the grid to the left, but that's OK. It's been entered). Now
you have some more data to work with. When you run the
query this time, it should look like Figure 8.5. I've adjusted
the column widths a bit so the full field names are readable.
You might want to do the same.

## ENTERING SOME CRITERIA

Now suppose you want to list only those people who live in California. To do this, you have to put a *criteria expression* in the State field.

**FIGURE 8.5:**

| First Name | Last Name | Company | City | State | Zip Code |
|---|---|---|---|---|---|
| Randolf | Robbins | Ralph Nicolby Inc. | Cornmont | CA | 94709 |
| Hank | Davies | Bass-O-Matic | West Goshen | SD | 43312 |
| Adriator | Wegwo | Rug Flox, Inc. | Sleepyhollow | CA | 02587 |
| Aretha | Phillipson | Soulariums-R-Us | Detroit | MI | 39482 |
| Randy | Batterydown | Voltaics | Carbondale | IL | 30129 |
| Nimrod | Neverberger | Bab's Fish N Chips | Khozad | CA | 89751 |
| Marcel | Phillip | Feline Frenzy | Paris | TX | 55493 |
| Valery | Kuletzski | Literary Allusions | Oakland | CA | 95420 |
| MARIAN | DAVIES | CITY OPERA CO. | NEW YORK | NY | 10021 |

Getting ready to execute conditional queries

1. Bring up the Query Design screen again by clicking on the Design button.

2. Click on the Criteria line of the State field in the QBE grid.

3. Since we want to list people who live in California (or CA) type **CA** in the State field, as in Figure 8.6.

If you've used other database programs before you might be concerned about how the *CA* is entered. Most other programs require special treatment of criteria, such as using quotation marks around words ("CA"). Access is very forgiving in this regard (a welcome feature), ensuring that your queries will usually work as you intended! You can enter criteria in any of these ways and Access will know what you mean:

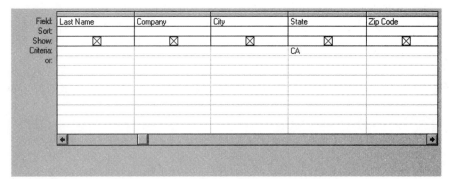

**FIGURE 8.6:**

Entering criteria for the State field so that the query creates a dynaset listing only residents of California

- CA

- =CA

- "CA"

- ="CA"

Of course, if you're searching for numerical data, you don't use quotation marks. That way, Access knows you are entering values, not characters. But I'll discuss numbers more later.

What about capitalization? You may recall from the last chapter when we tried to find MARIAN DAVIES's record using the Search command, capitalization usually isn't important. Similarly, it's not important to distinguish between uppercase and lowercase letters in queries. Confusion because of incorrect case specification in records or queries, though often a problem with other programs, isn't with Access. So you could have entered any of these:

- Ca

- =Ca

- "Ca"

- ="Ca"

- ca

- =ca

- "ca"

- ="ca"

and gotten away with it.

Now click on the Datasheet button again to run the query. The listing should look like Figure 8.7. Again, I've adjusted the field widths a bit for visibility. Incidentally, the field sizes that Access uses

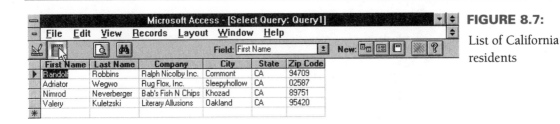

**FIGURE 8.7:**

List of California residents

when running a query are taken from the source table. Since we adjusted the sizes there, they keep being reflected in our query datasheets.

## IF ACCESS CAN'T FIND ANY RECORDS

If Access can't find any records that meet your criteria, you'll see a screenful of nothing. Just one empty record shows up on the screen. This means that Access searched the whole file, from the end to the beginning, but couldn't find any records that met your criteria.

For example, try entering **ZZ** into the State field to see what happens:

**1.** Return to the QBE design screen.

**2.** Enter **ZZ** into the State criteria line.

**3.** Run the query. You'll see the following:

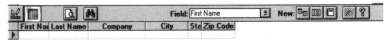

## USING LIKE AND WILDCARDS IN A QUERY

Now let's try a search that's a little trickier. Suppose you want to look up one person to find an address. For example, how would you find

Marcel Phillip's address? Create the query yourself, and then compare your solution with the one presented here.

1. Return to the Query Design screen and erase the *CA* by selecting it and pressing Del.

2. Move the highlight to the Last Name field and type **Phillip**.

3. Click on the Datasheet button to see the data:

| Marcel | Phillip | Feline Frenzy | Paris | TX | 55493 |
|--------|---------|---------------|-------|-----|-------|

Now what if you want Aretha Phillipson's record to show up too, since the first seven letters of Marcel and Aretha's last names are the same? For this sort of query, you need to use a wildcard. (Recall from the last chapter that Access uses * and ? as wildcards.) A match using wildcards, sometimes called an *inexact match,* is useful, for example, if you want to list all people whose last names begin with a certain letter. Here's how to perform an inexact match.

1. Return to the Query Design screen.

2. In the Last Name field, erase the old filter and then enter

   **Phillip***

   to tell Access to display any name beginning with Phillip and followed by any other characters.

3. Click on the Datasheet button to see the effects. Two records appear:

| Aretha | Phillipson | Soulariums-R-Us | Detroit | MI | 39482 |
|--------|------------|------------------|---------|-----|-------|
| Marcel | Phillip | Feline Frenzy | Paris | TX | 55493 |

**4.** Return to the Query Design screen. Notice that the criteria you typed in now reads

**like "Phillip*"**

The word *like* is Access's pattern-match operator. It tells the query that you're going to use the wildcard * or ? (or both) in your query example for that field. Access adds the *like* in order to process the request. You can type it in if you like, but either way works.

You can also use the ? wildcard in queries. For example, you might want to find all people living in zip code areas beginning with the numbers 947:

**947??**

Similarly, you could use the ? to find all people whose last names are five letters long and begin with the letter *S*:

**S????**

Remember that the ? represents one character (letter or number in a character field), and the * represents any number of characters.

Here's the list of wildcards you can use, and what they find:

| | |
|---|---|
| * | Zero or more characters |
| ? | A single character of any type |
| # | Any single numeral (0 through 9) |

Unlike some database programs, Access unfortunately doesn't have a "sounds-like" function, sometimes called a "soundex" search. So you can't set up a query that will search for, say, Marcel by accidentally spelling it Marselle, Marsel, Marcelle, or even, as a long shot, Marshall. Or to list Bernsteins along with Bernstiens. You'll have to use wildcards in such cases where spellings might vary or when you can't remember the exact spelling.

## IF YOU MAKE A MISTAKE ENTERING CRITERIA

Sometimes Access will barf on what you've entered into a query criteria line. You've probably had this happen to you already, during these experiments. Before Access tries to run a query, or even lets you move to another field to enter more criteria, it checks the validity of the most recently entered criteria. If Access can't recognize what you've typed, you'll see this message:

Just click on OK. Then go back and fix up the criteria. You entered something wrong. The word that Access had trouble with will be highlighted to help you figure it out.

## How to Save a Query

Before ending this chapter's exercises, we'll save the query you've designed so you'll have it on disk for later use. Remember, query files aren't another copy of the database; they simply store the conditions you defined when you designed the query. As mentioned earlier, a given database can have many queries associated with it.

To save this query:

**1.** Choose File ➤ Save, or if you're on the Datasheet view of the query, choose File ➤ Save Query.

2. A dialog opens asking for the name of the query:

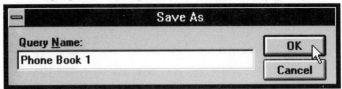

3. Type **Phone Book 1** as you see here and click OK. The query is saved. When you're taking a lot of time to create a query, don't forget to do this saving process early on, and repeat it while you're working to prevent accidental loss of the query should something untoward occur.

4. Close the Query window and return to the Database window by choosing File ➤ Close. Notice that the Database window now lists Phone Book 1 in the Queries list. Your query has been added to the PHONEBK database.

The advantage of saving a query is that you can quickly have Access display the various permutations of a database that you use regularly, without having to wade through all your records. All you have to do is select it from the Database window.

For example, suppose you want to put the names and addresses of both your friends and business customers in the Name and Address table. You could add another field that indicates whether the person is a friend, a customer, or both. Then you could create two queries, one for friends and one for customers, and save them to disk. Once that's done, you can easily select the part of the database that you want to use while still keeping all the data together, so you don't have to duplicate the records of people who are both friends and customers.

FEATURING

**Combined Search Conditions**

**Finding Records with Empty or Full Fields**

**Finding Unique Values**

▼

# Combining Search Criteria

n the last chapter, we explored some of the simpler approaches to retrieving information from a typical table using queries based on data in a single field. In this chapter, we'll try some more sophisticated techniques, many of which involve using criteria from more than one field.

# How to Combine Search Criteria

The Query Design screen lets you combine criteria in single or multiple fields without much difficulty. Using a single field, for example, you can have Access not only pick out people who live in California, but also list the people who live in California or Nevada or Colorado. Using two fields, you can create a query to have Access list any New York residents who also have the last name of Davies. Because you can combine as many fields as you want, the possibilities are virtually endless, particularly when you are working with complex tables consisting of many fields, or when you're drawing upon fields from several tables.

The first step in creating complex queries is to understand how Access analyzes your requests. The rules that Access uses to analyze your criteria use *relational operators,* so called because their job is to relate the data to the criteria and to produce a result. This result is always a yes or a no: Does this person live in New York (yes or no)? Is this customer's balance more than $1000 (yes or no)? Of the several different kinds of operators, you'll have to choose the one that best fits the situation.

For example, when you're working with numbers, chances are you'll be using a group of relational operators called *comparison* operators. These are listed here.

| | |
|---|---|
| = | Equal to |
| <= | Less than or equal to |
| < | Less than |
| > | Greater than |
| >= | Greater than or equal to |
| <> | Not equal to |

So far the only operator we've used is the equal-to operator. The equal-to operator is useful when you are looking for a particular string of characters, such as a name or a state. Access used the equal-to operator to search for the records we specified in the last chapter. For example, when we queried the table for everyone who lived in California, Access internally used the formula *State = "CA"* to find the records. However, all you had to do was type CA in the State field on the query screen; Access did the rest.

# USING LOGICAL OPERATORS TO COMBINE RELATIONAL EXPRESSIONS

In complex queries with criteria in several fields, or several criteria in a single field, you can tell Access to combine your criteria using *logical operators*. The three logical operators are AND, OR, and NOT. Don't worry that this sounds like computer gobbledygook. It's not really that complicated. Here's what the operators do:

- You use AND to combine two expressions when both must be true for a record to qualify—for example, when you want to select only records with the last name Smith *and* the city New York.

- You use OR when only one or the other expression must be true for a record to qualify—for example, when you want to select records with the state either New York *or* California.

- You use NOT to display all the records that do not meet the criteria—for example, all people who live in a state that is *not* California.

The names of these operators aren't that important to know. What is important is to realize that you'll be using these concepts to root out records from your table. We actually use these concepts every day, so don't let them throw you. Here are some examples of the AND and OR operators in action.

## Combining Criteria with AND

Suppose you want to see all the records of people who have a zip code between 30129 and 60000. Such a query would require combining two criteria: For a record to qualify, its zip code must be both greater than 30129 *and* less than 60000. You must use two relational operators (greater than and less than) and one logical operator (AND). Here's how to create this query:

1. If you have taken a break, get to the Database window and click the Queries button.

2. With the highlight on the Phone Book 1 query, click the Design button just above it. This opens the query on the Query Design screen. You use this button when you want to modify a query without first running it.

3. Clear out anything left in the criteria row of the QBE grid from last session. The easiest way to do this for all the fields, even ones you can't see, is to position the pointer on the left edge of the leftmost column (First Name) and move it slightly until it turns into a right-facing arrow. Then click. The whole row will become selected. Press Del to clear it.

4. Tab to the Zip Code field and enter

    **>30129 and <60000**

    Be sure to include a space before and after the AND. Quotation marks will appear after you move off the field by clicking elsewhere or when you run the query. This is because even though the Zip Code field has numbers in it, it's a Character field. Your screen should look like Figure 9.1.

5. Click on the Datasheet button to see the result of the query. You should see the records shown in Figure 9.2.

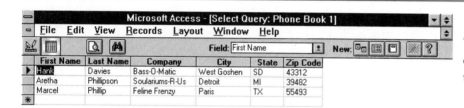

**FIGURE 9.1:**
Query for a zip code between 30129 and 60000. Notice that you use the AND operator to select a range of records.

**FIGURE 9.2:**
The result of the query in Figure 9.1

See how the combined search criteria worked? The AND between the two expressions told Access that a record's zip code must be greater than 30129 *and* less than 60000.

Here's a little shortcut for the same result. Access has a built-in operator called BETWEEN...AND that makes finding a range of records a little easier. Instead of using the formula you just entered, you could have used this one in the Zip Code column.

**between 30130 and 60000**

Since it's a little more like English and a little less like math, you might prefer this approach. However, because the endpoints in this command are inclusive, you have to adjust them a bit. This command is really analogous to

**=>30130 AND =<59999**

## Using OR

Now let's look at the OR operator. Instead of both requirements having to be true for a record to be listed, only one has to be true. For instance, suppose you want to list either people who live in Illinois *or* people who live in Texas. You could create two lists, one for each state, just as in the last chapter we listed people living in California. But Access provides a faster way. All you have to do is enter the two conditions separated by the OR operator, like this:

1. Return to the Query Design screen.

2. Clear the criteria in the Zip Code field by selecting it and pressing Del. You can drag the text cursor across the text to select it just as in a word processor, but here's an easier way to clear a field. Just click on the field. Then press F2. This changes the way the cursor works. It doesn't let you edit any fields, but it selects the whole field so you can replace it by typing, or delete it by pressing Del. Incidentally, pressing F2 again puts the cursor back in normal editing mode. Keep this trick in mind when editing data in your tables, because it works the same way.

3. Move to the State field and type

   **IL or TX**

   Your screen should look like Figure 9.3.

4. Click the Datasheet button to see the results. Your screen should look like Figure 9.4.

By now you should be getting the idea. When you want to use the AND operator in a single field, you list the criteria separated by an AND, such as we did in the previous section when we entered >30129 AND <60000. When you want to use the OR operator, you enter the criteria separated by an OR.

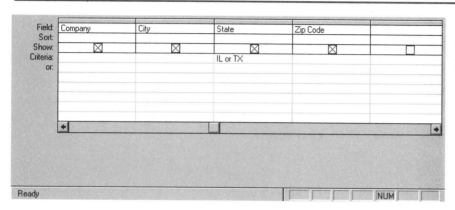

**FIGURE 9.3:**

Querying for Illinois or Texas

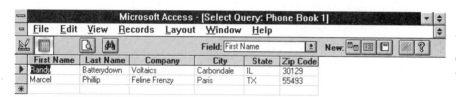

**FIGURE 9.4:**

The result of the query in Figure 9.3

Things get trickier when you want to use more than one field, as you'll see in the next section.

## Using AND and OR in Different Fields

Suppose you want to use AND and OR with criteria that apply to two different fields rather than a single field. For example, suppose you want Access to list everyone whose first name starts with A *and* whose zip code falls between 30129 and 60000. To do this, you put the criteria for both fields on the same line. Only the First Name and Zip Code fields contain data; all other fields are blank. Thus, the query would take the following form:

| First Name | Zip Code |
|---|---|
| A* | between 30129 and 60000 |

Remember, the * is a wildcard, as discussed in Chapter 7.

By contrast, when you want to find records with one criterion *or* another criterion (in different fields), you put the second criterion on a separate line. For example, to list everyone whose first name is Adriator or whose last name is Phillipson, you set up the query like this:

**First Name**      **Last Name**

**Adriator**

                    **Phillipson**

Take this last one out for a spin:

1. Get back to the Query Design screen.

2. Fill it in as you see in Figure 9.5.

Running this query will result in the following records, as you may have guessed:

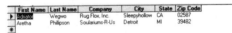

The Query Design screen's logical operators are especially helpful when you are working with a large table. For example, suppose that our table gets very large, and we want to look up Sally Jones.

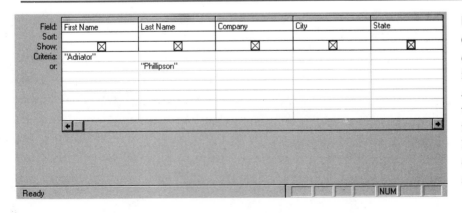

**FIGURE 9.5:**

Querying for everyone whose first name is Adriator *or* whose last name is Phillipson. Notice that the criteria go *on separate lines.*

Chances are good that there is more than one Sally and more than one Jones. Typing the names on the same line under their respective fields solves the problem. Simply tell Access to look for a first name of Sally *and* a last name of Jones:

**First Name**    **Last Name**

**Sally**          **Jones**

## Using the NOT Operator

Use the NOT operator to root out records that *don't* fit the criteria to stipulate. For example, you might want to list everyone *except* those living in a certain state, having certain phone number area codes, or

| Field: | First Name | Last Name | Company | City | State |
|---|---|---|---|---|---|
| Sort: | | | | | |
| Show: | ☒ | ☒ | ☒ | ☒ | ☒ |
| Criteria: | | Not "davies" | | | |
| or: | | | | | |

something similar. To use the NOT operator, type **not** or put the <> signs in front of the criteria, like this:

| Field: | First Name | Last Name | Company | City | State |
|---|---|---|---|---|---|
| Sort: | | | | | |
| Show: | ☒ | ☒ | ☒ | ☒ | ☒ |
| Criteria: | | <>"davies" | | | |

Either of these examples would list all people except those whose last name is Davies. Another way to think of it is that it will list everyone whose name is *not* Davies. (Of course, the quotes are not necessary, and capitalization isn't important.) The result is shown in Figure 9.6.

# COMPLEX QUERIES

Some combinations are too complex for the normal QBE format to handle. For example, suppose that you're conducting an environmental impact study and are using a table to store all your findings. Suppose, after all the data is in, that you want to know all the sites where there are oil pipelines, natural gas pipelines, *or* nuclear power plants, *and* where there are deer, elk, *or* bison that might be affected by these installations. Or suppose, using our phone list, you want to

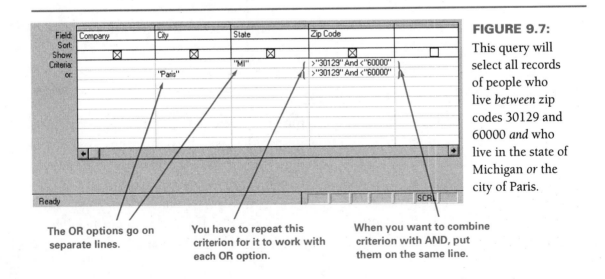

**FIGURE 9.6:**
You use the NOT operator to list records that do *not* meet the criteria you specify.

query for anyone *between* zip codes 30129 and 60000 *and* who live in the state of Michigan *or* the city of Cornmont?

For these types of queries, you have to get creative on the QBE grid. This often requires some repetitive typing, duplicating some entries on several lines. Figure 9.7 shows an example, with the results in Figure 9.8. (I've used the < and > operators in the Zip Code field so the whole formula shows but of course the BETWEEN operator would have worked too.)

In general, there's no easy way to remember how to combine ANDs and ORs like this except by a little practice, or by trial and error. Trial and error is risky on large databases though, since you

**FIGURE 9.7:**
This query will select all records of people who live *between* zip codes 30129 and 60000 *and* who live in the state of Michigan *or* the city of Paris.

The OR options go on separate lines.

You have to repeat this criterion for it to work with each OR option.

When you want to combine criterion with AND, put them on the same line.

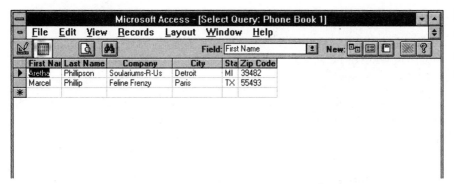

don't always know if a query is giving you all the records you requested. The best bet is to review some book examples when you're constructing your queries, and to follow these rules:

- If you want to select records meeting this OR that criteria in a single field, put it on the first Criteria line in a single box like this: **MI or NY**.

- If you want to select records meeting this AND that criteria, and the criteria are from separate fields (e.g., "payment overdue" AND "lives in New York"), put the criteria on the same line (the Criteria line) in different columns. If the criteria are from a single field (e.g., >30129 AND <60000), they both go in the same box.

- If you have to combine ORs and ANDs, they have to go on separate lines. This usually means you have to repeat a condition. For example, if we hadn't repeated the Zip Code criteria on the second line in Figure 9.7, it wouldn't have been applied to Paris.

## Listing Only Records Whose Fields Are Filled In

Sometimes you'll want to select only records that have a certain field filled in. For example, perhaps you have a database with a field indicating whether a person has a work phone number so that they can be called during the day, or you have a field indicating how much they have donated to your church in the past year. In the first case, you don't want to list people who don't have work phones. In the second case, you may want to list everyone who hasn't donated, so you can call them, with the hope of a donation.

Access has a built-in operator that looks for blank fields. You can put this operator to use in queries. Here's how it works.

Suppose you wanted to see all the records for people who don't have any notes typed into their Memo fields. Here's what you would do.

1. Clear out any existing query information.

2. Add the Notes field to the query design by moving into the upper area of the query and double-clicking on Notes.

3. Enter the following into the Note column in the query.

   **Is Null**

   *Is null* means "is empty."

4. Now run the query.

Figure 9.9 shows the query in the upper half with the results in the lower half.

When you want to do just the reverse—that is, you want to select records in which a specific field does contain some data (any data), use the criteria

   **Not Null**

instead of Is Null.

# Listing Only Records Whose Fields Are Unique

One more trick. Occasionally you'll want to select only records that have a unique value in a given field. For example, say you have a table of inventory items. The table contains a field listing the company that supplies each part. One day you want to see a list of all the companies you deal with, but not every inventory part. No problem. You just use the Unique Values Only option in the Query Properties dialog box.

Here's an example we can run using the Name and Address list. Suppose you want to see which states your people are in, but don't care how many of them there are, just how many different states.

**1.** Remove all the fields except the one you want to show unique values for. This is because the whole displayed row has to be unique for this to work. Since we have several people in the same state, but their names are different, all the records will show up if you don't eliminate all the fields except State from

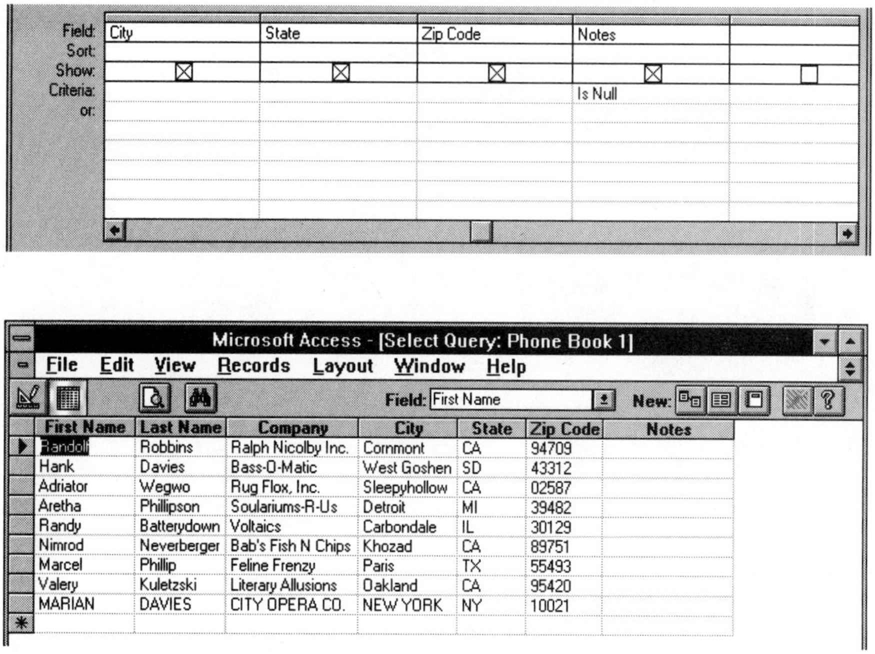

**FIGURE 9.9:**

You can find records with an empty field using the IS NULL criteria in the appropriate field. All records with an empty Notes field will appear, as you see in the lower half of this figure.

the query. You remove a field by moving the cursor to the top of the field until you see the down arrow. Then click and press Del.

**2.** Use the → and ← keys to make sure that only State is in the QBE grid.

**3.** Now click on the Query Properties button or choose View ➤ Query Properties. The pointer is on the button in Figure 9.10.

**4.** Turn on the Unique Values Only check box by clicking on it.

**5.** Click OK in the dialog box.

**6.** Run the query. The results are shown in Figure 9.11.

**7.** You'll want to make sure to turn off the Unique Values setting unless you really want it. It will screw up future modifications to this query if you are not careful. So, return to

**FIGURE 9.10:**

To see unique values for a field, create a query with the unique field(s).

**FIGURE 9.11:**

The results of the query. Note that no state names are repeated.

the design screen, open the dialog box again and turn the setting off.

**8.** Now close the query from the File menu, and choose No when asked about saving changes. I don't want you to save the changes since we've removed most of the fields.

FEATURING

Primary Keys

Sorting Records
from a Query

Sorting Records
with a Filter

Creating Indexes
to Speed Up
Sorts

▼

# Sorting Records for Faster Access

The order of the records in most tables, even our short phone book table, is often haphazard. For example, you didn't enter the phone book records in alphabetical order, or even in zip code order. And when you displayed your data, it simply appeared on the screen in the order in which you had entered it, as follows.

| ID | FIRST NAME | LAST NAME | STREET ADDRESS | ZIP CODE |
|----|-----------|-----------|----------------|----------|
| 1 | Randolf | Robbins | 374 Tipplemeyer Ave. | 94709 |
| 2 | Hank | Davies | 333 33rd. St. | 43312 |
| 3 | Adriator | Wegwo | 158 Snorewell Blvd. | 02587 |
| 4 | Aretha | Phillipson | 999 Motor City Ave. | 39482 |
| 5 | Randy | Batterydown | 495 Anode St. | 30129 |
| 6 | Nimrod | Neverburger | 77 Easy Street | 89751 |
| 7 | Marcel | Phillip | 456 Fresno St. | 55493 |
| 8 | Valery | Kuletski | 451 Fahrenheit Ct. | 95420 |
| 9 | MARIAN | DAVIES | 344 MARKET ST | 10021 |

Typically, records are added to databases as they become available, and as a result, they are stored in a more or less random order. However, there are times when you will want to rearrange an entire table into an order that suits a specific purpose. For example, consider the telephone book you receive from the phone company. Once all new data has been added for a year, the phone company prints its table in alphabetical order according to name, and that is the listing you see in your phone book. This form of organization lets you easily look up people's phone numbers.

Access provides a couple means of reordering your records:

- You can change the primary key from the Table Design window.

- You can sort the table using the Sort line on the Query Design window.

■ You can sort using a filter (from a Form window).

We'll experiment with all of these.

## Making a New Table for Sorting Experiments

The previous chapters used a telephone book table for examples. But for this chapter, let's create a new table that contains a list of items to take along on a camping trip.

1. Create a new database by getting to the Database window and choosing File ➤ New Database. If you're having trouble getting to the Database window, try opening the Window menu and choosing Database from there. Also, pressing Ctrl+F6 will jump you from window to window in a round-robin fashion in Access, just the way it does in many other Windows programs, such as 1-2-3 or Microsoft Word.

2. In the resulting file box, name the database **Camping** and press ⏎. You may be asked about saving changes to your Name and Address table, and to any open queries. This is because only one set of tables and queries (one database) can be open at a time. Since you're creating a new one, Access is doing the housekeeping of closing up PHONEBK. You can answer no to these questions.

3. When the new Database window appears, check that the Tables button is depressed and click on New.

4. For the new table, enter the structure shown in Figure 10.1. Notice that Weight is a Number field and Cost is a Currency field, the first ones so far in this book.

5. After entering the field names, types, and descriptions, go back and edit the field properties so that Item and Owner have a field size of 10.

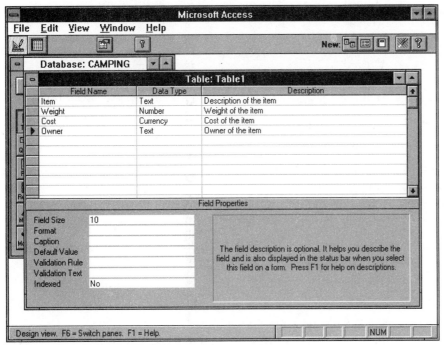

Forget how to change the settings? Click on the appropriate field name in the upper half of the window, then on the Field Size or Decimal Places lines in the lower half of the window. Then type in the property, or choose it from the drop-down list. (Open the list by clicking on the little drop-down list box button that appears after you click on the Field Size or Decimal Places lines.)

**6.** Choose File ➤ Save. Type in a description such as this:

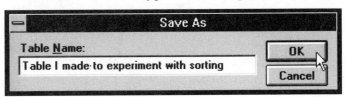

**7.** Click No when asked about creating a primary key.

**8.** Click on the Datasheet button and add the following records:

| ITEM | WEIGHT | COST | OWNER |
|------|--------|------|-------|
| Backpack | 10 | 60.00 | Rich |
| Stove | 25 | 85.00 | Rich |
| Tent | 12 | 62.33 | Lisa B. |
| Food | 30 | 45.27 | Group |
| Rain Gear | 7 | 12.95 | Renee |
| Flashlight | 2 | 7.50 | Jean |
| Hammock | 5 | 15.00 | John |

**9.** When you're finished, your screen should look like Figure 10.2.

Well, almost like Figure 10.2. Actually, I've made my screen a bit more readable by changing the font, or typeface, the data is displayed in. You can do the same if you like, by opening the Layout menu and choosing Font. Then choose the font you like. I've chosen Arial 10-point Bold, as you can see in Figure 10.3. Enlarging the font makes sense only when you don't have too much data to fit on the screen. Otherwise, unless you have a large monitor (screen), you'll have to scroll around too much.

You may have noticed that you didn't have to enter the dollar signs or the final zeros in numbers like $60.00 or $7.50 in the Cost field. Since the Cost field has a Currency data type, Access can do that for you. All you have to type is 60 or 7.5 and move on to the next field, and all is done for you. Just be sure to enter the decimal point yourself (e.g., 7.5) before moving on. Entering the decimal point manually ensures that it gets placed properly.

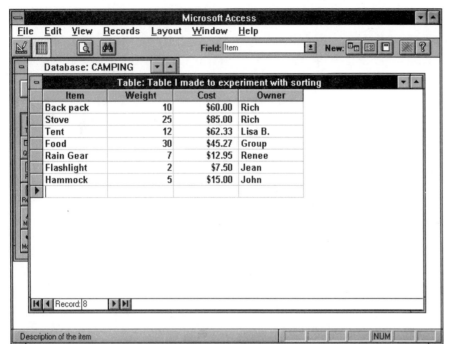

**FIGURE 10.2:**

The CAMPING data

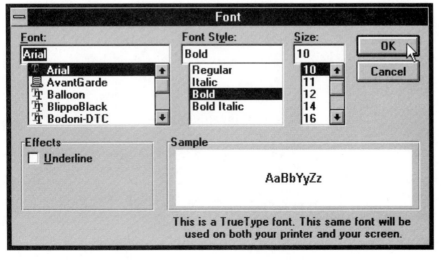

**FIGURE 10.3:**

You can change the font of displayed data using the Layout ➤ Font command.

## Sorting Records by Assigning a Primary Key

As I said earlier, one way to order the database is to assign a primary key. Recall that when you created the Name and Address list, we had Access create a primary key, which it used to order the records. As a rule, Access wants at least one primary key, though actually, if you aren't doing anything fancy, a key isn't necessary. But once you start linking tables together, keys become more important. Also, if you are working with large tables and you're regularly searching for information from a given field, such as Last Name, then you'll want to make that field the primary key—it will speed up your searches. In the meantime, you can use the key to order your records in a simple table such as the Camping list.

Suppose you want to organize the file so that it lists the items in order of weight. Here's what you do:

**1.** Click on the Design button.

**2.** In the Table Design window, click anywhere on the Weight row.

**3.** Now click on the Key icon in the Toolbar.

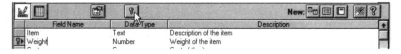

This puts a little key to the left of the field name, meaning it's now the primary key.

**4.** Click on the Datasheet button to see the effects.

**5.** Oops! You got a message saying you have to save the table first, right? This is because assigning a key actually changes the database structure. That's OK. Just click on OK. Now your records are sorted by order of weight, as in Figure 10.4.

**6.** Click on the Design button to bring up the Table Design window again.

**7.** Choose View ➤ Table Properties. Now look at Figure 10.5. The Table Properties box lists important things about the ordering of the table. The primary key is listed there as Weight.

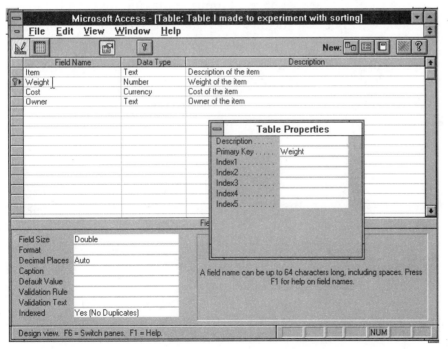

**FIGURE 10.4:**

Saving the modified structure with a new primary key on the Weight field lists the records in order of weight.

**FIGURE 10.5:**

The Table Properties box reports the primary key.

**8.** Now switch to the datasheet.

**9.** Try changing the weight of the hammock to 2 (double-click on 5 in the Weight column and type in **2**). You can enter the numeral, but when you click on another record or field, Access checks the value against the key values in other records and alerts you with the following:

**10.** Click on OK and change the value back to 5.

So, what happened? To work correctly, a primary key must be based on a field that will have a unique value in it for each record. A common example is a social-security number, or a part number. By not allowing duplicates, Access prevents mishaps that can result when two identical records exist in a table. For example, you've probably heard about people's credit records getting mixed up when they have the same name and same birth date. This kind of mistake can be prevented by using an intelligently designed key, based on multiple fields.

Getting back to our Camping list, it's obvious that using a primary key for sorting has some limitations. We would be prevented from entering two items with the same weight, or if the key was on Cost, two items of the same cost, and so on. Likewise, if all the data is already entered and you try to create a key after the fact, there can be problems: If the field you choose has duplicate values in it, Access will report that it can't create the key.

## Sorting Records with a Query

So what about sorting a table on a *non-unique* field, one containing say, many Joneses, or Smiths, or identical weights? First, you have to remove the key from the Weight field because that would prevent such an entry:

1. Get back to the Table Design window.

2. If the Properties box isn't on screen, choose View ➤ Table Properties again to bring it up.

3. Click on the Weight row.

4. In the Table Properties box, Weight should be listed as the primary key. In that box, double-click on Weight and press Del.

5. Click anywhere in the Table Design window again. This updates the Design window, removing the key. The little key symbol to the left of Weight should have disappeared.

6. Click the Datasheet button in the Toolbar. When asked about saving changes, click OK. When asked about assigning a primary key, click Yes. Now Access creates a new primary key similar to the ID field in our Name and Address list. Your table now looks like Figure 10.6.

| ID | Item | Weight | Cost | Owner |
|---|---|---|---|---|
| 1 | Back pack | 10 | $60.00 | Rich |
| 2 | Stove | 25 | $85.00 | Rich |
| 3 | Tent | 12 | $62.33 | Lisa B. |
| 4 | Food | 30 | $45.27 | Group |
| 5 | Rain Gear | 7 | $12.95 | Renee |
| 6 | Flashlight | 2 | $7.50 | Jean |
| 7 | Hammock | 5 | $15.00 | John |
| (Counter) | | | | |

Microsoft Access - [Table: Table I made to experiment with sorting]

File   Edit   View   Records   Layout   Window   Help

Field: ID     New:

**FIGURE 10.6:**

A primary key is added to the table

OK. With that out of the way, let's do some more sorting.

1. You should still be on the Datasheet screen. If you aren't, get to it.

2. Choose File ➤ New ➤ Query. A new query window comes up. Note that this is a more direct path to creating a query for a specific table than the approach we used last time (clicking on the Query button in the Database window). It automatically adds the field list from the current table.

3. Add all the fields to the QBE grid. Double-click on them, one at a time.

Now let's play with the sorting order. As you know, if you don't do anything, the records will normally be displayed in the order of the ID field (the key). This is also the same order as you entered the records. Suppose you want to see them in the order of Weight.

1. Click on the second line in the Weight column (the Sort row). A drop-down list button appears to the right.

2. Open the drop-down list and choose Ascending, as you see in Figure 10.7.

3. Run the query by clicking on the Datasheet View button. Records are now listed in order of increasing weight as shown in Figure 10.8.

# ASCENDING VERSUS DESCENDING ORDER

So much for ordering records according to increasing weight. What if we want to see heavier weights first? As you may have suspected, it's easy to reverse the order using the Descending option on the drop-down list. Let's sort the records again.

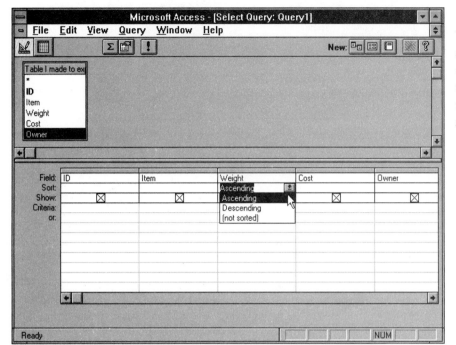

**FIGURE 10.7:**

To sort a table on a given field, click in the Sort row for the field, then choose the sort type.

**1.** Get back to the QBE Design window.

**2.** Click in the Weight field's Sort row again, but open the list and choose Descending as the sort type.

**3.** Click on the Datasheet button to see the results. Your screen should look like Figure 10.9.

Note the ID numbers, and see that the record numbers are out of order, even though the records appear in order of increasing weight. Why is this? Because Access has rearranged the records to match the request you made in the query. Recall that a query doesn't actually make any modifications to the source table. It just lists the chosen fields and records according to your specifications. Since the order of the records has been modified for the listing (to list weights in descending order), naturally the ID numbers will be in a new order too.

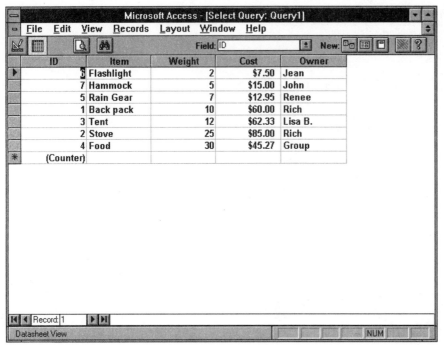

## HOW ACCESS SORTS

More often than not, you'll want to sort records in ascending order, as we did earlier. Different programs are a little different from one another in what they consider an ascending sort to be. In Access, ascending- and descending-order sorts organize items in the following ways:

| ASCENDING | DESCENDING |
|-----------|------------|
| 199       | Zephyr     |
| 200       | zany       |
| Anteater  | apple      |
| apple     | Anteater   |

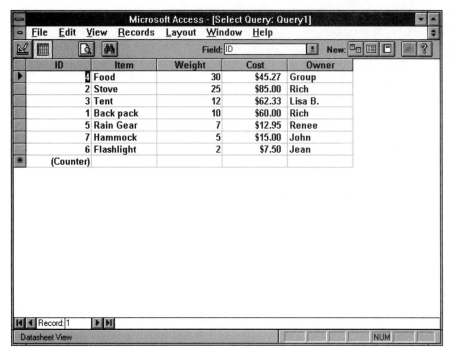

**FIGURE 10.9:**

The result of sorting by weight in descending order

| ID | Item | Weight | Cost | Owner |
|---|---|---|---|---|
| 4 | Food | 30 | $45.27 | Group |
| 2 | Stove | 25 | $85.00 | Rich |
| 3 | Tent | 12 | $62.33 | Lisa B. |
| 1 | Back pack | 10 | $60.00 | Rich |
| 5 | Rain Gear | 7 | $12.95 | Renee |
| 7 | Hammock | 5 | $15.00 | John |
| 6 | Flashlight | 2 | $7.50 | Jean |
| (Counter) | | | | |

| ASCENDING | DESCENDING |
|---|---|
| zany | 200 |
| Zephyr | 199 |

Note that numbers always come before letters and that *a* comes before *Z*, regardless of case, when sorting in ascending order. Descending order has the opposite effect: *Z* before *a*, and numbers last.

## SORTING ON A TEXT FIELD

Now that you have sorted on a Number field, let's try sorting on a Text field.

**1.** Return to the QBE Design screen.

2. Clear the Weight field's Sort row and erase Descending.

3. Click in the Sort box for the Item field, and choose Ascending from the drop-down list.

4. View the datasheet. The items are now arranged in alphabetical order, as shown in Figure 10.10.

## CREATING A MULTILEVEL SORT

Another useful feature of the Sort option is that it allows you to sort databases on more than one field. This is called a *multilevel sort*. The Name and Address table provides a good example of a multilevel sort. Suppose you sorted according to last name, but within each last name you wanted first names alphabetized (for example, you want Suzy

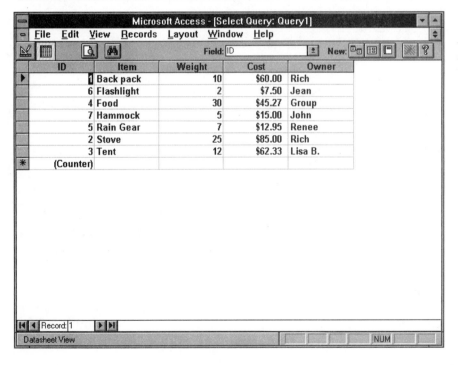

**FIGURE 10.10:**

An ascending sort based on the Item field

Raymond listed before Tina Raymond). To achieve this, you sort on the more significant field first (Last Name) and then the less significant field (First Name).

Let's turn to our Camping list again. Assume that under each owner, we want the items themselves alphabetized by name. We want a multilevel sort using Owner as the most significant key and Item as the secondary key. To do this, you add sort criteria to each of the fields, just as we've been doing. But instead of using only one field, you set up the sort for both fields. There is one trick, though. Access sorts fields from left to right on the QBE grid. So, the most significant key will be the one closest to the left of the grid. The next significant field will be to the right of that, separated by other fields if you want, and so on. Since we want Owner to be most significant, we'll have to do some moving. Here are the steps:

1. First, let's move Owner to the leftmost position in the grid. Click on its column selector tile (just above the word *Owner*; wait till the pointer turns into a down arrow, then click and release).

2. Position the pointer right on the tile again, and click and hold the mouse button down. Then drag the column to the leftmost position on the grid, and release.

3. Clear out anything left in the Sort row for any of the fields.

4. Set the Owner field for an ascending sort. Here's a trick: you can just type the letter *A* into the Sort box and then click on another field. Access fills in the rest of *Ascending*. Likewise, *D* will fill in *Descending*.

5. Set the Item field for an ascending sort. Your grid looks like this:

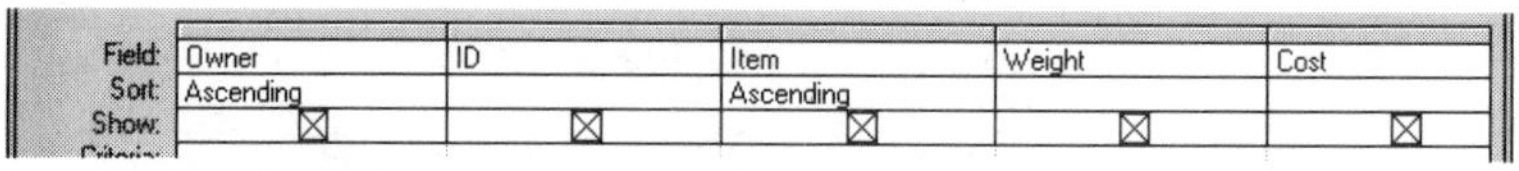

| Field: | Owner | ID | Item | Weight | Cost |
|---|---|---|---|---|---|
| Sort: | Ascending | | Ascending | | |
| Show: | ☒ | ☒ | ☒ | ☒ | ☒ |

6. View the datasheet. The results are shown in Figure 10.11.

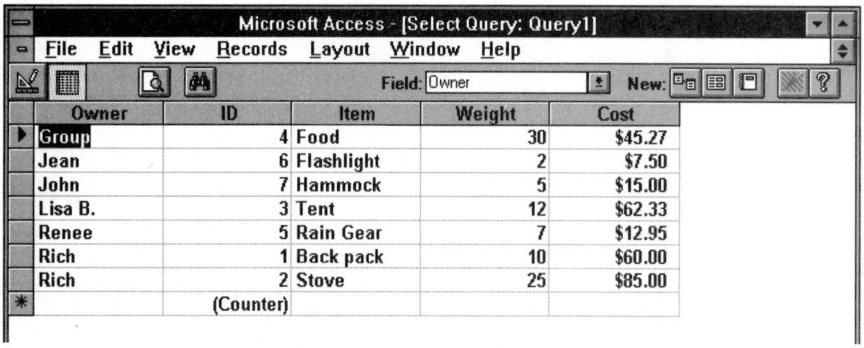

**FIGURE 10.11:** Results of a multilevel sort using Owner and Item. Items are alphabetized within owner groups.

Note that only Rich's records are relevant in the example since only he owns more than one item. His backpack is listed before his stove, since alphabetically, *B* comes before *S*.

## SAVING AND REUSING YOUR SORTED VIEWS

As you can see, it's easy to create many differently organized tables from one master table. Once you have the sort criteria set and are happy with the results, you can switch to the datasheet and see the file in its new sorted order. You can also save the query for future use, just as we did with earlier queries. So, you could have one query that shows a name and address list in last-name order, and another in first-name order. And you can have them both available at the same time. Just save each query with a different name (such as "In Last-Name order," "In First-Name order") and open them both from the Database window. Adjust their windows as necessary to see them both, or jump between them with Ctrl+F6.

Keep in mind that you can mix sort types (ascending and descending) within a query. But on large databases, sorting on a number of fields could take some time, so be prepared to wait. Typically, though, sorts use only one or two levels and shouldn't be cause for a coffee break.

Also, since you do a sort from a Query grid, you can apply all the rules you learned in earlier chapters that pertain to queries. For example, you can add criteria on the Criteria and Or lines while you do a sort—all in one fell swoop.

You can also choose not to have certain fields show up in the datasheet, even though they're on the QBE grid. You do this by clicking on the check box in the Show line of the grid. When the box has an X in it, the field will show up in the query. When it's off, it won't. Of course, you could argue that if you don't want a field to show up on the datasheet, then you shouldn't include it in the grid in the first place. True, but sometimes you'll want to use data in the field as criteria for the query while not displaying the contents of the field itself. Here, for example, Item will still affect the sort order, but it won't display.

| Field:   | Owner     | ID | Item      | Weight | Cost |
|----------|-----------|-----|-----------|--------|------|
| Sort:    | Ascending |     | Ascending |        |      |
| Show:    | ☒         | ☒   |           | ☒      | ☒    |
| Criteria:|           |     |           |        |      |

Finally, don't forget that sorts can apply to Form view as well as to Datasheet view. Just create a query with the desired sort criteria. Then create a form. When asked what table/query you want to use for the basis of the form, choose the one with correct sorted order.

## How to Sort Tables Using a Filter

The third option for sorting tables uses filters. We haven't talked about filters much yet, but we will now by way of sorting. Filters are like little ad hoc queries. However, you can't save a filter for later use, and they only work from forms. But for one-shot deals they're pretty useful.

As a rule, when you'll want to view a table in a certain order frequently, you should do your sort from a query and save it for later use. By contrast, you'll want to use a filter when

- You want to temporarily filter out certain records from view. For example, you can filter out people who have already paid their bills, while leaving the remaining records in view so you can work with them one at a time, using your form.

- You want to quickly sort the records in a table while using the form—without hassling yourself by designing a query.

Since we already have a form designed for the Name and Address list, let's use that one for the next example.

1. Choose File ➤ Close to close the query. Answer No to the resulting dialog box.

2. Open the Window menu. This menu provides an easy way to switch between various open windows. Choose Database: CAMPING.

3. Once the Database window returns, choose File ➤ Close Database. This closes the open database (CAMPING) and anything associated with it, such as forms, queries, reports, and so forth.

4. Choose File ➤ Open Database and double-click on phonebk.

**5.** Now open the form we made several chapters back. Click on the Form button, then double-click on Basic Single-column Form. Up comes the Name and Address form.

Now let's create the filter that will sort records:

**1.** Click on the Edit Filter button, as shown here:

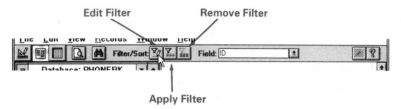

A standard QBE window appears, just like when you're creating a query.

**2.** Let's sort the table by First Name, in descending order.

Note that you don't have to put all the fields on the grid to see them. The form takes care of that. You only have to specify the sort order (and/or other criteria if you want to filter out certain records rather than just sort them all).

**3.** Click on the Apply Filter button on the Toolbar. The filter is applied, and you see what's shown in Figure 10.12. Notice what's happened. What was normally listed as the eighth record (as indicated by the ID number) is now Record 1 (as shown in the status line).

**4.** Press PgDn several times to verify that, indeed, the records are coming up in descending alphabetical order based on First Name.

**5.** Click on the Remove Filter button. The records return to their original order.

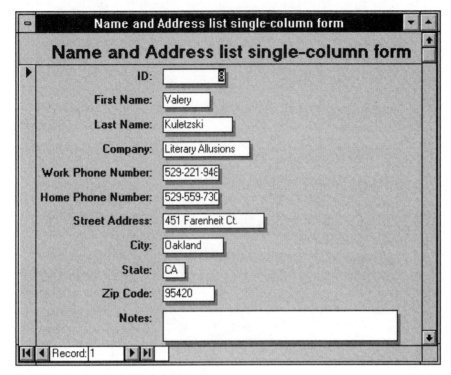

**FIGURE 10.12:**

Applying the filter shows Valerie's record.

# About Indexes

Finally, let's discuss *indexes*. You may recall that when you were designing the structure of tables, there was an option for indexing in the Field Properties box:

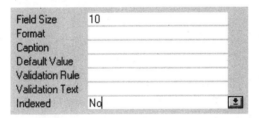

If used, the Indexed line tells Access to create and maintain a *pointer list* (index) based on the field(s) you choose. This pointer list works like a card catalog in a library. Instead of searching through all the books in a library, you can turn to a card catalog (author, title, and subject) to point you to the book you want. Since the catalogs are in alphabetical order, searching them is usually a quick and simple process.

Microsoft Access indexes work the same way, only faster, thanks to your computer. If you regularly do sorts or queries using a certain field, it pays to create an index for that field, because it will speed up searches or sorting procedures. For example, if you have an index on Last Name, then searching for, say, *Jablonski* will be much faster, particularly in a large table. As a default, the primary key is always indexed.

So you might wonder "Why shouldn't I index all my fields?" Because, on the downside, using indexes can slow you down when you edit or add records. This is because Access has to update the indexes as well as the table whenever changes are made.

So, you should consider indexing a field *only* if all of the following conditions apply:

■ It's not the primary key (that's already indexed).

■ The field is a Text, Number, Currency, or Date/Time type.

■ You expect to be sorting or searching the field.

■ The contents of the field are going to vary from record to record, rather than contain values repeated from record to record.

Once you've created some indexes, Access is smart enough to know when to use them to speed things up, and doesn't bother you with having to remember they exist, or turning them on or off, or updating them, as other programs often require.

To see how indexing is done, let's create an index on the Last Name field for the Name and Address list.

1. The single-column form is still open. You have to close it before Access will allow you to change the underlying

table's structure. A quick way to close any window is to double-click on the window's Control box. So to close the Form window, double-click here:

Double-click here.

2. Back at the Database window, click on Table, make sure Name and Address list is highlighted, and click on the Design button. This brings up the familiar Table Design window.

3. Click anywhere on the Last Name row.

4. In the Field Properties section, click on the Indexed line.

5. Click on the little drop-down list button:

6. Choose Yes (Duplicates OK). You use this setting when you don't care if two records with the same value are entered (e.g., two Joneses). For fields where you want to ensure this *doesn't* happen, choose Yes (No duplicates). As I mentioned earlier, use *No Duplicates* for things like serial numbers and part numbers.

7. Choose File ➤ Save to save the changes you've made to the structure.

## CREATING MULTIFIELD INDEXES

Just as with sorting, you can create a single index based on several fields. If you often create queries using the same couple of fields together (such as first and last name), then you'll speed up the processing of such queries by creating an index based on the two fields. Access then uses this index whenever you set up a query that has criteria in both First Name and Last Name.

Here are the steps for creating a multifield index (though we're not actually going to do it).

**1.** Open the table and get to the Table Design window.

**2.** Choose View ➤ Table Properties. The Properties box opens.

**3.** On the Index1 line, type in the field names you want to index, separated by a semicolon. For example:

| Table Properties | |
|---|---|
| Description . . . . . | |
| Primary Key . . . . . | ID |
| Index1 . . . . . . . . . | Last Name; First Name |
| Index2 . . . . . . . . . | |
| Index3 . . . . . . . . . | |
| Index4 . . . . . . . . . | |
| Index5 . . . . . . . . . | |

# CLOSING UP THE DATABASE

Now you can close the database.

**1.** Check to see that Last Name has an index on it, allowing duplicates.

**2.** Check that First Name doesn't have an index on it.

**3.** Check the Table Properties box to see that there are no additional indexes other than the primary key.

**4.** Use the Window menu to get back to the Database window.

**5.** Choose File ➤ Close Database. When asked about saving changes, click Yes. You're returned to a blank Access window. You can quit Access now if you want to take a break.

**FEATURING**

**Editing Memos**

**Copying, Cutting, and Pasting Records**

**Adding Records**

**Deleting Records**

▼

# Updating Your Records

There will probably come a time when you'll want to alter some of the records stored in your tables. Consider your phone book table; people may change jobs or move. Or consider an accounting or inventory table. These tables, by their nature, change frequently.

Microsoft Access allows you to edit your records easily. You can edit your tables in two basic ways: manually or automatically. With manual editing, you look up a record, display it on your screen, and type the changes by hand. With automatic editing, using *update queries*, you make changes to an entire table all at once. For example, you can have your inventory list updated at night, to reflect the sales records gathered at cash registers during the day. Chapter 15 discusses update queries. This chapter explains the manual approach to editing records.

We'll be using the PHONEBK table for this section, so

1. Run Access if it isn't already going.

2. Use the File menu to open the PHONEBK database, either with the Open command or by clicking on PHONEBK if it's on the menu.

## How to Edit Data in a Form Window

As you may have suspected from earlier use of the Datasheet and Form windows for entering new records, you can also edit your data from these windows. First let's experiment with the Form window.

1. In the Database window, click on the Forms button.

2. Make sure *Basic single-column form* is highlighted (it probably will be).

3. Click the Open button.

The Form window appears, as in Figure 11.1.

Notice that the record number on the status line indicates Record 1. This means the file isn't sorted, which makes sense since we're not using a query—but just looking at the records in the order they were entered. The Form window should look very familiar since you've seen it several times before.

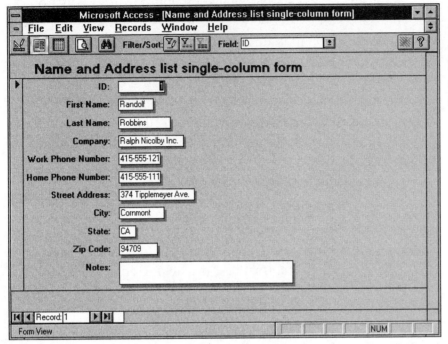

**FIGURE 11.1:**

The Form window: used for editing as well as adding new records

You can add and edit data in a Form window using the commands listed in Table 11.1. These commands apply to datasheets, too. Now let's try some editing techniques on the Name and Address list.

1. Try pressing PgDn once to see what happens. You should see Hank Davies's data.

2. Now press PgUp to return to Randolf's record.

3. Press ↓ twice to highlight the Last Name field.

4. Press Ctrl+PgDn. Notice that the same field is highlighted in the next record. This makes it easy to edit the same field in successive records while in a form.

| KEY | EFFECT |
|---|---|
| Tab or ↵ | Moves to the next field |
| Shift+Tab | Moves to the previous field |
| F2 | Switches from Select Field mode to Edit mode |
| Typing | Inserts text at the insertion point (blinking cursor), or replaces selected data |
| Backspace | Deletes one character to left of insertion point |
| → | Moves one character to the right; if at the end of a field, moves to the next field |
| ← | Moves one character to the left; if at the beginning of a field, moves to the previous field |
| ↑ | Moves up one row (Browse screen), or to the previous field (Edit screen) |
| ↓ | Moves down one row (Browse screen), or to the next field (Edit screen) |
| Shift | When used with arrow keys, extends the text selection in the direction of cursor motion |
| PgUp | Moves to the previous record on a form, or to the previous page of records on a datasheet |
| PgDn | Moves to the next record on a form, or to the next page of records on a datasheet |
| Home | Moves to the first field of the current record |
| End | Moves to the last field of the current record |
| Esc | Undoes changes to the current field |
| Ctrl+→ | Moves to the beginning of the next word |
| Ctrl+← | Moves to the beginning of the previous word |
| Ctrl+PgUp | Moves to the same field in the previous record in a form |
| Ctrl+PgDn | Moves to the same field in the next record in a form |
| Ctrl+Home | Moves to the first field in the first record |

**TABLE 11.1:**

Navigating, Editing, and Data-Entry Commands in Form and Datasheet Windows

| KEY | EFFECT |
|-----|--------|
| Ctrl+End | Moves to the last field in the last record |
| Backspace | Deletes letter to left of insertion point |
| Del | Deletes character to right of insertion point, or selected data |
| Ins | Turns Insert mode (Overwrite mode) on or off |
| Ctrl+↵ | Enters a new line into a Memo field |
| Ctrl+" | Copies data from the corresponding field of the previous record to the current field |
| Shift+↵ | Saves changes to current record (moving to next record has same effect) |
| Ctrl+Alt+Spacebar | Replaces the value of a field with its default value |
| Alt+↓ | Opens a drop-down list box from the keyboard |

**TABLE 11.1:**

Navigating, Editing, and Data-Entry Commands in Form and Datasheet Windows (continued)

5. Press Ctrl+Home and then Ctrl+End. Notice how you move to the beginning of record 1 and then to the end of record 9 (the last record in the table).

6. Press Home. The first field is highlighted.

7. Press End. The last field is highlighted.

## JUMPING TO THE DESIRED RECORD

To display the record you want to modify, you simply use the various commands you've learned in previous chapters. For example, suppose you've just received a letter from the famous writer Randolf Robbins announcing that he will be working under a new pen name: Wackford Squeers. Naturally, you'll want to change his name in your table, but you have to call up his record first. You can do this in any of three ways:

- You can press the PgDn key until you find the right record, but this can be time-consuming, especially if you are working with a large table.

- If you know the record number, you can get to the record directly by using the Records ➤ Go To command or the Record box at the bottom of the window. Chances are, however, that you don't know it.

- You can use the Edit ➤ Find command to go directly to the record.

The last choice is usually the fastest, particularly in a large table, and especially if you have created an index on the field you're searching in. Since our table is already indexed on Last Name, we'll take advantage of that index. (Actually with this small a table, the improvement won't be significant, but later if you add more names to your list, it will be.)

1. Click on First Name field in the current record (should be 9).

2. Choose Edit ➤ Find.

3. Enter **Randolf** and press ↵. Access jumps to Randolf's record (record 1), and the status line says "Search succeeded." Press Esc—it's the fastest way to get the dialog box off the screen.

4. Edit the record. Since the First Name field is already highlighted, just type in **Wackford**. If, by chance, the field is not highlighted, just click on the field name (e.g. First Name). This selects the whole field.

**5.** Press ↵ once to move to the Last Name field. Enter **Squeers**. Your screen should look like Figure 11.2. Notice the little pencil in the left margin of the window, just to the left of the ID field. This means the record has been edited, but the changes haven't been recorded yet.

**6.** Before moving off the Last Name field, press Esc. *Robbins* returns. This is how you undo your changes to a field. But it only works on the field you're on. That's why the First Name field didn't revert to Randolf.

**7.** Since we really do want to change Robbins to Squeers, change it back by typing **Squeers** again.

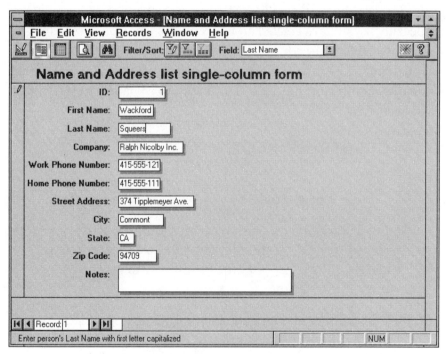

**FIGURE 11.2:**

The edited record

# USING THE MEMO EDITOR

Memo fields are excellent for storing auxiliary information pertaining to a record—information that may vary in length from very short to very long. As you may recall, you can type up to about 32,000 characters (letters and spaces) into a Memo field.

Unlike some other programs, such as dBASE, Access stores Memo field data right in the database file along with forms, reports, queries, and so forth. Only the space actually consumed by your memos is stored, so there's no wasted disk space even if you leave Memo fields blank, despite the fact that you can store 32,000 characters in a fully packed Memo field.

When you enter or edit data in a Memo field, the keys on the keyboard work a little differently, letting you move around more easily, as though you were using a word processor. Most of the commands are the same as for editing other fields, but a few are different. Table 11.2 lists the commands.

You can also execute searches based on words in the Memo field to find records in the table. Simply use the Find command. Make sure to set the Where option to Any Part of Field rather than Whole Field; otherwise your search isn't likely to succeed.

1. For future reference, let's make a note about why we changed Robbins's name. Click in the Notes field. You are now in the memo editor.

2. Now type the notes about why and when the name was changed, as shown below. (The typing mistake in the word *publication* is intentional.)

> **Randolf Robbins changed his name to Wackford Squeers on January 13, 1993. This new name was assumed for publicatoin purposes. He still answers to the names of Randolf or Randy, but now prefers to be hailed as Wacko.**

| KEY | EFFECT |
|---|---|
| F2 | Switches from Select Field mode to Edit mode |
| Typing | Inserts text at the insertion point (blinking cursor), or replaces selected data |
| Backspace | Deletes one character to left of insertion point |
| Ctrl+Backspace | Deletes word to left of cursor |
| → | Moves one character to the right |
| ← | Moves one character to the left |
| ↑ | Moves up one line |
| ↓ | Moves down one line |
| Shift | When used with arrow keys, extends the text selection in the direction of cursor motion |
| PgUp | Moves up one windowful of text |
| PgDn | Moves down one windowful of text |
| Home | Moves to the start of the line |
| End | Moves to the end of the line |
| Ctrl+→ | Moves one word to the right |
| Ctrl+← | Moves one word to the left |
| Ctrl+Home | Moves to the beginning of the memo |
| Ctrl+End | Moves to the end of the memo |
| Backspace | Deletes letter to left of insertion point |
| Del | Deletes character to right of insertion point, or selected data |
| Ins | Turns Insert mode (Overwrite mode) on or off |
| Ctrl+↵ | Starts a new line in the Memo field (if you don't want normal wrapping) |
| Esc | Undoes changes to the Memo field |

**TABLE 11.2:**

Navigating, Editing, and Data-Entry Commands in Memo Fields

Notice that as you reach the right side of the field, words will wrap to the next line. You don't have to press ↵ to move the cursor down. By the time you're done, you can't see anything but the last line or two of text, but that's OK.

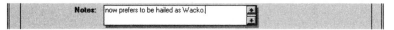

Moving around within a memo to make changes can be done simply by clicking on the desired position with the mouse, but don't overlook using the keys listed in Table 11.2. Here are some exercises to try.

1. The cursor is now at the end of the memo. Press Ctrl+←. The cursor moves backward by one word.

2. Press Ctrl+→ for the opposite effect.

3. Press ↑ twice. The little Notes window scrolls up a line.

4. Click on the little up and down buttons to scroll the window. Scroll until you can see the misspelled word *publicatoin*.

5. Press the Ins key several times while looking at the far right side of the status line. The letters *OVR* toggle on and off with each keypress. Try this again, looking at the cursor. Notice that the shape of the cursor changes from a thin line to a block that covers a letter when the OVR indicator is on. You're toggling the memo editor between Insert and Overwrite modes of typing. In Insert mode, any typing you do will push existing text to the right. In Overwrite mode, Access types over any existing text. This process applies to other fields in your table, too, as you may recall from earlier chapters.

6. Make sure Insert mode is on and the cursor is on the *p* of *publicatoin*. Now type **publication**. Notice that the last two lines of text wrapped around to the next line as you added text.

**7.** Now press the mouse button and drag the mouse to the right. As you do, the text beneath the cursor becomes highlighted. Highlight just the remaining part of the word.

**8.** Press Del. This kills the selected letters. If you need to, press the spacebar to separate the words *publication* and *purposes*.

Now that you've gotten a taste of memo editing, you can experiment with the other editing commands on your own. If you're familiar with editing in Windows programs, there is nothing much new here. You could also have fixed the misspelling by double-clicking the word and typing in the new word. Or, you could have clicked at the end of the misspelled word, pressed the Backspace key several times, and then retyped. Any of these techniques will work—and they apply to most text or data editing tasks in Access.

## SAVING YOUR EDITS

Now that you've made edits to several fields in the record, you'll want to save them. There are several ways to do this. As mentioned earlier, one thoughtful feature of Access is that it takes some of the onus of saving your work off of you—either with reminders in dialog boxes, or by automatically saving a record when you move to the next record.

Still, as long as the little pencil it still on the form or in the leftmost column of a datasheet, that particular record hasn't been saved. To save the record, do one of the following:

- Move to another record.

- Choose File ➤ Save Record.

- Press Shift+↵.

- Close the form or datasheet.

The most common way is to move to another record.

## UNDOING EDITS

There are a couple of tricks you might want to know about undoing edits you've made to fields and records:

| TO UNDO | DO THIS |
|---------|---------|
| The last typing you've done | Choose Edit ➤ Undo Typing. |
| Edits to a field | Press Esc before leaving the field, or choose Edit ➤ Undo Current Field. |
| All edited fields in a record | Choose Edit ➤ Undo Current Record. |

The options on the Edit menu change, depending on what you've done most recently, and on how many fields you've edited in the record. Also, remember that pressing Esc while on a field undoes the changes you made to the field, but *to that field only*.

But wait. There's more. If you act fast, you can undo a record even *after* you move on to another record! Access remembers the changes you made to the last record until you start editing the next record, you apply or remove a filter, or you switch to another window. So, if you panic, thinking you've blown away someone's address or lost that one order you had for your home made atomic clock, there's hope. Just open the Edit menu and choose Undo Saved Record (or press Ctrl+Z). The previous record will come up on screen with its old data intact. Test it out:

1. Click on the Last Name field in your current record, and type in something strange and unwanted. It doesn't matter what. Just simulate some kind of mistake.

2. Press PgDn to move to the next record. If you watch your computer's hard disk light, you'll see it come on, indicating the record was saved.

3. Open the Edit menu and choose Undo Saved Record. You're returned to the previous record and the strange and unwanted text is removed.

## How to Modify Data on a Datasheet

Depending on the task at hand, you may find that editing in the datasheet is easier than using a form. This really depends on how many fields you have, and whether you want to see fields in other records at the same time. If you need to see all the fields in a record at once, a form is the better choice. If you want to edit the same couple of fields in lots of records, you might as well use a datasheet. Recall that a datasheet lets you scroll through your table as though you were reading a newspaper with a magnifying glass. You can use the mouse and keyboard commands to edit as you go. You can also add or delete records in this mode.

## MOVING AND EDITING ON A DATASHEET

Navigating and editing on a datasheet is pretty much identical to editing in Form mode. I don't want to belabor the issue, so we won't bother doing any actual editing since you should have that under your belt by now. You can refer to the keyboard commands summarized in Table 11.1 if you have questions.

One trick to keep in mind while editing a datasheet concerns the F2 key. While the cursor is in a field, pressing F2 selects the whole field. This is like clicking on the field's name when you're using a form. Whatever you type will replace the field's contents. Pressing F2 again returns to normal editing, where characters you type are inserted at the cursor.

Because of the advantages of each type of data presentation, it's often worth shuttling back and forth between Form and Datasheet views of your data when editing. Here's a little shortcut for switching between Form or Datasheet views:

1. First you create a form that suits your needs. Put all your fields on it, so you can see them easily, preferably in one screenful.

2. To see things in Datasheet view, click on the Datasheet button on the Form window's Toolbar:

   This will bring up the datasheet.

3. Make adjustments as necessary, using the options covered in Chapter 7:

   ■ Hiding columns you want to temporarily disappear
   ■ Changing the order of columns
   ■ Resizing columns to get more data on the screen at one time
   ■ Changing the font size for easier viewing or to get more data on-screen

Also, if you want to filter the view, sort records, see specific fields only, or what not, just click on the Edit Filter button and create a filter, as you learned to do in the last chapter.

To move back to the Form view, simply click on the Form button:

# FREEZING AND UNFREEZING COLUMNS

One last option worth knowing about while using a datasheet to edit your data is the Layout ➤ Freeze Columns command. This is a command common in spreadsheets, so you may be familiar with it. It lets you specify one or more columns on the left of the screen that will not scroll when you move to fields on the right side. This is particularly useful for tables that have lots of columns that you want to edit while still seeing an identification column on the left margin.

Let's say, for purposes of illustration, that you want to keep the First Name and Last Name visible while you're working on the other columns, particularly when you scroll over to the Notes field for each person.

1. Bring up a datasheet of the Name and Address list, either from the form or by opening the table from the Database window.

2. Select the First Name and Last Name columns. You can select multiple columns by holding down the Shift key and clicking first on the First Name column tile and then on the Last Name column tile.

3. Choose Layout ➤ Freeze Columns. This freezes those columns from moving when you scroll right.

4. Press Tab several times to see what happens. When you get to the Zip Code column, you'll notice that the two frozen columns don't move. The Notes column comes into view, as in Figure 11.3. I've widened the Notes column a bit so that more can be seen.

5. To unfreeze the columns, choose Layout ➤ Unfreeze All Columns.

**FIGURE 11.3:**

Freezing the First Name and Last Name columns lets other columns scroll.

# How to Add New Records

Of course, a common task with most tables will be that of adding new records. How do you do this?

Both the Form view and Datasheet views of your tables always have a blank record in them as the last record. In the Datasheet view, the last record has an asterisk in it:

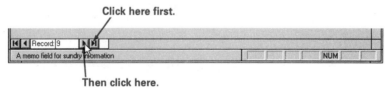

Just click in the first field and start entering information.

On a form, you get to the last record by pressing Ctrl+End or by clicking on the Last Record button in the Record Number box at the bottom of the window. Then press ↓ once or click on the Next Record button at the bottom of the window:

Click here first.

Then click here.

Up comes a blank record in the form, ready to be filled in, as you see in Figure 11.4. As soon as you begin entering information in the first field of the blank record, Access adds another new blank record so you can keep up the process of adding records.

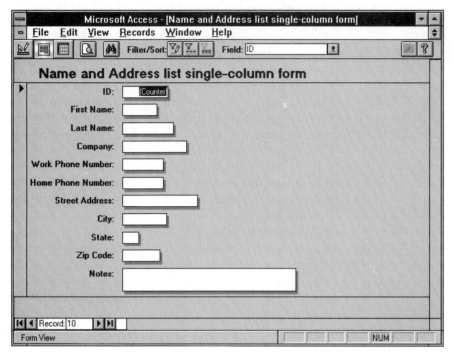

You can also enter new records by choosing Records ➤ Data
Entry, which will remove all but the empty record from view. When
you've finished adding, you choose Records ➤ Show All Records to
see old as well as newly entered records.

A batch of records can be added to a table from another table,
too. This is called batch updating and is done using *update* or *action*
*queries*. We'll discuss these in Chapter 15.

# Copying, Cutting, and Pasting Data

Microsoft Access, as a Windows program, adheres to the common
Windows rules for cutting, copying, and pasting data. These operations allow you to move information around within Access tables and
share data with other Windows programs. You simply select the data,

then choose Cut or Copy from the Edit menu. Then locate the cursor in the destination spot (window, field, etc.) by clicking, and choose Edit ➤ Paste.

# COPYING A RECORD IN A DATASHEET

You already used the Copy and Paste commands when you added the Work Phone field. This was done in the Database Design window. We just copied the Home Phone field, inserted a blank row, clicked in the row, and pasted. Copying records works the same way. Let's try a quick experiment, copying the last record into the blank record at the end of the Name and Address list.

1. Get to the datasheet of people's names.

2. Click on the record selector at the left of record 9.

3. Choose Edit ➤ Copy. This puts the data on the Windows *Clipboard*, the temporary holding tank built into all Windows programs.

4. Click on the blank record's selector button (the asterisk). This selects the destination record.

5. Choose Edit ➤ Paste. The record is copied, as you see in Figure 11.5.

---

**FIGURE 11.5:**

To copy a record, select it and choose Edit ➤ Copy. Then click on the blank record's * selector button and choose Edit ➤Paste.

| First Nam | Last Name | Company | Work Phone | Home Phone | Street Address | City | Sta | Zip C |
|---|---|---|---|---|---|---|---|---|
| Wackford | Squeers | Ralph Nicolby Inc. | 415-555-1212 | 415-555-1111 | 374 Tipplemeyer Ave | Cornmont | CA | 94709 |
| Hank | Davies | Bass-O-Matic | 909-549-3787 | 909-398-2563 | 333 33rd St. | West Goshen | SD | 43312 |
| Adriator | Wegwo | Rug Flox, Inc. | 321-889-3674 | 321-883-9821 | 158 Snorewell Blvd. | Sleepyhollow | CA | 02587 |
| Aretha | Phillipson | Soulariums-R-Us | 908-776-5298 | 908-337-8194 | 999 Motor City Ave. | Detroit | MI | 39482 |
| Randy | Batterydown | Voltaics | 809-675-4532 | 809-777-3300 | 495 Anode St. | Carbondale | IL | 30129 |
| Nimrod | Neverberger | Bab's Fish N Chips | 822-991-2861 | 822-675-4500 | 77 Easy Street | Khozad | CA | 89751 |
| Marcel | Phillip | Feline Frenzy | 310-563-0987 | 310-265-7560 | 456 Fresno St. | Paris | TX | 55493 |
| Valery | Kuletzski | Literary Allusions | 529-221-9480 | 529-559-7300 | 451 Farenheit Ct. | Oakland | CA | 95420 |
| MARIAN | DAVIES | CITY OPERA CO. | 211-334-9876 | 211-411-6111 | 344 MARKET ST | NEW YORK | NY | 10021 |
| MARIAN | DAVIES | CITY OPERA CO. | 211-334-9876 | 211-411-6111 | 344 MARKET ST | NEW YORK | NY | 10021 |

Microsoft Access - [Name and Address list single-column form]

File  Edit  View  Records  Layout  Window  Help

Filter/Sort:  Field: First Name

Of course, if you want the original record to disappear, you can use the Cut command instead of Copy. This deletes the original.

What if you want to copy just a single field, not the whole record? You use the same technique. Let's say we want to alter the new record to put Marian Davies at her second job, since she's joined the ranks of Bass-O-Matic:

1. Click in the Bass-O-Matic field (record 2).

2. Press F2 to highlight the whole field.

3. Choose Edit ➤ Copy.

4. Click in the last record's Company field.

5. Press F2 to highlight the whole field.

6. Choose Edit ➤ Paste. Bass-O-Matic replaces CITY OPERA COMPANY.

If you wanted to add the new data to the existing data in the destination field, you'd just position the cursor first (don't press F2), then choose Paste.

## COPYING MULTIPLE RECORDS IN A DATASHEET

Sometimes you'll want to copy more than one record at a time, either within a single table, or between separate tables. For example, you might want to have two copies of your customer list for different uses.

1. Drag the pointer (with mouse button depressed) down the left edge of the Datasheet window, over the record selectors, to select the source records. If you want to select all the records in a table, choose Edit ➤ Select All Records or click in the upper left corner of the datasheet.

**2.** Move to the destination table. The columns should be in the same order as the source information. The field names can be different. Rearrange the columns if you need to match them up.

**3.** To replace records in the destination table, select them before pasting. Then when you paste, they'll be replaced by the new records when you choose Edit ➤ Paste. If you want to *add* the records to the destination table, choose Edit ➤ Paste Append. The records will be added to the end of the table.

## CUTTING, COPYING, AND PASTING RECORDS IN FORMS

What about cutting, copying, and pasting records by using forms? It's pretty much the same as with records, though selecting records is different.

**1.** Move to the record you want to copy.

**2.** Click on the left margin of the form, in the vertical bar under the pointer, as you see in Figure 11.6. If you want to select multiple records in a form, press and hold down the Shift key. Then press PgUp or PgDn to get the next record, and click again on the left margin. Repeat this for each record you want to select.

**3.** Choose Edit ➤ Copy.

**4.** Open the form or datasheet you want to copy into.

**5.** To replace records in the destination form, select them before pasting. When you paste, they'll be replaced by the new records when you choose Edit ➤ Paste. If you want to *add* the records to the destination table, choose Edit ➤ Paste Append. The records will be added to the end of the table.

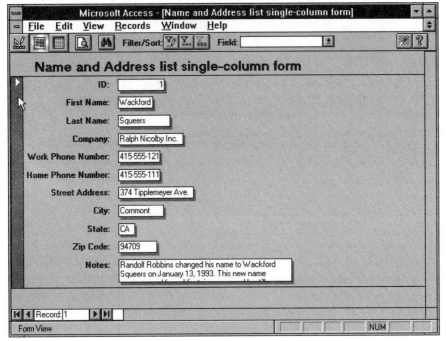

**FIGURE 11.6:**

Clicking here selects the whole record.

In general, it's much easier to go about performing these tasks in a datasheet. Sometimes data will be lost or fields will be mixed up when you paste into a form, because of the "tab order" of the fields on the form. With a datasheet you're much more likely to get what you intended, since data is dropped into the sheet in the same order as the columns appear on the screen.

If you want to copy into Access from another program, the data has to be stored in spreadsheet fashion, or fields have to be separated by tabs. Otherwise, Access doesn't know where one field begins and another ends.

# How to Remove Records from a Table

Keeping your table clean and uncluttered is central to optimizing Microsoft Access. Duplicate, incomplete, erroneous, and outdated records can slow down many Access processes. They can also lead to other types of data contamination and potentially embarrassing situations, such as invoices sent and phone calls made to the wrong people. Therefore, it is good practice to purge your table of unwanted records regularly.

How is this done? There are two ways: manual and automatic. Just as with batch appending, mentioned above, you can have Access do some updating for you, using action queries. But that's a little complicated. The manual approach works fine for most day-to-day tasks. Simply put, you just delete records as you come across them, or you create a query that will show all the records you want to trash, then you select them all and delete them.

## DELETING SINGLE RECORDS

Since we've duplicated Marian Davies's record, we'll want to get rid of that one, right? OK. Let's do it.

1. Get your datasheet on-screen.

2. Select the last record, record 10, which is the duplicate.

3. Choose Edit ➤ Delete. A dialog box asks if you really want to delete the record. Say No, since we're going to use the record in a minute.

OK. You get the idea. Now let's try it from a form.

1. Switch to Form view.

2. Move to record 10 (check the status bar).

3. Click in the left margin of the form (where the little triangle is). This selects the record.

**4.** Choose Edit ➤ Delete. The dialog box asks for confirmation. Click OK.

**5.** Return to the datasheet and see that the record is gone.

A good technique for determining whether your table needs to be cleaned up is to print it on paper and examine it. You can do this with the File ➤ Print command in the Form or Datasheet window. Once the table is printed, mark all the records that need modification or deletion. Then return to the computer and make the changes.

## USING A QUERY TO DELETE MULTIPLE RECORDS

Sometimes you'll want to delete a whole series of records from a table, for example, records for all people from New Jersey, former clients, out-of-date orders, and so on. Chapter 14 presents an efficient way to do this. For small jobs, though, you can use the method described here.

First you create a query that shows only records that meet the criteria. In other words, you fill in the QBE grid with the necessary filter information as described in Chapters 7 and 8.

Next, you display those records. Examine them to see that they are all records you want to trash. In Datasheet view, click in the upper left corner of the window, or choose Edit ➤ Select All Records.

Finally, choose Edit ➤ Delete or press Del. You'll get a dialog box reporting how many records you're about to kill. Just click on OK. Access does the rest.

Note that when you delete records, any primary key that Access has created (such as our ID field) may have nonconsecutive numbers in it. For example, if you deleted record 4, the ID numbers would jump from 3 to 5. Access doesn't reassign the numbers. This prevents tables that are linked together using the ID number from getting out of sync. You'll see how that works later. In the meantime, just don't be thrown if your record numbers and your primary field or ID numbers don't always match.

FEATURING

**Simple Printing**

**Creating a Report with ReportWizards**

**Modifying a Report**

**Including Calculated Fields**

**Setting Control Properties**

▼

# Creating Reports

Congratulations! If you've followed along thus far without serious incident, you should now know the basic techniques for creating and maintaining databases. Now you can take the next step: creating some reports from data you have entered. If you're like most people, that's one of the primary reasons you bought a database program in the first place—for printouts and reports.

In a sense, you've already created some simple reports, using queries. And for many day-to-day needs, printing right from those queries—whether viewing the data in a simple datasheet or on a form—will meet your needs for printed output.

Other times you'll want to create more formal listings, with explanatory column headings, a title at the top, subtotals, grand totals, and with records grouped together in relevant ways to convey additional information to the reader.

In any case, this kind of listing is called a *report*, and reports are one of the primary reasons for the existence of database management systems like Microsoft Access. Whether you call them invoices, mailing labels, phone lists, or fancy market research summaries, these are all examples of printed data and qualify as reports.

In this chapter, you'll experiment with the "canned" reports that come with Access, and then work a bit with some custom report design basics.

## Simple Printing from Forms and Datasheets

Let's start with simple printing of a database table. So you've got your names and addresses, or PTA list, or parts inventory typed into your first database table. It's great having it on the screen where you can search around for things, but you have to fire up the computer each time to do it, which is a hassle. Why not print it out several ways, make copies, and put them around the house or hang them on the wall at work? Having lists around is great. I do this with my phone and address list.

If you haven't already tried some printing, follow along and print out your Name and Address list a couple of different ways.

1. Open the PHONEBK database. If you are using another database, you will have to close it, since Access lets you have only a single database open at a time.

2. Open the single-column form, since a form will let us switch back and forth between Datasheet and Form views easily.

3. Switch to Datasheet view and maximize the window, so you can see as much stuff as possible.

4. Click on the Print Preview button, or choose File ➤ Print Preview.

The result is a small facsimile of a printed page, like the one in Figure 12.1.

5. Press PgDn to see the next page. Hmmm. Why is there material on the second page? Because not all the fields could fit on the first page. Instead of wrapping the data down to the bottom of the page, Access puts it on the next

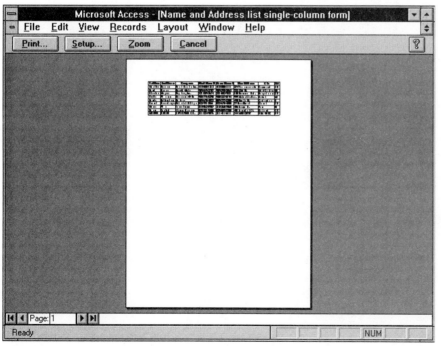

**FIGURE 12.1:**

A Print Preview page. If you click on Print, this is how it will come out on paper.

page. Then you can tape the pages together, side by side. If you had many more records in the table, this would make sense.

6. Move the pointer around and notice it becomes a little magnifying glass shape when it's over the printed page. Position the magnifying-glass cursor over some of the data and click. This has the same effect as clicking on the Zoom button. You get a close-up of the data under the cursor, as you see in Figure 12.2.

7. Click again, and the whole page preview returns.

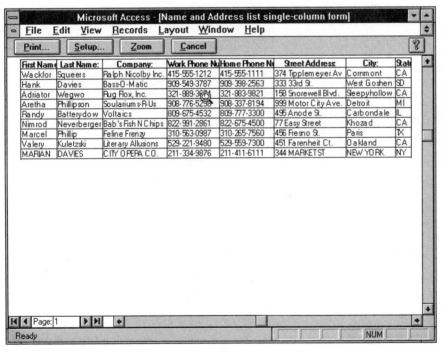

**FIGURE 12.2:**

Clicking on the Zoom button or on the page zooms in so you can get a closer look at your proposed printout.

## SQUEEZING MORE DATA ONTO A PRINTED PAGE

OK. Now what can you do about the fact that your table won't fit on a single page? Well, you could...

- Decrease the font size of all the fields, using the Layout ➤ Fonts dialog box.

- Eliminate some columns that you can do without on the particular printout.

- Change the paper layout from Portrait to Landscape.

The third choice is the best one here, since it will let us keep all the columns. Check it out:

1. Click on the Setup button. This is for making changes to the printer setup. You'll see a screen something like the one in Figure 12.3. It may be a little different, depending on what kind of printer you have, and what printer drivers you installed into your Windows setup.

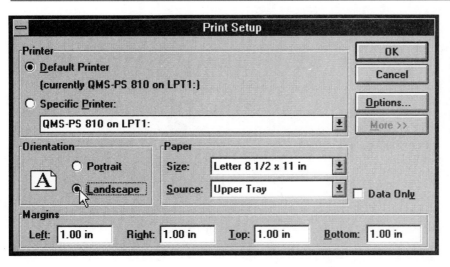

**FIGURE 12.3:**

Changing the printing orientation to Landscape helps get more columns on a page.

**2.** Click on Landscape, then on OK. Now the view changes. Looks like all your fields fit now, as shown in Figure 12.4.

**3.** Click on Cancel to return to the datasheet.

**4.** Now let's try a change. Choose Layout ➤ Gridlines. This turns off the gridlines, just to make things look a tad less busy.

**5.** Click on the Preview button again.

**6.** Turn on your printer. Make sure it's plugged into your computer, it has paper, and it's online.

**7.** Click on the Print button. Your data should come rolling out.

Of course, you can adjust the column widths or select a different font type and size before printing. You can also print from a query if

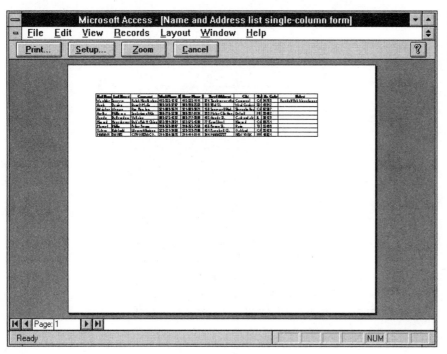

**FIGURE 12.4:**

Now all the fields fit.

you want to, say, sort the records first by Last Name or print only people with certain area codes.

## PRINTING IN FORM VIEW

So much for printing from a datasheet. Access lets you print forms, too. We'll talk about printing mailing labels later in the book. But for right now, try printing out the simple single-column form.

1. After your printing is done, switch to Form view.

2. Once again, click on the Print Preview button.

3. Click on Setup and change the page orientation back to Portrait. Your preview screen should look something like Figure 12.5.

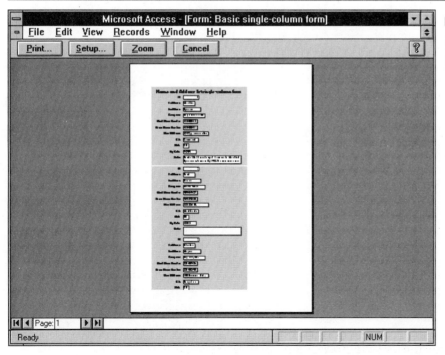

**FIGURE 12.5:**

Preparing to print forms

**4.** Press PgDn a few times to see how many pages you'll get. You can see that Access divides up the pages a bit oddly, sometimes breaking a form into two pieces to take best advantage of the space on a page. This is unfortunate, but nonetheless that is how it works.

**5.** Ready the printer and click on Print. You'll see the Print dialog box, asking which pages to print and giving you a few other options that depend on your printer. Here's what mine looks like:

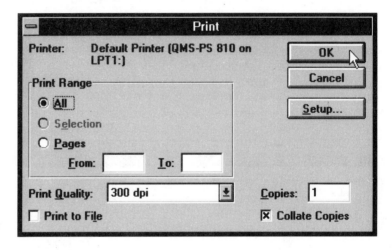

**6.** Click on OK and the pages should start rolling out.

Access, like most Windows programs, uses the Windows Print Manager to handle the task of sending information to the printer. If you decide you want to cancel a print job in the middle, you have to switch to the Print Manager and cancel the job. A quick-and-dirty way of doing this is to turn off your printer, though doing this with some laser printers can leave a piece of paper inside the machine if you do it at the wrong time. Then Print Manager will put a dialog box on the screen reporting a printer problem and asking if you want to retry. At that point, you can just click on Cancel, then switch to Print Manager and close it, which will erase the print file.

If you have other print jobs pending, you won't want to use this approach. You should use the normal technique for canceling a print job from Print Manager (highlight the job and click on Delete). See your Windows manual for details on using Print Manager.

# Printing Fancier Reports

In addition to printing simple jobs like the one above, Microsoft Access can, in only a few minutes, create fairly sophisticated report printouts (either on screen or on paper) based on information in a database. Reports like a general ledger, a list of sales figures for the year, mailing labels, or an inventory list can be created quite easily using ReportWizards, though highly complex reports require some manual intervention using the Report Design window.

With Microsoft Access's report capabilities, you can

- Group similar or related data together

- Perform arithmetic operations like calculating subtotals, totals, and averages on fields

- Add headings, footings, and page numbers to each page

- Print field data exactly where you want it on a page

- Cosmetically improve your presentation with attractive fonts

- Even include graphics, pictures, logos, or charts in your reports

Once created, reports—like other Access objects—can be saved for reuse. If the data in the underlying tables changes after you run the first report, the next report you run will reflect the changes.

Before experimenting with reports, you will need some new material to work with. Although we could use the CAMPING or

PHONEBK database, a slightly more complex table, typical of a business environment, would be better.

1. Close the PHONEBK database by first closing the form, then choosing File ➤ Close Database. When asked about saving changes, click No. The only change that Access was asking about is the page orientation.

2. Create a new database and call it **STEREO**. The database will contain an inventory list from a stereo shop that you just inherited: Uncle Bob's Hi-Fi Anachronisms.

3. Click on the Table button, then on New, to create a new table. Give it the following structure:

| FIELD NAME | DATA TYPE | FIELD SIZE | INDEXED |
| --- | --- | --- | --- |
| Category | Text | 10 | No |
| Brand | Text | 10 | No |
| Model | Text | 6 | No |
| Quantity | Number | | No |
| Wholesale | Currency | | No |
| Retail | Currency | | No |

4. When asked, do not have Access create a primary key.

5. Give the table the name

   **Stereo Equipment**

6. Now fill the new table with the data shown here.

| REC# | CATEGORY | BRAND | MODEL | QUANTITY | WHOLESALE | RETAIL |
| --- | --- | --- | --- | --- | --- | --- |
| 1 | Receiver | Nizo | T-33 | 5 | 225.49 | 350.49 |
| 2 | Receiver | Nizo | T-35 | 4 | 312.00 | 425.25 |

| REC# | CATEGORY | BRAND | MODEL | QUANTITY | WHOLESALE | RETAIL |
|------|----------|-------|-------|----------|-----------|--------|
| 3 | Receiver | Acme | R25-MT | 13 | 19.99 | 49.99 |
| 4 | Receiver | Nadir | 2-CHP | 50 | 12.95 | 29.95 |
| 5 | Speakers | Razco | L-55 | 30 | 199.00 | 249.00 |
| 6 | Speakers | Talbest | BG-20 | 6 | 250.00 | 350.88 |
| 7 | Tape Deck | Rollem | CAS-3 | 10 | 125.65 | 212.99 |
| 8 | Tape Deck | Flowutter | WBL-5 | 5 | 149.33 | 250.77 |
| 9 | Turntable | Xirtam | 25-L | 5 | 99.99 | 149.99 |
| 10 | Turntable | Raluric | RND-1 | 3 | 595.00 | 850.00 |

Browse the data to check its accuracy. Your screen should look like Figure 12.6. If it doesn't, then edit the structure or the records until it does.

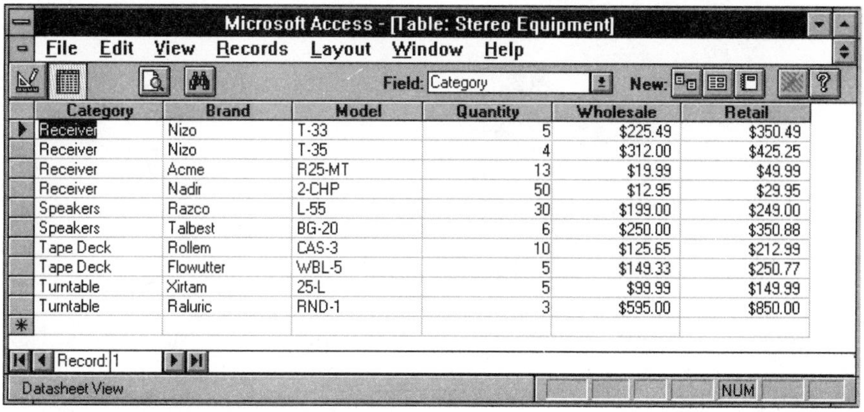

**FIGURE 12.6:**

The Stereo Equipment table

## How to Create a Quick Report with Wizards

Access gives you tons of room for creativity when it comes to designing and printing reports. In fact, you could probably make a living just specializing in fancy report writing. Luckily for most of us, Access also has some built-in standard reports (Wizards, again) that will fit most needs. Let's start with them to see what they can do.

**1.** Get back to the Database window. You can leave the table open if you want. Just open the Window menu and select Database: STEREO.

**2.** Click on the large Report button.

**3.** Click on New.

**4.** A dialog box comes up. Use the drop-down list to select the table we're going to use. Then click on ReportWizards:

**5.** Access now displays the Wizards menu. You may remember it from when you created a form. Choose Single-Column for our first report, and click on OK.

**6.** The Fields dialog box comes up, asking which fields you want in the report. Let's add all the fields. Just double-click on each one, and they'll jump over to the right side as in Figure 12.7.

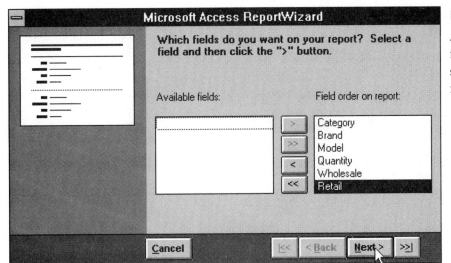

**FIGURE 12.7:**

Adding all the fields to the single-column report layout

**7.** Click on Next to get to the next dialog box.

**8.** Now the Wizard wants to know how you want to sort your data in the report. Let's say we want to see the inventory sorted by Category, with brand names alphabetized within each category. Double-click first on Category, then on Brand. The result should look like Figure 12.8.

**9.** Click on Next. Now you get to choose between three "looks" the data can be given. Click on each little button to see the effect. I'm going to choose Ledger for clarity, since it adds grid lines.

**10.** Click on Next. Now you're asked what title you want printed at the top of the report. Enter the following, as a reminder for future reference of what the report does.

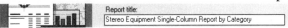

**11.** Click on the Print Preview button. Now the computer magic happens (this is the stuff you'd have to do manually without Wizards) as Access designs the report for you and

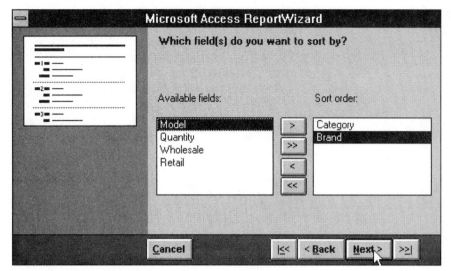

**FIGURE 12.8:**

Choosing the sort order for records in the report

displays it in a window. You'll only be able to see a portion of the window, so maximize it. It should look like Figure 12.9.

**12.** Click on Zoom, or click the magnifying glass cursor on the page if you want to see the little tiny full-page view. If you printed the report, the first page would look like Figure 12.10.

You might recognize that this is not much more than what you got when you printed from a Form screen, but now you have grid lines and the data is sorted. You could achieve the sorting, of course, with a filter from your form. Single-column reports really aren't much more than a listing of the data in your fields, but at least Report-Wizards adds page numbers and dates.

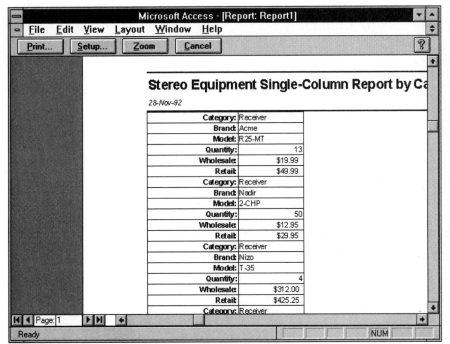

**FIGURE 12.9:**

The preview of the single-column report. You have to maximize the window to see it.

## MAKING WIZARD REPORTS WITH SUBGROUPING

Let's see if the Wizard will give us something a little more interesting. Suppose we want items listed by category, with subtotals for each category indicating how much investment we have tied up in receivers, speakers, and so on. Access can calculate subtotals on any numerical field. For example, it can calculate the total wholesale cost just for receivers. You can also group all products from the same manufacturer together and perform calculations, and so on.

Unfortunately there's no easy way to "re-Wizard" your current report. You have to start from scratch. Let's close the single-column report and quickly make up the next one.

## Stereo Equipment Single-Column Report by Category

28-Nov-92

| | |
|---|---|
| Category: | Receiver |
| Brand: | Acme |
| Model: | R25-MT |
| Quantity: | 13 |
| Wholesale: | $19.99 |
| Retail: | $49.99 |
| Category: | Receiver |
| Brand: | Nadir |
| Model: | 2-CHP |
| Quantity: | 50 |
| Wholesale: | $12.95 |
| Retail: | $29.95 |
| Category: | Receiver |
| Brand: | Nizo |
| Model: | T-35 |
| Quantity: | 4 |
| Wholesale: | $312.00 |
| Retail: | $425.25 |
| Category: | Receiver |
| Brand: | Nizo |
| Model: | T-33 |
| Quantity: | 5 |
| Wholesale: | $225.49 |
| Retail: | $350.49 |
| Category: | Speakers |
| Brand: | Razco |
| Model: | L-55 |
| Quantity: | 30 |
| Wholesale: | $199.00 |
| Retail: | $249.00 |
| Category: | Speakers |
| Brand: | Talbest |
| Model: | BG-20 |
| Quantity: | 6 |
| Wholesale: | $250.00 |
| Retail: | $350.88 |
| Category: | Tape Deck |
| Brand: | Flowutter |
| Model: | WBL-5 |
| Quantity: | 5 |
| Wholesale: | $149.33 |
| Retail: | $250.77 |
| Category: | Tape Deck |
| Brand: | Rollem |
| Model: | CAS-3 |
| Quantity: | 10 |
| Wholesale: | $125.65 |
| Retail: | $212.99 |

**FIGURE 12.10:**

A typical single-column report. Not too fancy, but at least all the data is there.

1. In the Print Preview screen (if you're still on it), click Cancel. From the Report Design window, choose File ➤ Close.

2. You'll be asked about saving the report. Click on Yes. A Save As box will ask what name you want to give it. Call it Single-Column by Category, and click on OK. You're returned to the Database window. Your new report is now listed there.

3. Click on New to start a new report.

4. Select Stereo Equipment again and click on Wizards.

5. Choose Groups/Totals this time.

6. Add all the fields just like you did last time. This time do it the easy way, by clicking on the >> button.

7. Click on Next. Now you see a new dialog box, asking how you want to "group" your data.

What does this mean? Well, since you're going to do subtotaling, you have to tell Access which fields to look at to find records that have something in common. For example, suppose you want to subtotal the inventory investment separately for each category of stereo equipment: for receivers, speakers, tape decks, and turntables. Here is how you want Access to group the records for subtotaling:

| BRAND | CATEGORY | MODEL | QUANTITY | WHOLESALE | RETAIL |
|-------|----------|-------|----------|-----------|--------|
| Nizo | Receiver | T-33 | 5 | 225.49 | 350.49 |
| Nizo | Receiver | T-35 | 4 | 312.00 | 425.25 |
| Acme | Receiver | R25-MT | 13 | 19.99 | 49.99 |
| Nadir | Receiver | 2-CHP | 50 | 12.95 | 29.95 |
| Razco | Speakers | L-55 | 30 | 199.00 | 249.00 |
| Talbest | Speakers | BG-20 | 6 | 250.00 | 350.88 |

| BRAND | CATEGORY | MODEL | QUANTITY | WHOLESALE | RETAIL |
|-------|----------|-------|----------|-----------|--------|
| Rollem | Tape Deck | CAS-3 | 10 | 125.65 | 212.99 |
| Flowutter | Tape Deck | WBL-5 | 5 | 149.33 | 250.77 |
| Xirtam | Turntable | 25-L | 5 | 99.99 | 149.99 |
| Raluric | Turntable | RND-1 | 3 | 595.00 | 850.00 |

You can use up to three fields as the basis for grouping. Most often you'll use one field. If you use additional fields, each group is further broken down with subtotals for, say, each brand.

The field we want to group on is Category, since we want all speakers together, all receivers together, and so on.

1. In the Group By dialog box, choose Category. Then click Next.

2. Now that you've told Access to look in the Category field to figure out how to group your records, you need to tell it exactly how to analyze what it finds in that field. For example, should it group records only when the complete field is identical (e.g., records containing *Receiver*), or when just the first three letters are identical (*Receiver* and *Rec*), in case someone has abbreviated during data entry? This option also allows you to group, say, people who have the same first letter of their last name, or those with zip codes starting with the same first three digits. Since we want an exact match, choose Normal, then click Next.

3. The next box asks which field(s) you want to sort by. Since we're grouping on Category, that's already assumed and isn't available as a choice. The report will already be sorted by Category. Just as we did before, let's sort by Brand, so add that field to the box at the right. Then click Next.

**4.** Let's choose Executive this time for the report's look. Select that option and click Next.

**5.** Finally, give the report the name:

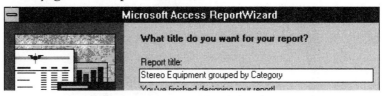

**6.** Click on Preview and then watch the Wizard create the report. It may take as long as 30 seconds, so just wait until the hour-glass cursor goes away. Then adjust your window and scroll a bit so you can see the first of the groupings, as in Figure 12.11. Notice that Access automatically assumed you wanted subtotals and a grand total on all numeric or currency fields. Thus, you have calculated totals under Quantity, Wholesale, and Retail.

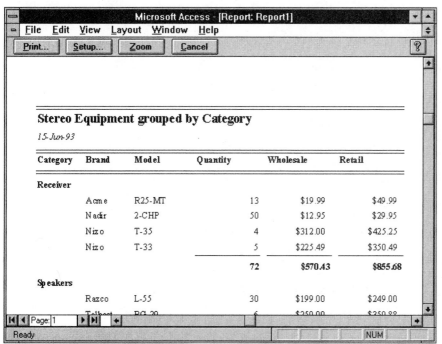

**FIGURE 12.11:**
The first of the groupings as shown in the Print Preview window. Each group will look like this.

**7.** Go ahead and print out your report to see the whole effect. It should look like Figure 12.12. It's not a bad report, I'd say. For next to no work, it looks pretty good! Having been a database programmer, I can say this with some authority. Two points for the engineers at Microsoft (an unpaid commercial announcement).

## Stereo Equipment grouped by Category

*15-Jun-93*

| Category | Brand | Model | Quantity | Wholesale | Retail |
|---|---|---|---|---|---|
| **Receiver** | | | | | |
| | Acme | R25-MT | 13 | $19.99 | $49.99 |
| | Nadir | 2-CHP | 50 | $12.95 | $29.95 |
| | Nizo | T-35 | 4 | $312.00 | $425.25 |
| | Nizo | T-33 | 5 | $225.49 | $350.49 |
| | | | 72 | $570.43 | $855.68 |
| **Speakers** | | | | | |
| | Razco | L-55 | 30 | $199.00 | $249.00 |
| | Talbest | BG-20 | 6 | $250.00 | $350.88 |
| | | | 36 | $449.00 | $599.88 |
| **Tape Dec** | | | | | |
| | Flowutter | WBL-5 | 5 | $149.33 | $250.77 |
| | Rollem | CAS-3 | 10 | $125.65 | $212.99 |
| | | | 15 | $274.98 | $463.76 |
| **Turntable** | | | | | |
| | Raluric | RND-1 | 3 | $595.00 | $850.00 |
| | Xirtam | 25-L | 5 | $99.99 | $149.99 |
| | | | 8 | $694.99 | $999.99 |
| | | **Grand Total :** | 131 | $1,989.40 | $2,919.31 |

**FIGURE 12.12:**

The report with subtotals

## How to Create a Custom Report

Now let's create a more complex report, customizing it to better suit our needs. So far the report lists all the products you stock and calculates your total number of items, total investment in inventory (your total wholesale cost), and total retail value for the items you have on hand, separated by category. But does it? Oops. Notice that the totals under Wholesale and Retail only add the single-unit prices, not reflecting the number of units in stock. Look at the first line. Thirteen Acme receivers didn't really cost you $19.99; they cost $13 \times$ $19.99.

In addition to fixing that, suppose you'd also like to calculate your gross margin for each item, so you can see the anticipated gross margins associated with your various inventory investments. Using Access's brain power, these calculations should be a cinch. But for these modifications, you'll have to use the Report Design window and get a little dirty. Luckily the report already includes the basics. We'll just have to modify it a bit by adding a couple of fields, removing the bogus totals, and squishing things together a little tighter across the page.

Before moving ahead to create a more complex report using the Stereo Equipment table, let's have a look at the Report Design window. Click Cancel in the Print Preview window to return to the Report Design window. Your screen should look like Figure 12.13. So that you can see the names of the sections (horizontal strips of the window), I've dragged the Toolbox to the right side of the screen.

As you can see, the Report Design screen's Toolbar has many buttons, more than other screens thus far. With them, you can easily group items, look up field names, change colors of objects, change font and size, set text in bold or italics, and change alignment of text.

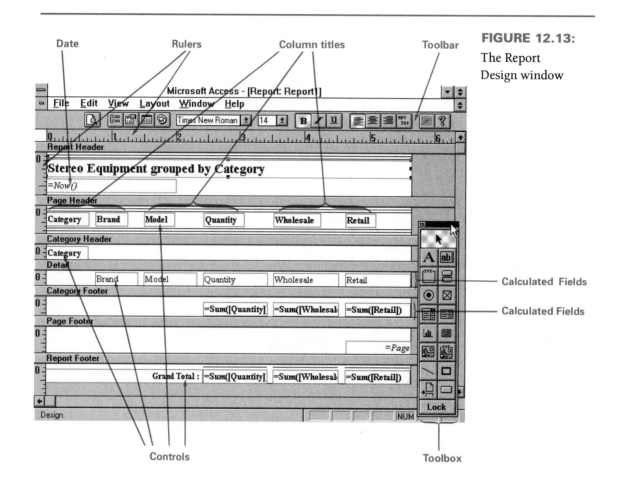

**FIGURE 12.13:**
The Report
Design window

# UNDERSTANDING THE SECTIONS OF A REPORT

Now let's take a moment to look at the various sections of the Report Design window. Understanding what's going on here is the biggest key to modifying your reports.

Because the Report Design window cannot display a whole printed page of your final report on your screen all at once, Access breaks each page of your report into distinct parts called *sections,* some of which are smaller than they will be when printed. The sections are delineated by solid lines that extend across the window.

For example, in Figure 12.13 you see the Report Header section at the top of the screen. Within this section are the date and the name of the report. Below this section is the Page Header section, which has the column names in it. In designing a report, all you really have to do is decide what you want to include in each section of your printed pages.

For example, you can put the following things into a section:

- Fields from the current table or view that display the report data

- Text you type from the keyboard, such as explanatory notes or a form letter, called *labels*

- Special fields you create on the report screen, called *calculated fields,* that do calculations on the fly to report such things as totals

- Boxes and lines you create on the report screen to emphasize parts of your report

- Graphs or pictures

- Buttons, check boxes, and list boxes that indicate how a given field is filled in (e.g., a check box for Paid or Overdue)

Each report has seven sections. Each section consists of the space between the name of the section and the next solid horizontal line below it. The three center sections are the really important ones, because they pertain to the data. The top and bottom sections (the Report and Page Footers and Headers) are just icing on the cake. For some reports, you may not need all the sections. You can turn off the Report Header and Page Headers via the Layout menu if you don't need them.

In our example, the three central sections are called

**Category Header**
**Detail**
**Category Footer**

The header and footer have the prefix *Category* because Category is the name of the field we're grouping on. The name of the header and footer sections would be different if we were grouping on another field (e.g., Last Name Header).

Now compare these three sections (Category, Header, Detail, Category Footer) to your printed output or to Figure 12.14 to see the task that they have dutifully performed:

- The Category header simply prints out the first category, second category, and so on (e.g., Receiver, Speaker, etc.).

- The Detail section reports the data in the table's fields just as they are listed in the section, from left to right.

- The Category footer has printed three calculated fields (each has a fancy formula in it to calculate the subtotals).

Our report is missing calculated fields that will multiply the quantity of each item by its wholesale price. Something like Figure 12.14 would be better.

As with most things in Access, there are numerous ways to solve this problem. The calculated fields we want could come from another source—a query. We could add a calculated field to a query or even to the main table that the report is based on and simply plop them into the report with no report modifications necessary. This is one solution to the problem. On the other hand, if you don't often need to look at that data, then why have it cluttering up your query? Better to add it to a report. Access will do the calculations, using the latest prices in the table, whenever you run the report. For the purpose of learning about reports, we'll do it here. (You'll learn about adding calculated fields to queries and tables later.)

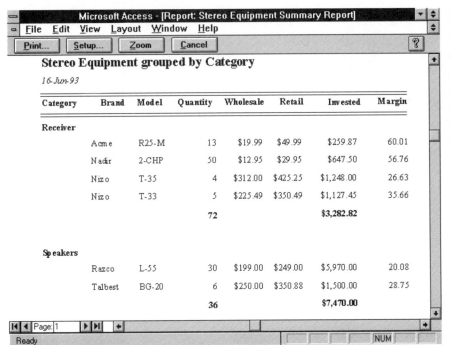

**FIGURE 12.14:**

Correctly calculated fields and the removal of two erroneously calculated fields improve this report.

# MAKING SOME ROOM FOR ADDITIONAL FIELDS

First we'll condense things, remove the incorrect calculated fields, and add some room to clean things up a bit in the report. Then we'll add two calculated fields that work correctly.

Each of the little boxes on the screen with thin lines around it is called a *text box*, or *control*. You can move these boxes around on the screen and resize them. You just click on the control and drag it left or right, up or down. When you click on a control, *handles* appear (little black boxes in its corners or on its sides). You can click on the object's handles and drag them to alter the object's size.

Sizing handles: Click here to resize.

Move handles: Drag from here to move.

Depending on where you click on a control, the cursor will take a different shape. Experiment with subtle movements of the mouse on a control to see these effects:

- When placed over the move handle, it takes the shape of a pointing finger.

- When over text, it becomes the blinking text cursor (I-beam).

- When on the perimeter (faint line) of the object, it turns to a hand.

- When on the sizing handles, it turns into a two-headed arrow.

If you double-click on a control, its Properties box comes up, listing all kinds of weird stuff about the item, most of which we don't care about at this time. If this happens, just drag the Properties box by its title bar (topmost line) to a corner of the screen or double-click its Control box to remove it.

When you're moving controls around, the rulers at the top and left edges of the window can help you more accurately position them. You can also select a number of items and move them as a unit. Hold down the Shift key and click on each item to add to the group. When you drag one of them, they'll all move. (This is called Shift-dragging.)

When things get out of alignment (such as a number of controls on one row), select them all and choose Layout ➤ Align.

Sometimes it's really a hassle to select a control in a way that gets its handles to show. The easiest thing is to click on another control, then on the one you want to select.

Got the ground rules? OK. Let's get down to business.

1. Check out Figure 12.15 to see what I've done. Rather than tell you every move, which is a bore, just copy the figure, noting that I've

   - decreased the Model field in the Detail section by clicking on it, moving the pointer by its lower right handle, and dragging it to a smaller size.
   - moved the Quantity, Wholesale, and Retail columns to the left. This required decreasing the size of the Grand Total control in the Report Footer a bit. I moved each one as a group by Shift-dragging. It was much easier that way.
   - downsized the Quantity fields. Even if the formula is cut off, it still works. Don't worry about it.

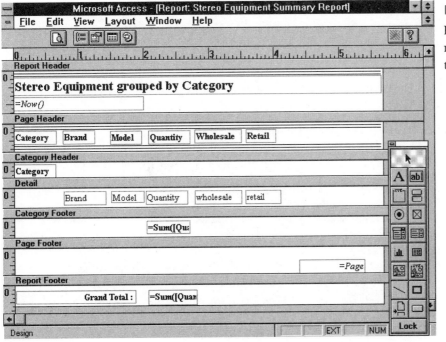

**FIGURE 12.15:**

First set of modifications to the report

- deleted the Wholesale and Retail subtotal calculated fields in the Category Footer section, because their calculations were incorrect. Just click on the fields and press Del.
- deleted the three little lines above the grand totals.

Don't worry if your screen doesn't look identical to the figure. Believe me, it took a lot of work to get it as neat as this! You need the patience of Job and the dexterity of an artist to really get good at this.

2. While you're working, don't forget to save. Choose File ➤ Save and save your work as Stereo Equipment Summary Report.

# ADDING THE CALCULATED FIELDS

Next we'll want to add two more columns to the report. They'll show the total amount invested for each item's inventory and the gross margin for each item (that is, the markup as a percentage of the retail price). Access will calculate the values in the fields from the figures in your table and then print them in the report. If the figures in the table change, the calculated fields will reflect the changes.

Here's how to add the two new fields.

1. In the Page Header section create a little box (control) that reads **Invested**. Here's how. In the Toolbar, there's a tool for adding a new control. It's the one that looks like a big A. It's called the Label tool.

Once you click, the cursor changes shape. Position the cursor as you see above and click. This places the new control, which will look like a little vertical line. This means the box will grow as you type into it.

**2.** Since this is to be the column head for the column showing your investment, type **Invested**.

**3.** Repeat steps 1 and 2 for the second heading, which should read **Margin**. Now your screen should look like Figure 12.16.

**4.** To create the calculated fields, use the AB tool to the right of the A tool. It's called the Text tool. You use this tool to place a field rather than just display a label. But this time, position the field box just to the right of Retail down in the Detail section of the report.

**5.** Click inside the new box to make the word *Unbound* disappear, and type this formula into the field box:

**=[Quantity]*[Wholesale]**

**FIGURE 12.16:**

The two column heads added

(If you don't enter the brackets, it won't work.)

6. Add another field to its right, down under Margin, using the same technique. Enter the formula

**=((Retail-Wholesale)/(Retail))*100**

Note that Access will stick in square brackets when you move off the field.

## ADDING THE SUBTOTAL FIELDS

Lastly, we have to add the subtotal field that will report the amount invested for each category of product and the grand total field for investment in all products.

1. Create a new field in the Category Footer (same row as the Quantity subtotal is in) in the Invested column. This will tell us the total amount invested for each category of product. Use the Text (AB) tool again. Enter the formula

**=SUM(Quantity*Wholesale)**

2. Next, create the last field (whew!). This one will live down in the Grand Total line at the bottom of the form. It will report the *total* invested in all the equipment inventory, summing up all the figures in the Invested column. Use the text (AB) tool again. Give it the same formula as the last one:

**=SUM(Quantity*Wholesale)**

*Note:* When you create a SUM field, you have to specify the entire formula used in the detail section of the same column, and add SUM to the start of the formula.

3. Adjust the width of the new field boxes so their right edges are aligned exactly where you want the right edge of the

numbers to start (the numbers sort of print from right to left). This is how you line up printed numbers, since they are right-aligned. Otherwise numbers will be hanging out in the breeze too far to the right.

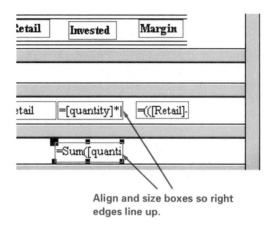

Align and size boxes so right edges line up.

# FINAL PREPARATIONS

Just a few touch ups, now. Here's a quick way to line up the fields.

1. Shift-select all the fields in one row, say the Page Header row.

2. Choose Layout ➤ Align ➤ Top. The fields will align horizontally.

3. Shift-select all the fields will in a row, say the Invested row.

4. Choose Layout ➤ Align ➤ Right. The fields align vertically along their right edges, which is what we want for number fields.

5. Finally, notice that the new summary fields aren't formatted as bold, though the other summary fields are. Select each field and click on the Bold tool in the Toolbar at the top of the window (the one that looks like a big, bold B). This will cause their numbers to be formatted as bold when printed.

6. Check your screen against Figure 12.17, and adjust as necessary. Don't sweat the small stuff. But at least the formulas have to be right.

7. Save your work.

8. Click on the Print Preview button in the Toolbar. Hmmm. Things don't look quite right. (See Figure 12.18. If you got an error message, skip to "If You Got an Error Message While Running a Report.")

9. The values look right, but a couple need to be formatted as currency, and the Margin fields could use fewer decimal places. Choose View ➤ Properties to bring up the Properties dialog box.

10. Select the first of the Invested fields (the top one with the formula in it).

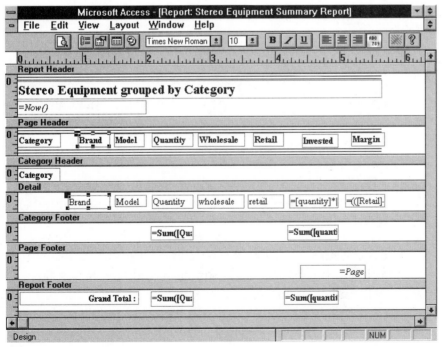

**FIGURE 12.17:**

The final layout

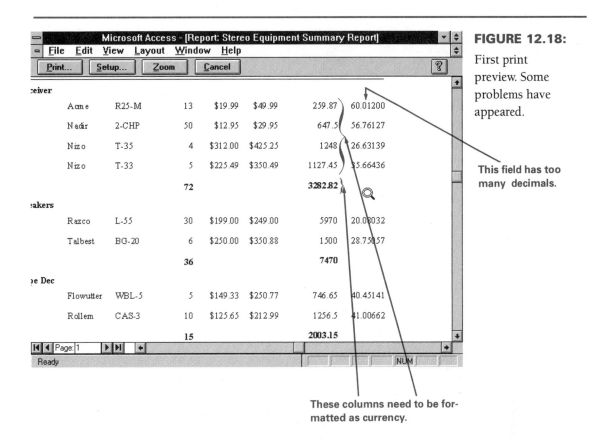

FIGURE 12.18:

First print preview. Some problems have appeared.

This field has too many decimals.

These columns need to be formatted as currency.

**11.** In the Properties box, click on the Format line and then on the little drop-down list button, as you see in Figure 12.19.

**12.** Choose Currency.

**13.** Click on the next field down (same column—the one that starts with SUM). The properties for it are immediately reported, without having to double-click. Repeat this process for the remaining SUM field below that one.

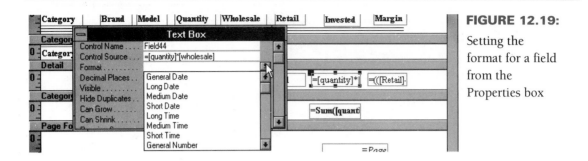

**FIGURE 12.19:**

Setting the
format for a field
from the
Properties box

**14.** Now, using the same technique, set the format for one field in the Margin column to Fixed.

**15.** Save your work with File ➤ Save.

**16.** Preview the report. Then print it. The results are shown in Figure 12.20. If you want to add more space between categories, increase the size of the Category Footer section by dragging its lower edge down. Remember, any of the sections' sizes can be increased this way, including spacing between each item in the detail section. I've adjusted spacing a bit for the print out.

One thing that could go wrong has to do with the size of your text and label boxes. I told you earlier to make some of them smaller in order to fit more in across the page. If you make them too small you could cause Access not to print the entire contents of the field. This is pretty obvious if you see something like *Tape Dec* in the Print Preview window, but it is not always as obvious in other places. For instance, if you see a dollar sign in a Currency field where the amount is in the hundreds, but no dollar signs appear if the amount is in the thousands, then you need to go back into the Report Design window and stretch that box a bit.

FIGURE 12.20:

The final report

## Stereo Equipment grouped by Category

*15-Jun-93*

| Category | Brand | Model | Quantity | Wholesale | Retail | Invested | Margin |
|---|---|---|---|---|---|---|---|
| **Receiver** | | | | | | | |
| | Acme | R25-M | 13 | $19.99 | $49.99 | $259.87 | 60.01 |
| | Nadir | 2-CHP | 50 | $12.95 | $29.95 | $647.50 | 56.76 |
| | Nizo | T-35 | 4 | $312.00 | $425.25 | $1,248.00 | 26.63 |
| | Nizo | T-33 | 5 | $225.49 | $350.49 | $1,127.45 | 35.66 |
| | | | **72** | | | **$3,282.82** | |
| **Speakers** | | | | | | | |
| | Razco | L-55 | 30 | $199.00 | $249.00 | $5,970.00 | 20.08 |
| | Talbest | BG-20 | 6 | $250.00 | $350.88 | $1,500.00 | 28.75 |
| | | | **36** | | | **$7,470.00** | |
| **Tape Deck** | | | | | | | |
| | Flowutter | WBL-5 | 5 | $149.33 | $250.77 | $746.65 | 40.45 |
| | Rollem | CAS-3 | 10 | $125.65 | $212.99 | $1,256.50 | 41.01 |
| | | | **15** | | | **$2,003.15** | |
| **Turntable** | | | | | | | |
| | Raluric | RND-1 | 3 | $595.00 | $850.00 | $1,785.00 | 30.00 |
| | Xirtam | 25-L | 5 | $99.99 | $149.99 | $499.95 | 33.34 |
| | | | **8** | | | **$2,284.95** | |
| | **Grand Total :** | | **131** | | | **$15,040.92** | |

# IF YOU GOT AN ERROR MESSAGE WHILE RUNNING A REPORT

Having trouble running a report? Fine-tuning custom reports often takes many tries. Luckily the Preview option cuts down on the pain and the wasted paper of aborted report attempts.

You'll see lots of error messages in the course of creating complex reports. More often than not, the culprit will be formula errors. Since it's impossible to see the formulas in the somewhat truncated field boxes, it's better to check them in the Control Properties box.

Just open the Properties box for a control by double-clicking on the control, or by selecting the control (handles have to appear) and choosing View ➤ Properties. Then check the first couple of lines of the box (there are many settings in the box, but most don't matter), particularly the formula. Stretch the box to the right by dragging its right edge to see the whole formula if you need to. Once open, you can click on one control after another to see what the settings look like and if the formulas look good. Don't hesitate to search around in Help or consult a more thorough Access book (such as SYBEX's *Understanding Microsoft Access,* by Alan Simpson) or manual for details on formulas. Remember,

- Parentheses have to be used as they would in algebra to group expressions, as in the following:

  **=(([Retail]-[Wholesale])/([Retail])*100**

- Field names should have brackets on both sides.

- Formulas should start with an equals sign.

# About Custom Forms

Incidentally, the skills you've just learned by modifying a report also apply to the design and modification of custom forms, which use similar controls. Using what you now know, along with Access's built-in Help system, you should be able to make custom data-entry forms with such features as easy-to-read fonts, list boxes, and radio buttons. You can even add pictures to forms. All of these features will make data entry easier for you or your data-entry staff.

CHAPTER

FEATURING

**Standard Labels**
**Custom Formats**
**Printing**
▼

# Printing Mailing Labels

A common use for a database management system is to create mailing labels for bulk mailings—one of the classic computerized time-savers. With Access's ReportWizards report generator, you can print addresses easily and neatly on various sizes of commercially available mailing labels, just by choosing the source table, the Avery label number or equivalent for labels, and a few other odds and ends.

Some of the supported label sizes are large, so you can design and print other types of labels too, like labels for shipping cartons, envelopes, or anything else—from leftovers to library books. You can create custom labels as well, by adding graphics, changing fonts, and so forth.

You can print labels on a printer with a tractor (sprockets) that can feed the labels accurately or on a laser printer. In either case, you'll need special labels designed for that type of printer. Only these types of printers have an accurate enough paper-feed arrangement for labels. Just a little "creep" from page to page will soon cause the labels to print off-center. Eventually the address will "walk" off the end of one label and onto the next, so regular friction-feed printers don't cut the mustard for label printing.

Designing labels is a little like creating the report we made in the last chapter, only a lot easier in most cases, since there's typically less data on a label than a report. ReportWizards does most of the work for you, anyway.

Here are the basic steps for creating mailing labels:

1. Decide which table or query the labels will use for data.

2. Choose which fields you want on the label, and in what order they should print.

3. Choose which fields the list should be sorted on.

4. Load up the labels and print.

## How to Design a Label

To see how label design works, we're going to create typical mailing labels that you could use for bulk mailing. We'll use the PHONEBK table's records.

1. Close the STEREO database if it was open when you started this chapter.

2. Open the PHONEBK database.

**3.** Click on the Reports button, and then click on New.

**4.** Choose the Name and Address list table from the drop-down list, and click on ReportWizards, since we want Access to design the labels if possible. (You'd only click on Blank Report if you wanted to design a label or report from scratch.)

**5.** Choose Mailing Label from the resulting dialog box and click on OK, as you see in Figure 13.1.

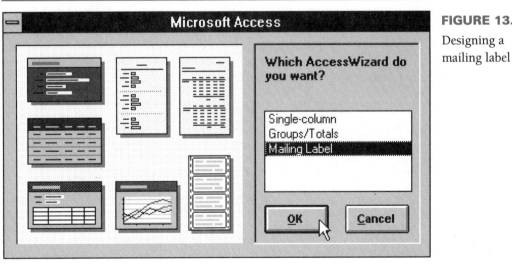

**FIGURE 13.1:**

Designing a mailing label

# CHOOSING THE FIELDS

If there's a tricky part to designing the label, this is it. What you have to do now is to set the label design. How many lines will the label have? Which fields are on what lines? How about the line that contains the city, state, and zip: Are there commas and spaces between the fields? If so, how many?

Luckily, the dialog box makes this all pretty simple to specify. Once you do it, it'll be a breeze the second time you print labels. Take a look at the dialog box that's on your screen now. It should look like Figure 13.2.

What you're going to do is choose the relevant fields from the box on the left and move them to the right side. The little buttons that look like punctuation marks are for adding spaces, commas, and other punctuation marks between fields on the labels.

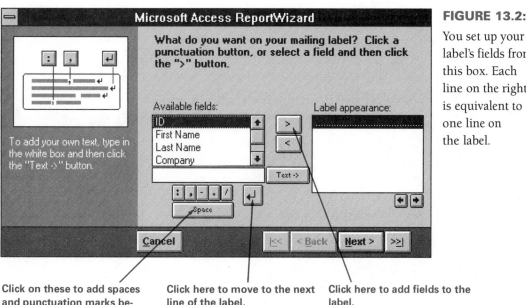

**FIGURE 13.2:**

You set up your label's fields from this box. Each line on the right is equivalent to one line on the label.

Click on these to add spaces and punctuation marks between fields.

Click here to move to the next line of the label.

Click here to add fields to the label.

1. The first line on the label should have the person's first name and last name separated by a space, right? So, click on First Name over on the left side.

2. Click on the > button to add it to the label.

3. Click on the Space button. This adds a space.

4. Click on Last Name, followed by the > button.

The first line of the label is done. The dialog box should look like Figure 13.3.

Now we'll add the rest of the lines.

1. Click once the ↵ button. This drops you down to the next line on the label. (*Don't press ↵ on your keyboard!* If you do, you'll go to the next dialog box. If that happens, click on Back to return to this one.)

2. Click on Company, followed by > . This places the company name on line 2.

3. Click the ↵ button again to add the next line.

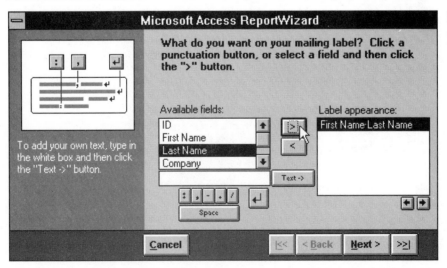

**FIGURE 13.3:**

The first line of the label defined

**4.** Click on Street Address, followed by > . This places the street address on line 3.

**5.** Click the ↵ button again to add the fourth line.

**6.** Now place the City, State, and Zip Code fields on the last line. Start by clicking on City, followed by > .

**7.** Since we want a comma and a space after the city name, as in

**Missoula, MT**

click on the comma button. Then click the Space button once.

**8.** Click on State, followed by >.

**9.** Click on the Space button four times to add some space between the state and the zip code:

**King of Prussia, PA    19088**

**9.** Finally, add the Zip field. Now the label should look like Figure 13.4.

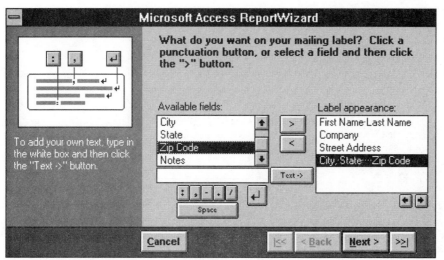

**FIGURE 13.4:**

All the fields placed on the label

**10.** Click on Next to get to the next dialog box.

**11.** Now you have to choose which field you want to sort the list on. Since the U.S. Postal Service requires zip code sorting for bulk mailing, let's choose Zip Code. Click on Zip Code followed by the > button, as you see in Figure 13.5.

## CHOOSING THE LABEL SIZE

Now you have to choose which type of labels you're going to use.

**1.** Click on Next. A box appears, listing all the "canned" label sizes that Access knows about. This is great! In the old days, figuring this out meant measuring your labels and lots of guesswork. You can still measure if you want to, but if you have commercial labels that conform to the Avery label numbers (is Avery getting a kick-back from this?), you can just look at the box and make your choice. You can even click on English to see the Avery numbers available in Europe and Great Britain.

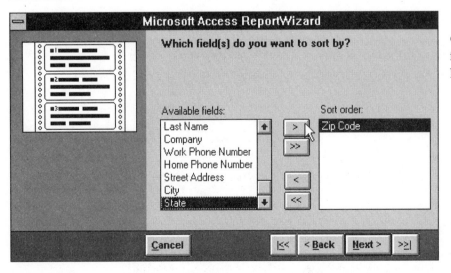

**FIGURE 13.5:**

Choosing the field to sort the labels on

2. The dimensions are listed with height first, then width. So the first label choice is 4" wide. Let's choose Avery number 4144 so we see three labels across the page. Your screen should look like Figure 13.6.

3. Now click on Next. From this point, you can modify the label, or go on to preview it. Click Preview. Up come your labels, as you see in Figure 13.7.

4. If you were really going to print at this point, you'd ready the printer, get the labels loaded, and print.

5. When you're done, don't forget to save your report and name it. Something like Mailing Labels for Name and Address list is fine.

## Modifying the Labels

If it turns out that things aren't quite right with your labels, you might want to adjust them slightly from the Design window. For example, I'd like to change the font on my mailing labels to something more interesting than the stock font that Access uses.

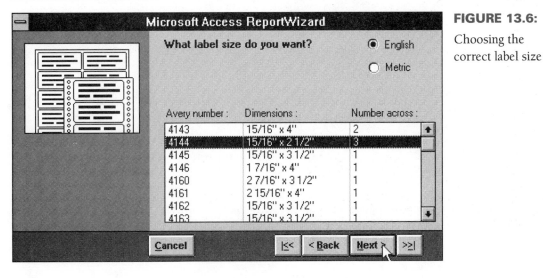

**FIGURE 13.6:**

Choosing the correct label size

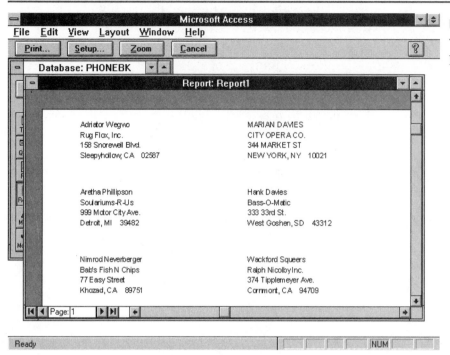

1. When you click on Cancel from the Print Preview dialog box, you're returned to the Design window. Before closing that window, take a look at it. Notice that it consists of one report section only. That section has four text boxes (controls) on it, just like the ones we used in the Stereo store report.

2. To change the font of, say, the first line (First Name and Last Name), select that box.

3. Click on the Font selector in the Toolbar and choose a new font, as shown in Figure 13.8. You can also choose a new font size from the drop-down list to the right of the font list, or you can choose other effects, such as bold or italic.

4. If you need to adjust the position of the controls, you can drag them, just as you did in Chapter 12. To alter the size of the label, just drag its right edge or bottom edge.

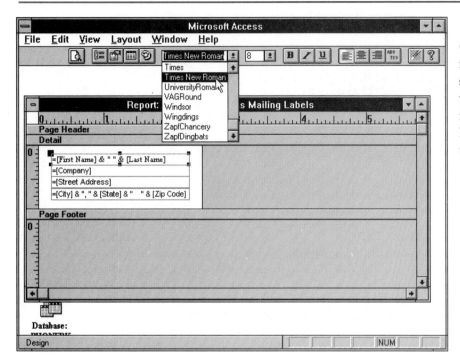

**FIGURE 13.8:**

Changing the font of the selected control will cause the first line of the label to print in the new font.

# Tips about Label Printing

Here are some more tips on printing labels. First, before rolling the presses big-time, print out one page of the labels, just to see if everything is lined up OK. It's a drag to come back after lunch to find 300 expensive labels printed off-kilter.

It's not uncommon for a label design to be off the first time around, and you may need to modify your design several times to get the exact dimensions right. Also, don't overlook the possibility that switches on your printer are not set properly, especially if blank lines appear between every printed line or if the label information is printing too wide. In the first instance, the printer's local line feed switch may be on. Try turning that off. If you are having the other problem, your printer may be set for too few characters per inch (for example, 10 characters per inch instead of 12), forcing the printing to be too wide. Set your printer to 12 characters per inch and try again. You may need to consult the operator's manual supplied with your printer to make these settings.

If you're using super-expensive laser-printer labels, (sometimes $50 a box!) try printing one page on normal paper and holding that sheet up to the light against a label sheet to check for proper alignment. If the alignment is off, you'll have to adjust the design (you probably chose the wrong type of label), either manually using the Report Design screen, or better yet, by creating the labels over again and choosing the correct stock size.

Here's one more little hint. Want to make up return address labels, or multiple labels that are all the same? Simple. Create a table where all the records are the same. Enter one record in a datasheet. Copy and paste it until you have as many records as you want labels for. Then use the table as the basis for your labels.

When I print a sheet of mailing labels on laser label stock and I don't have enough names to use the whole sheet, I use this technique so I don't have to throw away unused labels (you can't feed a half-used sheet back into the printer later without messing up the printer). I preview the label sheet on-screen, figure out how many empty labels I'll have, then add that many return addresses (my name and address) to the table before printing.

FEATURING

**Field Arithmetic**

**Comparison Operators**

**Aggregate Functions**

**Sums**

**Averages**

**Dates and Times**

**Update Queries**

▼

# Working with Numbers, Dates, and Yes/No Fields

We've already discussed numeric fields to some extent in previous chapters, using the CAMPING and STEREO databases. In this chapter, we'll explore some more techniques for managing numeric fields.

Microsoft Access allows you to ask some pretty sophisticated questions about the information in your table. You explored some of these capabilities in Chapters 7 and 8, which discussed queries. Access also provides other commands pertaining to numbers and numeric fields, which you can use to let Access shoulder even more of your work load. For instance, consider the CAMPING table for a moment. Even though it holds only a little data, you still might want to know the following:

- What do all the costs add up to?

- What is the total weight of all the items?

- Which items cost more than $20.00?

- Which items weigh less than 20 pounds, cost more than $12.50, and are owned by Mary?

These are examples of queries—requests for specific data—that Access can easily resolve for you with just a bit of work on your part.

# How to Use Arithmetic and Comparison Operators

You construct queries like those listed above using *operators*. Operators are symbols you can use to perform calculations on information in your table to produce a result. You may recall that you've already used relational operators when constructing queries. Two sets of operators that have relevance to numeric data manipulation are the arithmetic and comparison operators.

## ARITHMETIC OPERATORS

For many people, arithmetic operations are the more familiar of these two. Saying that Access has arithmetic operators is really a fancy way of saying it has a built-in four-function calculator with lots of memory for storing input and answers. You can add, subtract, multiply, or divide, just as if you were using a calculator, or you can use the operators

to ask Access questions about your tables. The arithmetic operators
are listed below.

| SYMBOL | MEANING | EXAMPLE |
|--------|---------|---------|
| + | Addition | 3 + 3 = 6 |
| − | Subtraction | 3 − 3 = 0 |
| * | Multiplication | 3 * 3 = 9 |
| / | Division of one floating point number by another | 3 / 3 = 1 |
| ^ | Exponentiation | 3 ^ 3 = 27 |

## USING CALCULATED FIELDS IN A QUERY

You don't have to create a report to get Access to perform some quick
calculations. You can perform arithmetic calculations via a query or
filter, too. The Query and Filter Design screens let you add *calculated
fields* to your datasheets—fields that are generated on the fly, much
like the Invested field we added to the Stereo Equipment inventory
report. Calculated fields are not added to the database table itself.
They just call on data stored in tables to give you results on-screen
when you run the query. The results of calculated fields can be used
in reports, datasheets, and forms, and even as the basis for other
queries. But they disappear when you close the query.

Let's try some examples.

1. Get to the Database window.

2. Close the PHONEBK database.

3. Open the STEREO database.

4. Click on Queries, then on New.

5. When the Add Table box appears, highlight Stereo Equipment and click on Add. Then click on Close.

6. In the Design window, add all the fields to the QBE grid. Remember how? Double-click each field in the field list, one at a time.

7. Using the scroll bar at the bottom of the QBE grid, scroll the grid over a bit to the left so you can see two more empty field columns.

Now we're ready to add the first calculated field. Let's add two fields that calculate the same things our report did. The first one is the amount tied up in inventory for each item in the store.

1. Click in the Field box in the first empty column to the right of Retail, and enter

    **Invested:wholesale*quantity**

    (Don't forget the colon after Invested.) Invested is the field's name. Without it Access would give it the name Expr1. Even though it's a temporary field, calculated just for display, it has to have a name. Note that the name and the formula go in the same box.

2. Add another field to the right of that one by entering

    **Margin:((retail–wholesale)/retail)*100**

    As you enter this long formula, it will scroll to the left. Mind your parentheses. Once you enter the formula and press ↵ or click on another field, Access adds square brackets around the field names. Your QBE grid should now look like this (I've enlarged the fields so you can see the complete formulas.):

| Field: | \ | Retail | Invested: [wholesale]*[quantity] | Margin: (([retail]-[wholesale])/[retail])*100 | |
|---|---|---|---|---|---|
| Sort: | | | | | |
| Show: | ☒ | ☒ | ☒ | ☒ | |
| Criteria: | | | | | |

3. View the datasheet by clicking on the Datasheet button. Adjust the column sizes to fit all columns on the screen. Figure 14.1 shows the results. Notice how Access quickly calculated the fields for you.

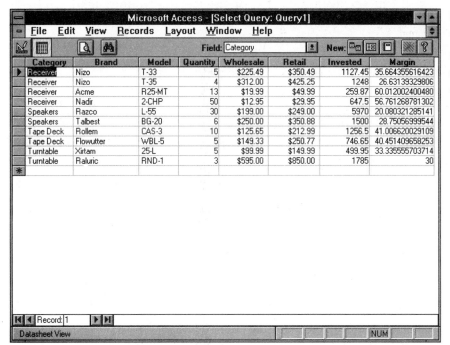

**FIGURE 14.1:**

The two calculated fields are added to the datasheet.

4. Oops. Looks like the formatting isn't correct. The Invested field should be formatted as currency, and Margin should have only two decimals.

5. Change the formatting for each field by returning to the Design screen. To do this, you have to alter the formula to contain a cryptic reference to the formatting style:

**Invested:CCUR([wholesale]*[quantity])**

For the Margin field (this one's pretty complicated since we want to format it as a percentage), add this formula:

**Margin: FORMAT((([retail]–[wholesale])/[retail]),"Percent")**

If you decide that you no longer need one of the calculated fields you created for your query, it's simple to remove it from view. Just click on the Show box to remove the X. For now, let's hide both of the new calculated fields. We're going to work with some other fields.

Note that Access offers numerous *functions* that you can use in calculated fields as well. Functions can be used, for example, to calculate the square roots of numbers. Also available are trigonometric functions for calculations such as tangents and arctangents. These functions are beyond the scope of this book. Refer to the *Microsoft Access Language Reference* for more information on their use, or use Help and search for "Functions, List of."

# USING COMPARISON OPERATORS WITH NUMERIC DATA

Recall from Chapter 8 that comparison operators compare two pieces of data and produce a result. When you were looking for people with specific names, Access used the equal-to operator to find matching records in the Name and Address list. In those cases, you were comparing character strings, not numbers. A character string consists of nonnumerical characters such as letters. But comparison operators can also be used to compare numbers. "Is *x* larger than *y*?" is an example of a numeric comparison operation. Here's the complete list of comparison operators available in Access:

| SYMBOL | MEANING |
|--------|---------|
| = | Equal to |
| > | Greater than |
| < | Less than |
| <= | Less than or equal to |
| >= | Greater than or equal to |
| <> | Not equal to |

You may recall having used the < and > operators for selecting a zip code range in Chapter 8. The <= and >= operators work similarly, but allow you to construct a search condition that includes the end points of a numeric range. For example, using the Stereo table, suppose we want to know the wholesale price of all products costing $250 or more:

1. Return to the Query Design screen and make sure the Invested and Margin fields are set to not show.

2. Scroll over to the Wholesale field.

3. On the Criteria line, enter **>=250.00**.

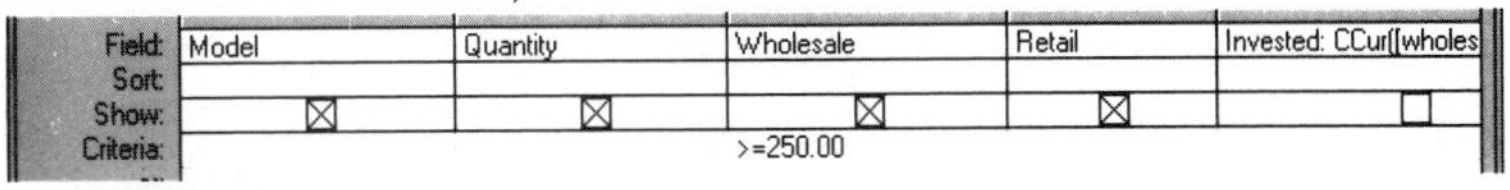

| Field: | Model | Quantity | Wholesale | Retail | Invested: CCur([wholes |
|---|---|---|---|---|---|
| Sort: | | | | | |
| Show: | ☒ | ☒ | ☒ | ☒ | ☐ |
| Criteria: | | | >=250.00 | | |

4. View the datasheet to see the effect of the query. You should see the records shown in Figure 14.2. Notice that record 6, for the Talbest speakers, was listed, because the wholesale price is exactly $250.00. The greater-than operator alone (>) would have excluded it.

Now let's use the not-equal-to operator. When would you want to know that an item or value *isn't* equal to something? Suppose you want to contact all of your clients except those living in the zip code

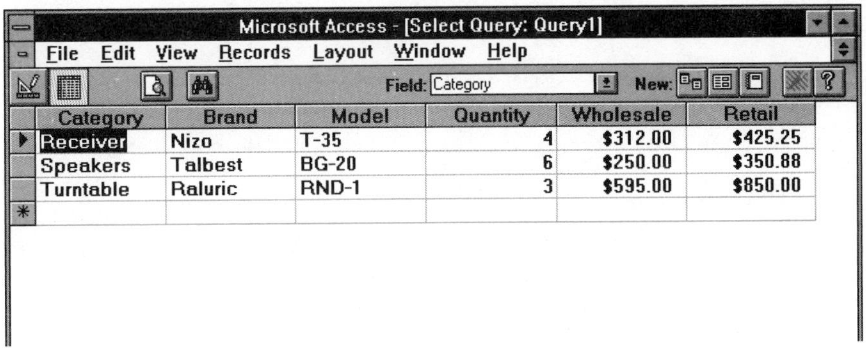

**FIGURE 14.2:**

Items with a wholesale price of $250 or more

| Category | Brand | Model | Quantity | Wholesale | Retail |
|---|---|---|---|---|---|
| Receiver | Nizo | T-35 | 4 | $312.00 | $425.25 |
| Speakers | Talbest | BG-20 | 6 | $250.00 | $350.88 |
| Turntable | Raluric | RND-1 | 3 | $595.00 | $850.00 |

Microsoft Access - [Select Query: Query1]
File Edit View Records Layout Window Help
Field: Category

area 89751, since you've already done a mailing to that area. Here's what you do:

1. Choose File ➤ Close to return to the Database window. Don't save the query.

2. Open the PHONEBK database.

3. Click on the Query button and click New. Choose Name and Address list as the source table, just as you did last time.

4. Add only the First Name, Last Name, Street, and Zip Code fields into the grid.

5. View the datasheet. Your screen should look like Figure 14.3. The figure shows all records, 1 through 9, just for illustration. (I've enlarged the type for you.) Note that Nimrod lives in the 89751 zip code area.

6. Return to the Query Design window. Tab to the Zip Code field, and then, down on the Criteria line, enter <>89751. The results are shown in Figure 14.4.

| First Name | Last Name | Street Address | Zip Code |
|---|---|---|---|
| Wackford | Squeers | 374 Tipplemeyer Ave. | 94709 |
| Hank | Davies | 333 33rd St. | 43312 |
| Adriator | Wegwo | 158 Snorewell Blvd. | 02587 |
| Aretha | Phillipson | 999 Motor City Ave. | 39482 |
| Randy | Batterydown | 495 Anode St. | 30129 |
| Nimrod | Neverberger | 77 Easy Street | 89751 |
| Marcel | Phillip | 456 Fresno St. | 55493 |
| Valery | Kuletzski | 451 Farenheit Ct. | 95420 |
| MARIAN | DAVIES | 344 MARKET ST | 10021 |

**FIGURE 14.3:**

All the records listed

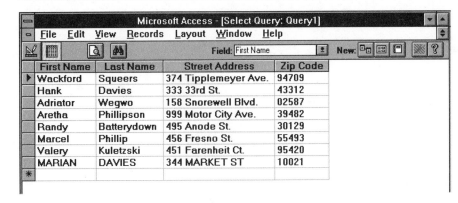

**FIGURE 14.4:**
Nimrod's record is eliminated by using the <> operator.

Notice that we eliminated Nimrod, record 6, from this listing, because his zip code is 89751.

# How to Use Aggregate Functions

The *aggregate functions* are also useful for working with numbers. You can use these functions to perform a calculation on all the values in a field for all the records in a table (or using criteria, only on certain records). For example, you might want to know the average price of items in the store, or the average number of days since your last reorder, or the number of units shipped last month. The nine aggregate functions are listed below, along with the meaning of each. Each of these functions can be used in a query.

| FUNCTION | MEANING |
| --- | --- |
| Avg (Average) | Computes the arithmetic mean of the fields |
| Sum | Adds the values of the fields |
| Min (Minimum) | Displays the lowest value found |
| Max (Maximum) | Displays the highest value found |
| Count | Counts the number of records meeting specific criteria |

| FUNCTION | MEANING |
|----------|---------|
| StDev | Standard deviation of values in the field |
| Var | Variance of values in the field |
| First | The value of the field in the first record in the table |
| Last | The value of the field in the last record of the table |

# USING SUM TO TOTAL DATA FROM DIFFERENT RECORDS

The Sum command adds data in a given field from all the records in the datasheet. Sum, like all the functions, operates on the whole table. If you want a calculation to be based on only specific records, you have to first create a query that limits the records. Then create a sum based on that table.

As an easy example that doesn't require this two-step process, suppose we want to add up the cost of all the items in the Camping list:

**1.** Close the current database. Don't save the query.

**2.** Open the Camping database.

**3.** Choose Tables and double-click the Camping list table. This data appears (if your records are ordered differently, don't worry):

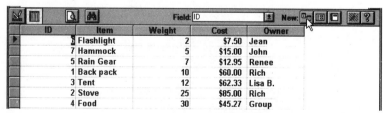

**4.** In the Toolbar, to the right of the word *New*, click the first button. This is the New Query button. It's a shortcut for opening a new query using the existing table.

5. Add only the Cost field to the grid. Here's another trick. You can drag the field to the destination column. Just click on Cost and keep the mouse button down. Then drag it to the first column in the grid. This technique makes placing fields in a specific order a bit easier.

6. When you want to use Sums, Averages, and so forth, you have to add another row to the grid. Choose View ➤ Totals or click on the summation button (Σ ) in the Toolbar. A new line appears in the grid, for totals.

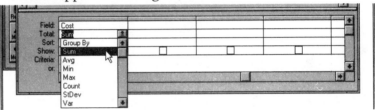

7. Click on the Cost column's Total row, open the drop-down list, and choose Sum:

8. There must not be any other fields in the QBE grid at this point. Now click the Datasheet button to see the result.

9. Get back to the QBE grid. Remove the Cost field and drag the Weight field into column 1. Choose Sum again from the drop-down list, and view the result. You'll be carrying 91 pounds on your camping trip.

The next example is more complex and also more practical. For this one, we'll use the STEREO inventory table. Suppose you want to see quickly, without running a report, the *total* amount of capital investment you have tied up in inventory. That is, you want to see the wholesale cost of each item times the quantity of that item on hand, for all items; then you want all those subtotals added for a grand total. Here's how to do it using Sum.

**1.** Get to the Database window and use File ➤ Close to close the CAMPING database. Open the STEREO database.

**2.** Double-click on the Stereo Equipment table to open it.

**3.** Click on the New Query button up in the right side of the Toolbar to start a new query.

**4.** Add the Totals line, since we're going to do some totals. Fill in the first column of the grid like this:

| Field: | [quantity]*[wholesale] | | | | |
|---|---|---|---|---|---|
| Total: | Sum | | | | |
| Sort: | | | | | |
| Show: | ☒ | ☐ | ☐ | ☐ | |

The first row reads *[quantity] * [wholesale]*. You don't have to enter the brackets, but if you do, they must be square brackets, not parentheses.

**5.** View the result. It's 15040.92 .

You now know that you have over $15,000 tied up in inventory. Let's see how much you have tied up in receivers alone. We'll have to use a criteria line for this.

**1.** Back at the Query Design screen, fill in column 1 like this:

| Field: | Expr1: [quantity]*[wholesale | Category | | | |
|---|---|---|---|---|---|
| Total: | Sum | Group By | | | |
| Sort: | | | | | |
| Show: | ☒ | ☒ | ☐ | ☐ | |
| Criteria: | | "Receiver" | | | |

Note that Access has given the first field a name: Expr1 (for *expression 1*).

**2.** View the result. Access reports that you have 3282.82 tied up in receivers.

Using the Sum option alone instructs Access to calculate a sum for the specific Numeric field. As you saw in the last example, you can also limit the summing to only specific records by entering filters in other fields of the query.

# USING AVG TO CALCULATE AVERAGES

Another very useful aggregate function is Avg, or the Average operator. Avg produces the arithmetic mean of one or more fields in the currently open database.

1. Clear out any operators and filters you have in the query. The easiest way is to click on the column selector tile to highlight the whole column, then press Del.

2. Add three fields to the grid: Quantity, Wholesale, and Retail. Then fill in the grid as Figure 14.5. The results are shown in Figure 14.6.

Since you did not type filter information into any of the fields, averages were calculated for all records in the table.

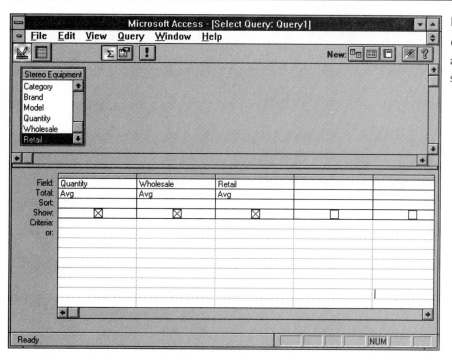

**FIGURE 14.5:**

Calculating averages for specific fields

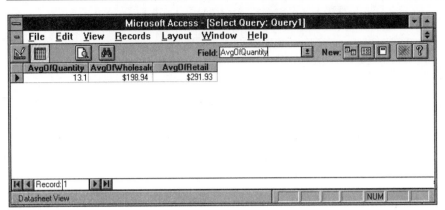

**FIGURE 14.6:**

The results of the averaging query in Figure 14.5

Now let's try something more practical. Suppose you're considering carrying a new brand of receiver, but the local sales representative for the line seems to be quoting too high a price for the product. A quick check of your table displays the average price you are currently paying for receivers:

1. Return to the Query Design screen.

2. Add the Category field to the grid. Type **Receiver** into the Criteria line of that column.

3. Type **Sum** in the Quantity field.

4. Leave **Avg** in the Wholesale and Retail fields. Notice that Access adds the words *Group by* on the Total line for Category.

| Field: | Quantity | Wholesale | Retail | Category | |
|---|---|---|---|---|---|
| Total: | Sum | Avg | Avg | Group By | |
| Sort: | | | | | |
| Show: | ☒ | ☒ | ☒ | ☒ | ☐ |
| Criteria: | | | | "Receiver" | |
| or: | | | | | |

5. View the query.

Your screen shows you that of 72 receivers you have on hand, the average wholesale cost is $142.61, and the average retail price is $213.92.

# COUNTING RECORDS THAT MEET CERTAIN CRITERIA

Occasionally, instead of adding or averaging numbers, you'll want to know how many records in your table meet a certain requirement. Suppose you have a mailing list and are planning to print mailing labels from it. You may need to know the number of labels that will be printed for a specific zip code or range of zip codes, so you can accurately calculate the number of labels to buy and the cost of the postage. To answer this type of "How many?" question, use the Count function.

1. Clear off the query grid.

2. Let's say you want to see how many types of receivers you stock. Fill in the grid like that in Figure 14.7.

**The Total line is set to Where.**

**The Show button is turned off in the Criteria column.**

**FIGURE 14.7:**

Counting the number of receivers only

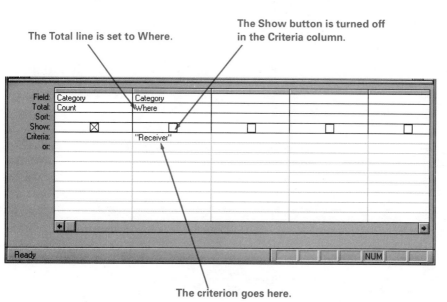

**The criterion goes here.**

Notice that to make this work, you have to add Category to the grid twice. The one on the left does a count of the whole table. The second, which is processed next by Access, limits the count to only those records whose Category equals Receivers.

Let's try out a more complex count, using the Name and Address list and the Zip Code field. Let's say you want to see how many labels you'll need for people living between zip code areas 90000 and 99999.

**1.** Jump to the Database window.

**2.** Close the current database (don't save the query).

**3.** Open the PHONEBK database, open the Name and Address list, and start a new query.

**4.** Click the Totals button to add the Totals row to the grid.

**5.** Set up the grid as shown in Figure 14.8. Notice that the Zip Code field has its Show check box turned off and the Total row is set to Where. When you use the Where option, you can't have the field showing in the datasheet. But there must be at least one field in the dynaset that results from a query. That's why the ID field is added, with its Total row set to Count.

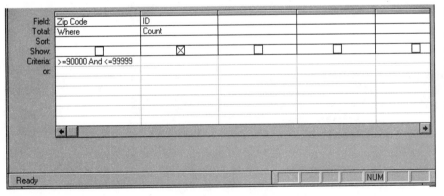

**FIGURE 14.8:**

Counting for people living in zip codes between 90000 and 99999

**6.** Display the datasheet, and you'll see the result, which is 2.

Suppose you wanted to count all tape decks and receivers? The query shown in Figure 14.9 would do it.

If you wanted to count all tape decks but only Nizo receivers, simply add a new column for Brand, choose Where, and type **Nizo** under in the criteria area for Brand, as in Figure 14.10.

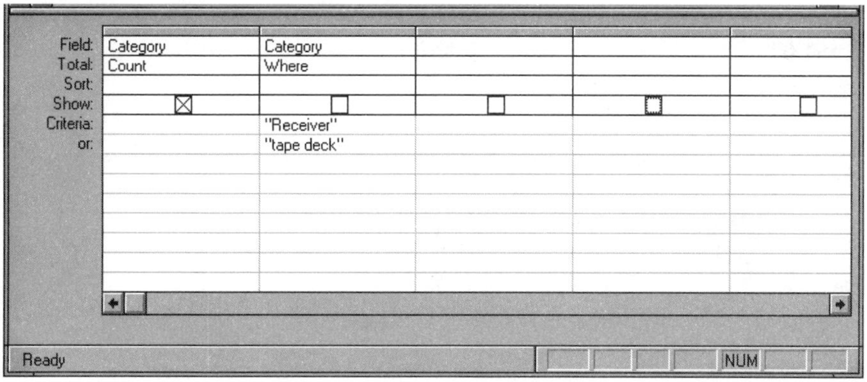

**FIGURE 14.9:**

Counting the number of receivers and tape decks

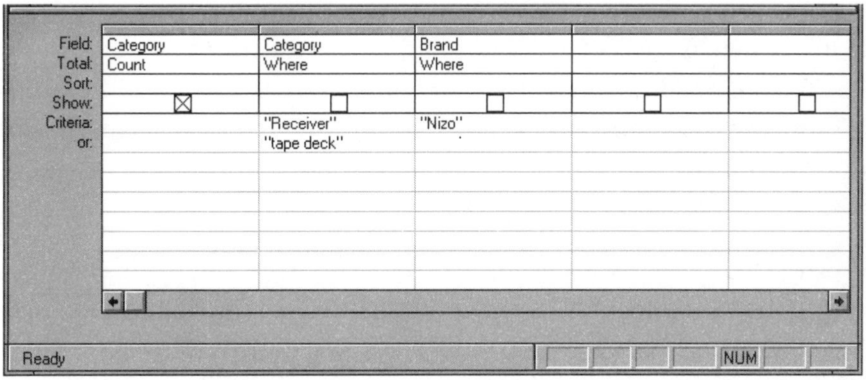

**FIGURE 14.10:**

Counting for all tape decks and only Nizo receivers

# FINDING MINIMUM AND MAXIMUM VALUES

Min and Max work much the same way as the other aggregate functions, but instead of calculating a number for you, they display the lowest or highest value encountered. A typical application of these functions is in a stock market or commodities table. To learn the highest and lowest closing prices of a particular item, place either Min or Max in the relevant field column of the query, and Access will do the rest.

Here's an example. To see the minimum number of units on hand for any receiver in the STEREO table, do the following:

**1.** Set up the query as shown:

| Field: | Quantity | Category | | | |
|---|---|---|---|---|---|
| Total: | Min | Where | | | |
| Sort: | | | | | |
| Show: | ☒ | ☐ | ☐ | ☐ | ☐ |
| Criteria: | | "Receiver" | | | |
| or: | | | | | |

**2.** Under Category, type **Receiver**; and under Quantity, type **Min**.

The answer is 4. Only four units of the Nizo T-35 are in stock. But keep in mind that the Min and Max operators aren't of much use if you want to know *which* item or record resulted in the finding. Don't bother using these operators if what you really want to know is, "What items have fewer than six units in stock?" You can find this information by simply entering <6 in the Quantity field, as discussed in earlier chapters:

| Field: | Quantity | Category | Brand | | |
|---|---|---|---|---|---|
| Sort: | | | | | |
| Show: | ☒ | ☒ | ☒ | ☐ | ☐ |
| Criteria: | <6 | | | | |
| or: | | | | | |

Both Min and Max can also be applied to Character and Date fields.

# How to Use Date/Time Fields

Dates and times are among the most important types of information in business databases. Whether you're keeping track of sales, payables and receivables, clients, or project schedules, you'll often want to store and retrieve information based on a certain period of time. Although dates and times are fairly easy for humans to deal with, computers occasionally need a helping hand. That is why Access has a specific field type dedicated to dates and times only, as well as some special tools for manipulating dates. Together, these allow you to perform a variety of calculations and to retrieve data based on time periods.

Date/Time fields can take a variety of formats. You set the format from the Field Properties box when designing or modifying a table's structure. Upon installation, the U.S. version of Microsoft Access is set to accept and display dates in the format *mm/dd/yy* (month/day/year) and times as *hh:mm:ss* (hours/minutes/seconds) AM/PM.

By using the Format line in the Field Properties box, you can set dates and times to display as shown in the following table. By default, Access is set to General Display, which shows both time and date. However, if the value is a date only, no time is displayed; if the value is time only, no date is displayed.

| FORMAT | EXAMPLE |
| --- | --- |
| General Date | 4/3/93 05:34 PM, 4/3/93, and 05:34 PM |
| Long Date | Saturday, April 4, 1993 |
| Medium Date | 03-Apr-93 |
| Short Date | 4/3/93 |
| Long Time | 5:34:23 PM |
| Medium Time | 05:34 PM |
| Short Time | 17:34 |

Note also that the Windows Control Panel's International settings affect whether dates have month or day first (e.g., 1/31/94 vs. 31/01/94).

## ADDING A DATE/TIME FIELD

We're just going to work with dates in this book, since they're more common than times in databases. Before we can experiment with dates though, we'll need some data to work with. Let's add a Date field to the STEREO database to indicate the date on which each product was last ordered.

1. Open the STEREO database.

2. Click on Stereo Equipment in the Database window, then on the Design button to modify its structure.

3. Add a new field below Retail called Last Order. Make it a Date/Time field.

4. Your structure should now look like this:

| Field Name | Data Type |
|---|---|
| Category | Text |
| Brand | Text |
| Model | Text |
| Quantity | Number |
| Wholesale | Currency |
| Retail | Currency |
| Last Order | Date/Time |

5. Save the modified structure by choosing File ➤ Close. Say Yes to saving the changes and No to any question you might see about creating a primary key.

6. Open the datasheet, adjust the column widths, and enter the dates you see in Figure 14.11. (I've set the font to bold.)

7. Just for fun, try moving down to the last line (the blank record) and entering the date 15/15/91 into the field. Then move off the field by pressing ↑. You get an error message.

| Category | Brand | Model | Quantity | Wholesale | Retail | Last Order |
|----------|-------|-------|----------|-----------|--------|-----------|
| Receiver | Nizo | T-33 | 5 | $225.49 | $350.49 | 1/12/94 |
| Receiver | Nizo | T-35 | 4 | $312.00 | $425.25 | 1/12/94 |
| Receiver | Acme | R25-MT | 13 | $19.99 | $49.99 | 8/15/94 |
| Receiver | Nadir | 2-CHP | 50 | $12.95 | $29.95 | 3/6/90 |
| Speakers | Razco | L-55 | 30 | $199.00 | $249.00 | 8/1/92 |
| Speakers | Talbest | BG-20 | 6 | $250.00 | $350.88 | 4/13/94 |
| Tape Deck | Rollem | CAS-3 | 10 | $125.65 | $212.99 | 9/1/93 |
| Tape Deck | Flowutter | WBL-5 | 5 | $149.33 | $250.77 | 9/15/93 |
| Turntable | Xirtam | 25-L | 5 | $99.99 | $149.99 | 2/28/92 |
| Turntable | Raluric | RND-1 | 3 | $595.00 | $850.00 | 8/13/92 |

Microsoft Access - [Table: Stereo Equipment]

File  Edit  View  Records  Layout  Window  Help

**FIGURE 14.11:**

Entering the dates

Access is smart enough to know there isn't a fifteenth month. Click on OK, and press Esc to undo the entry.

**8.** Choose File ➤ Close to close the file. Click Yes to save the changes.

**9.** Open the Design window for the table again, click on the Last Order field, then set the Format to Medium Date. Then save the structure (no primary key again) and view the data. The dates are all displayed like **12-Jan-94**. As you see, you can easily change the display of dates. Now even if you enter dates in the form 3/6/94, Access will convert them immediately to the longer format.

## USING THE DATE FIELD WITH QUERIES

Now let's create some queries based on dates. Let's check to see which items were last ordered in 1993.

**1.** The table's datasheet should be open for viewing.

**2.** Click on the New Query button.

**3.** Double-click on the asterisk (*) in the Field box in the top part of the window. This is a shortcut for entering all the fields into the query. The first column in the grid now reads

*Stereo Equipment* *. (This approach with the * doesn't work when you're doing totals like we did earlier, however.)

**4.** Now all you have to do is add the fields you want to list criteria for. Fill in the rest of the query as follows:

Notice that the Criteria line reads

### <#01/01/94# and >#12/31/92#

The pound signs (#) inform Access that you're entering dates, just as quotation marks inform Access that you're working with characters. Without them, Access will issue a message that it cannot proceed. However, you have to manually enter the slash marks; Access doesn't enter them for you in a query. Finally, don't forget to enter the *and* between the two criteria.

**5.** View the data to see the results. Your screen should show two records, both with dates in 1993.

In a nutshell, we asked Access to display all records whose dates are less than Jan 1, 1994 and greater than December 31, 1992. You can use this procedure to select records for quarterly sales reports, for preparing tax forms, or whenever you want to select data from a certain time period. Search conditions using Date/Time fields are particularly useful for printing reports. With a Date field in your file, you can print a report for, say, third quarter sales of 1994.

Incidentally, there are two other ways to select records falling between two dates. You could have used either of these approaches in the query with equal success:

### Between #1/1/93# And #12/31/93#

or

### Year([Last Order])=1993

Of course, sorting on Date fields can also be useful. Just use the Sort line in the QBE grid, as you learned in Chapter 10.

Here are some other examples of query or filter criteria that may be of use when you're querying date fields:

| QUERY CRITERIA | WILL SHOW RECORDS... |
|---|---|
| =#2/2/93# | Orders made on 2-Feb-1993 |
| Between #5-Aug-93# and #10-Aug-93# | Orders between 5-Aug-93 and 10-Aug-93, inclusive of end points |
| < Date( )− 30 | Orders more than 30 days old |
| Year([Last Order])=1994 | Orders with order dates in 1994 |
| DatePart("q", [Last Order])=4 | Orders for the fourth calendar quarter (for all years) |
| DateSerial(Year([Last Order]), Month([Last Order])+1, 1)−1 | Orders for the last day of each month |
| Date() | Orders made today (same day as computer's internal clock) |
| Between Date() and Date()−90 | Orders made in the last 90 days |
| Between Date() and DateAdd("m", −3,Date()) | Orders made in the last 3 months |

Now close up the query without saving it.

# Using Yes/No Fields

The only field type we haven't yet discussed is the Logical type. As you may recall, Logical fields are used exclusively for storing yes/no or true/false data. Therefore, Logical fields are useful for answering questions like these: "Is this donation tax deductible?" "Did this check bounce?" or "Did this recipe go over well enough at the last dinner party to bother making it again?"

On the face of it, the notion of dedicating a whole field type to yes and no answers might seem silly. You could store a yes or a no in a Character field. True enough. But using Logical fields makes data retrieval much easier, because Access already knows that Logical fields can hold only two values. When you search for records that meet a certain logical criterion, you don't have to enter quotation marks, type the word *Yes* or *No* in a search condition, or use any special data-entry strategies.

# ADDING A YES/NO FIELD TO A TABLE'S STRUCTURE

To illustrate the concept and utility of Logical fields, let's add one to our Stereo Equipment table. Let's assume that you sell certain items only via interstate marketing and shipping, and therefore don't collect state sales tax on these items. We will add a Logical field that will indicate whether sales tax should be added when figuring the total sales price of each product. We will also add a field to hold the total price, which will include the sales tax, where applicable. Then we can have Access compute the total price and display it in that field.

1. Close the Equipment list table. Then modify its structure by adding a new field called Tax. Make Tax a Yes/No type field.

2. Now add another field, called Total. Make it a Numeric field.

3. Choose Exit ➤ Close. Do save the changes, and once again, don't create a primary key.

4. Open the table for viewing, and adjust the columns so they fit. Notice that by default Yes/No fields are filled in with Nos.

**5.** Fill in the Tax field to indicate whether each item in a record is taxable, as shown below. Access will only accept Yes or No in this type of field.

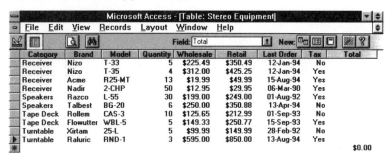

## USING LOGICAL FIELDS TO FIND DATA

Suppose now that you want a reminder of which items to add tax to. We need to create a query based on the Tax field.

**1.** Click on the New Query button to start a new query. Use the * shortcut to put all the fields in the query, then add the Tax field and fill in the grid like this (make sure Tax has its Show box turned off, or Tax will show up in the dynaset twice):

**2.** View the resulting data. Your dynaset should contain only records with Yes in the Tax field (6 records).

**3.** To see all the items that are *not* taxable, simply return to the Query Design window and enter **No** in the Tax field.

## BASING UPDATE QUERIES ON YES/NO FIELDS

Now let's ask Microsoft Access to calculate the values for the Total field on the basis of whether a record is taxable. Here's how it works in theory. First, we will create a query that says "Look at each record. If Tax is Yes, multiply the retail amount by eight percent (assuming that's the state sales tax rate) and store that amount in the Total column." Sound hard? Actually you already know all the rules for creating this type of select query. But you have to use another type of query to actually modify records. It's called an *action query*.

You use action queries when you want to make changes that affect an entire table rather than specific records, as manual editing does. Action queries save a lot of time and can be used for such chores as deleting all records meeting certain criteria, appending new records from one table to another, or creating a new table from a subset of records in the source table.

Here's a general rule of thumb: Before using an update query, or any kind of action query that will modify the precious data in your tables, it's good practice to create a select query to test out the criteria you're going to put into the action query. The select query will confirm whether the criteria you use will select the correct records to modify, or whether the criteria will need modification first.

In the last section, where we displayed the taxable and nontaxable records, we ensured that the criteria work, so we don't have to do that again. Now, here's how to create the kind of action query we need (called an *update query*) to fill the Total field. We'll need to run two update queries—one for taxable items and the other for nontaxable items.

1. Open the Query menu and notice that Select has a check mark next to it. This means the current query is a select query. Choose Update. The QBE grid changes somewhat to include a line called *Update To*.

2. Set up the following query. You can't have an asterisk (*) field in an update query, so you'll have to remove the first column if you're continuing from the last query. Notice the Tax field criteria is the same as what you did above, for showing taxable items.

| Field: | Tax | Total | | | |
|---|---|---|---|---|---|
| Update To: | | [retail]*1.08 | | | |
| Criteria: | Yes | | | | |
| or: | | | | | |

If you can't read the formula in the Total column's Update
To field, it's =[retail]*1.08. Note that Access is unforgiving
if you omit the square brackets.

**3.** Click on the Update button in the Toolbar. It's the one with
the big exclamation mark in the middle. This runs the update. Before the update will run, Access informs you how
many records (rows) will be altered if you go ahead. This is
a good time to cancel if the number seems off-kilter to you.
It should report that six records will be modified. Since we
got six records when running the select query, that sounds
good, so click on OK to have Access make the changes.

**4.** Let's look at the results before moving ahead. The easiest
way is to choose Window ➤ Table: Stereo Equipment to see
our source table. Your Total fields should be filled in, as in
Figure 14.12. Looks like the update worked.

Now we need to include the nontaxable records. We'll have to
create another update query for those, since the **No** in the Tax field
caused Access to skip them. Actually, for nontaxable items all we
need to do is copy the existing retail prices into the Total column.

**FIGURE 14.12:**

Only taxable
items are updated.

| Category | Brand | Model | Quantity | Wholesale | Retail | Last Order | Tax | Total |
|---|---|---|---|---|---|---|---|---|
| Receiver | Nizo | T-33 | 5 | $225.49 | $350.49 | 12-Jan-94 | No | |
| Receiver | Nizo | T-35 | 4 | $312.00 | $425.25 | 12-Jan-94 | Yes | $459.27 |
| Receiver | Acme | R25-MT | 13 | $19.99 | $49.99 | 15-Aug-94 | Yes | $53.99 |
| Receiver | Nadir | 2-CHP | 50 | $12.95 | $29.95 | 06-Mar-90 | Yes | $32.35 |
| Speakers | Razco | L-55 | 30 | $199.00 | $249.00 | 01-Aug-92 | Yes | $268.92 |
| Speakers | Talbest | BG-20 | 6 | $250.00 | $350.88 | 13-Apr-94 | No | |
| Tape Deck | Rollem | CAS-3 | 10 | $125.65 | $212.99 | 01-Sep-93 | No | |
| Tape Deck | Flowutter | WBL-5 | 5 | $149.33 | $250.77 | 15-Sep-93 | Yes | $270.83 |
| Turntable | Xirtam | 25-L | 5 | $99.99 | $149.99 | 28-Feb-92 | No | |
| Turntable | Raluric | RND-1 | 3 | $595.00 | $850.00 | 13-Aug-94 | Yes | $918.00 |
| | | | | | | | | $0.00 |

1. Use the Windows menu to get back to the Update Query window and modify it to look like this:

2. Perform the new update operation by clicking on the ! button again.

3. View the results. Now all the totals are filled in.

## COMBINING LOGICAL FIELDS WITH OTHER SEARCH CRITERIA

As with all the other field types and functions, you can use Logical fields in conjunction with other search criteria in queries. You can then save the query to use with reports, mailing labels, and other operations such as marking or unmarking records.

Here is an example combining Logical, Numeric, and Character fields in a single query. To list taxable receivers with a pretax retail price of more than $200.00, you would enter the following into the file skeleton of a query:

View the data. Only one record, the Nizo T-35 receiver, qualifies. Sometimes Access adds strangely named fields such as Field0 or StereoEquipment.Retail to a dynaset during such a query, and your results may show some such fields. You can prevent this by manually adding the fields you want to view rather than using the asterisk to add all fields to the grid. Either way works.

---

**A Tip about Expressions**

Sometimes you'll forget how to write certain expressions that you want in the Criteria field, particularly when you're concocting complex queries. Help is available in the form of examples that you can bring up on screen. A good Help screen I've found is the one called

"Criteria Expression Examples." Figure 14.13 shows the first part of that screen. You can get to lots of help about constructing expressions in queries and filters by choosing Help/Search, and searching for Criteria: Queries. Then in the Topics box, choose the topic that applies.

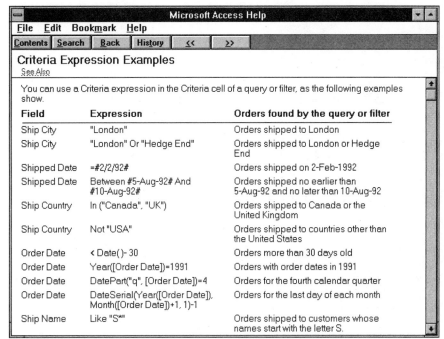

**FIGURE 14.13:**

Help contains examples of criteria expressions that may prove useful when you're constructing queries.

**Criteria Expression Examples**
See Also

You can use a Criteria expression in the Criteria cell of a query or filter, as the following examples show.

| Field | Expression | Orders found by the query or filter |
|---|---|---|
| Ship City | "London" | Orders shipped to London |
| Ship City | "London" Or "Hedge End" | Orders shipped to London or Hedge End |
| Shipped Date | =#2/2/92# | Orders shipped on 2-Feb-1992 |
| Shipped Date | Between #5-Aug-92# And #10-Aug-92# | Orders shipped no earlier than 5-Aug-92 and no later than 10-Aug-92 |
| Ship Country | In ("Canada", "UK") | Orders shipped to Canada or the United Kingdom |
| Ship Country | Not "USA" | Orders shipped to countries other than the United States |
| Order Date | < Date( )- 30 | Orders more than 30 days old |
| Order Date | Year([Order Date])=1991 | Orders with order dates in 1991 |
| Order Date | DatePart("q", [Order Date])=4 | Orders for the fourth calendar quarter |
| Order Date | DateSerial(Year([Order Date]), Month([Order Date])+1, 1)-1 | Orders for the last day of each month |
| Ship Name | Like "S*" | Orders shipped to customers whose names start with the letter S. |

FEATURING

**Appending
Tables**

**Dynasets Based
on Fields from
Two Tables**

**Using Criteria in
a Multitable
Query**

▼

# Working with
# Multiple Tables

S o far, all the commands and examples we've experimented with have used only a single table at a time. However, some situations call for the use of several tables together. You may simply need to merge two or more tables into one, or you may need to link several tables together to act as one, without actually merging the data.

This chapter explores two techniques for using multiple tables. First, it discusses how to merge data from one file into another. Then, you'll see how to use two or more tables at the same time.

Working with multiple tables can help eliminate unnecessary and time-consuming work and can also provide a means for combining your data in flexible ways for viewing and reporting. These procedures are a bit more complex than what we've done so far, but they offer strong dividends in flexibility and power. Becoming adept in their use may require some experimentation and patience. The best approach to mastering these commands is to find an appropriate database application, try implementing the necessary queries on your own, and then refer to the examples in this chapter for guidance.

# How to Append Data from Another Database

As you may recall, one of the types of update queries appends records from one table to another table. This is done using a type of action query called an *append query*. As you know, you can manually add records to your table one at a time. However, this isn't always the most prudent use of your time or energy when the records already exist in another table. In such cases, you can use an append query to quickly pull in the records, eliminating the extra typing. Here's an example.

Suppose you own two electronics stores, each with its own Access inventory list similar to the Stereo Equipment list. Both stores are doing a booming business, and floor space is getting cramped at both sites. To accommodate your growing operation, you negotiate a great deal on a large storefront property and merge the two stores into one big shop—including the inventory. Now you need to combine your inventory tables as well. But do you want to pay someone to type all the data from one file into another? You don't have to. Instead, you can use the Append command to have Access merge the tables.

Let's assume that the first table is the Stereo Equipment table as it stood at the end of Chapter 14. Now we need to create the table for the second store. Let's call it TV, since the other store sold televisions and related items.

1. Using the File ➤ New command from the Database window, create a new table (in the STEREO database) with the structure shown in Figure 15.1. Set the field sizes to 10, 10, 6, and 3 for the Text fields (in that order, top to bottom).

2. Click on the Datasheet button to save the new structure, and begin entering data. Name the table **TV**. When asked about a primary key, you can have Access create one for you.

3. On the datasheet, hide the ID column for the time being with the Layout ➤ Hide Columns command (look back to Chapter 7 if you've forgotten how to do it), and adjust column widths as necessary to see all the columns.

4. Choose File ➤ Save Layout to save the column settings.

5. Enter the data displayed in Figure 15.2.

## MERGING THE TABLES

Now we have two tables in the STEREO database. Notice that the structures are not exactly identical. The fields are not all in the same order, and not all fields are included in both tables. Fortunately, such discrepancies don't prevent the tables from working together.

We're going to use the Stereo Equipment table as the basis for the combined tables, so our first step in merging the two tables is to add the extra data in TV to the Stereo Equipment table.

| Field Name | Data Type | Description |
| --- | --- | --- |
| Category | Text | |
| Brand | Text | |
| Model | Text | |
| Size | Text | |
| Quantity | Number | |
| Retail | Currency | |
| Wholesale | Currency | |

**FIGURE 15.1:**

Structure for the TV table

Data for the TV table

1. Return to the Database window by using the Window menu or pressing Ctrl+F6.

2. Open the Stereo Equipment table.

3. Return to the Database window again. This time click on the large Query button and then on New to start a new query.

4. In the Tables dialog box, choose the table we're going to copy records *from* (the source table), which is TV, and click on Add. Then close the box.

5. Now you decide which fields you want appended into the destination (Stereo Equipment) table. We want them all except the ID field. So add them all (except ID) to the grid. Incidentally, at this point you could specify criteria if you wanted to append only specific records, such as records for TVs; but we want all the records, so we won't use criteria.

6. Click on the Datasheet button just to see that the query selects the records we really want appended. There should be five records.

7. Click the Design button to return to the Design screen.

**8.** Now you have to change the query to an append query. Choose Query ➤ Append. The following dialog box appears. Now Access needs to know the name of the destination table. Fill in the box like this:

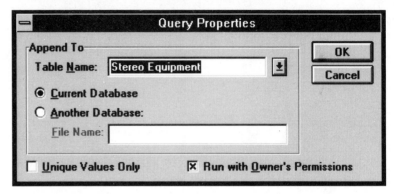

In the Append To area, you name the destination table. If the destination table is in another database (ours isn't), then you click on Another Database and type in the name of the database. Forget the other two options.

**9.** Click on OK. The query grid is modified to an Append Query grid like the one shown in Figure 15.3, and it looks a little different now, showing field names from both tables. You can see the names of the source and destination fields, indicating where data will land if you go ahead. Notice that Access is smart enough to pair up the fields, even though the two tables' columns and structures aren't in the same order. If you want to see the name of the source table, choose View ➤ Table Names. The source table's name appears in the grid. Notice that Size in the source (upper) table has no destination field, since the destination table doesn't contain such a field.

**10.** Click on the Run (!) button in the Toolbar to run the Append Query and actually add the records to the destination table. You're told how many rows (records) will be appended if you continue. Click OK.

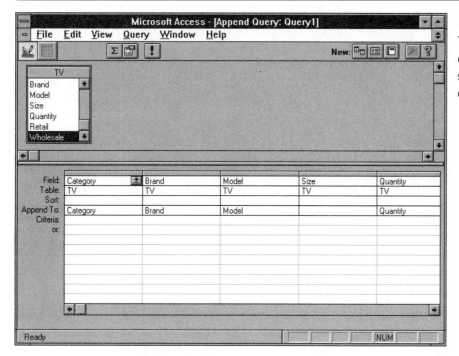

The Query grid displays the source and destination fields.

**11.** Use the Window menu to switch to the Stereo Equipment table. (If you don't see the new records, choose Records ➤ Show All Records.) Your screen should look like Figure 15.4. Notice that Access tacked the five new TV records onto the end of Stereo Equipment.

Appending five records was a swift process, but appending a few thousand would take considerably more time and disk space. Be sure you have enough of both in such cases.

# RULES FOR MERGING TABLES WITH APPEND

Now for a few technical points. Luckily your two tables had similar structures, field names, and field lengths; otherwise, the append

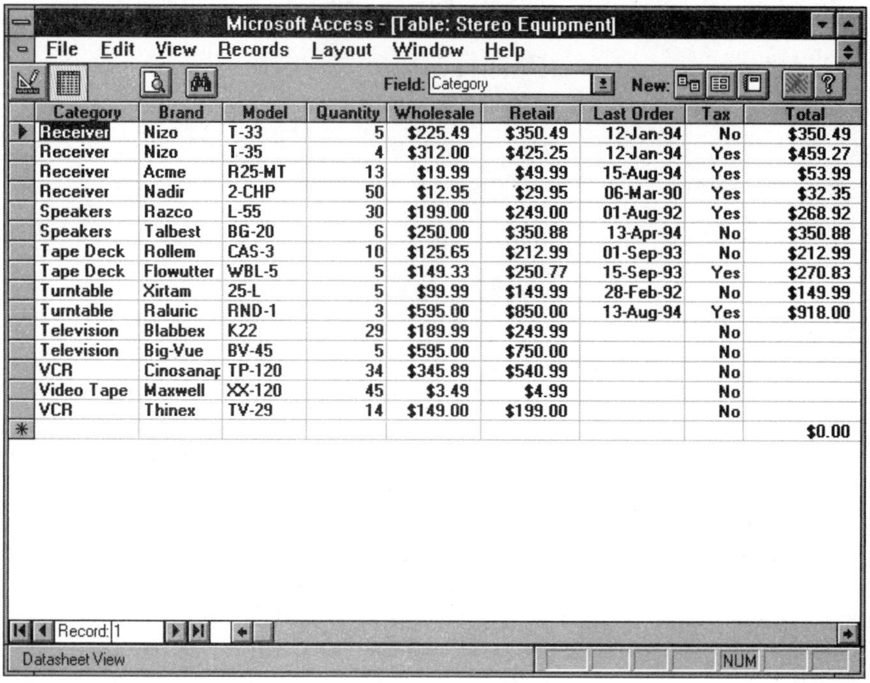


| Category | Brand | Model | Quantity | Wholesale | Retail | Last Order | Tax | Total |
|---|---|---|---|---|---|---|---|---|
| Receiver | Nizo | T-33 | 5 | $225.49 | $350.49 | 12-Jan-94 | No | $350.49 |
| Receiver | Nizo | T-35 | 4 | $312.00 | $425.25 | 12-Jan-94 | Yes | $459.27 |
| Receiver | Acme | R25-MT | 13 | $19.99 | $49.99 | 15-Aug-94 | Yes | $53.99 |
| Receiver | Nadir | 2-CHP | 50 | $12.95 | $29.95 | 06-Mar-90 | Yes | $32.35 |
| Speakers | Razco | L-55 | 30 | $199.00 | $249.00 | 01-Aug-92 | Yes | $268.92 |
| Speakers | Talbest | BG-20 | 6 | $250.00 | $350.88 | 13-Apr-94 | No | $350.88 |
| Tape Deck | Rollem | CAS-3 | 10 | $125.65 | $212.99 | 01-Sep-93 | No | $212.99 |
| Tape Deck | Flowutter | WBL-5 | 5 | $149.33 | $250.77 | 15-Sep-93 | Yes | $270.83 |
| Turntable | Xirtam | 25-L | 5 | $99.99 | $149.99 | 28-Feb-92 | No | $149.99 |
| Turntable | Raluric | RND-1 | 3 | $595.00 | $850.00 | 13-Aug-94 | Yes | $918.00 |
| Television | Blabbex | K22 | 29 | $189.99 | $249.99 | | No | |
| Television | Big-Vue | BV-45 | 5 | $595.00 | $750.00 | | No | |
| VCR | Cinosanar | TP-120 | 34 | $345.89 | $540.99 | | No | |
| Video Tape | Maxwell | XX-120 | 45 | $3.49 | $4.99 | | No | |
| VCR | Thinex | TV-29 | 14 | $149.00 | $199.00 | | No | |
| | | | | | | | | $0.00 |

**FIGURE 15.4:** Five new records from the TV table added to Stereo Equipment

operation would have been less successful. As it was, the only data that didn't transfer was that stored in the Size field. This is because there was no Size field in the target file's structure, so Access skipped this field during the appending process. If you had wanted to include the Size data, you would have had to modify the Stereo Equipment file structure to add a Size field prior to the appending process.

Note that even though the relative positions of Retail and Wholesale were reversed in the TV file, Access recognized the identical field names and reversed those fields' data before pulling them into the Stereo Equipment file. The Tax, Last Order, and Total fields were added as empty fields, since you hadn't typed or calculated anything in them.

To see how other discrepancies can cause problems, consider what Microsoft Access does when using this command. First, it compares the structures of the two tables concerned. It appends only source fields with the same names as target fields and skips any others. If the data in a source field is too long to fit in the target field, it is shortened, or *truncated*, until it fits. This means you may lose the right part of long entries.

For example, if the Last Name field in the new table has only a five-character width, the following truncation will occur when you append:

Source Table          John Smithsonian

Destination Table     John Smith

In our case, the names of fields were the same, so little intervention was necessary on the grid. If the names of fields are different, just enter the appropriate names in the source and destination sections on the grid. You can do this with the drop-down button that will appear when you click on the grid's Field and Append To lines.

And again, you can use complex criteria expressions to stipulate which records should be appended to the destination table. Just use the query rules you already know for designing the criteria.

One point concerns the inclusion of the Primary Key field in the grid. In our case, we didn't have a Primary Key field in the destination table. But if we had, we'd have had to include the field in the destination (bottom) section of the grid. The only exception to this is when the primary key is a Counter field type.

Finally, if you are only appending a few records, and both tables use the same field names and number of fields, you can use the Paste Append command. Just select the source records using the mouse (make a query to select specific records if you need to), then choose Copy. Switch to the destination table and choose Edit ➤ Paste Append.

# How to View Fields from Two or More Tables at Once

It's not uncommon in complex applications to need two tables open and available for data retrieval at the same time. Microsoft Access actually allows as many as 16 tables to be open at any given time, and it allows you to create dynasets that combine data from those tables, a process called *joining* the tables. (If you're familiar with dBASE terminology, this is called *linking*. Don't confuse this with dBASE's Join command, which is used for combining data from two tables.)

When you join tables, keep the following in mind:

- You are creating what appears to be one larger table. While the two tables are joined, you can work with their fields as though they were in the same table, which can be handy.

- The dynaset that results from the join can be stored as a query for later use.

- Reports, labels, and forms can be based on such a query, letting you include any of the dynaset's fields. When you save the report, form, or label, the associated query will be stored with it. The next time you run the report, print the labels, or use the form, the query is run so that any data changes that occurred in the interim are reflected.

The trick is to join the tables so that the records in each file line up correctly. Otherwise, Fred Schwartz might appear to have Bermuda Schwartz's social security number, or your luggage may get sent to Mesopotamia instead of Mozambique.

The link that connects tables is based on a common field in each table (other than a Logical or Memo field). Fields should contain unique, but similar, information. For example, a billing and a mailing list may have common customer ID numbers. If this number is unique for each person, and if it exists in both tables, it can be used to join the tables. Joined fields should have the same type, width, and contents in the two tables, though the field names do not have to be the same.

Here's another example of joined tables. For each item you sell in your electronics shop, there is a manufacturer's salesperson with whom you deal and from whom you order. When you look at your inventory table to see whether you'll need to order more items, you often want the names, addresses, and phone numbers of the various sales representatives readily available. Joining the inventory table to a second table containing the sales representative information can accomplish this.

## PREPARING THE JOIN

We'll use the PHONEBK table for the sales representatives' names and addresses. (I know you were wondering about those people.)

**1.** Open the PHONEBK database. When asked about saving the query, click No.

**2.** We'll have to add another field to join the Name and Address list table to the Stereo Equipment table. Alter the Name and Address list table structure to look like Figure 15.5. (Highlight Work Phone Number and choose Edit ➤ Insert Row to insert a new field.) Make the field two characters wide.

**3.** Switch to Datasheet view (save the structure) and enter the ID numbers for the sales representatives shown in Figure 15.6. The easiest way is to click in the Rep Number field for the first record and enter the number. Then press ↓ and enter the next number.

**4.** Now we have to add the same ID numbers to the Stereo Equipment inventory file. Close the PHONEBK database and open the STEREO database.

**5.** Modify the Stereo Equipment list structure by adding Rep Number (a text field with a width of 2) just before the Tax field.

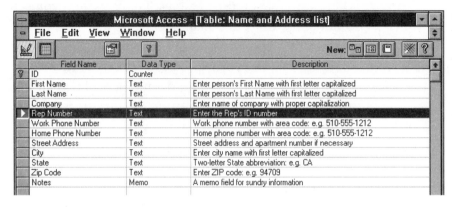

**FIGURE 15.5:**

Altering the Name and Address list structure to add a joining field

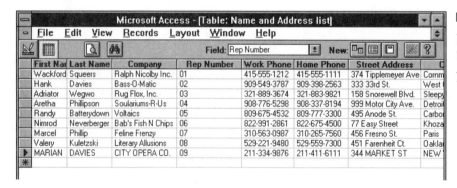

**FIGURE 15.6:**

Entering the Rep Number data into your table

**6.** Click on the Datasheet button to display the data. When asked about a primary key, click No once again.

**7.** Now we need to give sales rep numbers to each item in the inventory. Enter the numbers as shown in Figure 15.7.

| Category | Brand | Model | Quantity | Wholesale | Retail | Last Order | Rep Number | Tax |
|----------|-------|-------|----------|-----------|--------|------------|------------|-----|
| Receiver | Nizo | T-33 | 5 | $225.49 | $350.49 | 12-Jan-94 | 02 | No |
| Receiver | Nizo | T-35 | 4 | $312.00 | $425.25 | 12-Jan-94 | 02 | Yes |
| Receiver | Acme | R25-MT | 13 | $19.99 | $49.99 | 15-Aug-94 | 09 | Yes |
| Receiver | Nadir | 2-CHP | 50 | $12.95 | $29.95 | 06-Mar-90 | 01 | Yes |
| Speakers | Razco | L-55 | 30 | $199.00 | $249.00 | 01-Aug-92 | 03 | Yes |
| Speakers | Talbest | BG-20 | 6 | $250.00 | $350.88 | 13-Apr-94 | 04 | No |
| Tape Deck | Rollem | CAS-3 | 10 | $125.65 | $212.99 | 01-Sep-93 | 06 | No |
| Tape Deck | Flowutter | WBL-5 | 5 | $149.33 | $250.77 | 15-Sep-93 | 05 | Yes |
| Turntable | Xirtam | 25-L | 5 | $99.99 | $149.99 | 28-Feb-92 | 08 | No |
| Turntable | Raluric | RND-1 | 3 | $595.00 | $850.00 | 13-Aug-94 | 07 | Yes |
| Television | Blabbex | K22 | 29 | $189.99 | $249.99 | | 09 | No |
| Television | Big-Vue | BV-45 | 5 | $595.00 | $750.00 | | 09 | No |
| VCR | Cinosanap | TP-120 | 34 | $345.89 | $540.99 | | 09 | No |
| Video Tape | Maxwell | XX-120 | 45 | $3.49 | $4.99 | | 08 | No |
| VCR | Thinex | TV-29 | 14 | $149.00 | $199.00 | | 09 | No |

**FIGURE 15.7:**

Sales Rep ID numbers added to the Stereo Equipment inventory list

# CREATING THE JOIN

Now all you have to do is create the query that connects the tables. But first, there's one rule to be aware of: You can only join tables that are in the same database. Thus, we have a problem. How can we join our two tables? One is in the PHONEBK database, the other in the STEREO database. No problem. We'll just copy the current table (since we're in it now) to the PHONEBK database.

1. Close the current table, and return to the Database window.

2. With Stereo Equipment highlighted, choose Edit ➤ Copy. This puts the whole table on the Clipboard, ready to be pasted.

3. Choose File ➤ Open Database, and open the PHONEBK database.

4. In the PHONEBK Database window, click on Tables, then choose Edit ➤ Paste. You'll see a dialog box. Fill it in as

shown here:

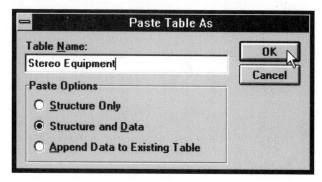

Access takes a few seconds to open the source database and then copies in the table's data. Now Stereo Equipment is listed as one of the tables in the PHONEBK database window.

**5.** Now click on Query and on New to create a new query.

**6.** When the Add Table dialog box comes up, add Name and Address list and Stereo Equipment (double-click on one, then on the next, then on Close).

**7.** Notice that the Query window now contains field lists from both tables:

I've scrolled the lists so you can see the Rep Number field in both.

**8.** Now you have to tell Access to link the tables using the Rep Number field. Scroll the lists so you can see Rep Number in both.

**9.** Drag Rep Number from the left list onto the Rep Number in the right list, and release. A line appears between the two lists, pointing to the linked fields.

**10.** If you scroll either list now, the link line will zig-zag to follow the field name.

# CHOOSING WHICH FIELDS TO DISPLAY

Next, you have to specify the fields from each table you want in the dynaset.

**1.** The normal steps for placing fields into the query apply here—either double-click on a field name or drag it from the list to the grid. Let's use the following fields:

    Brand   Model   Quantity   First Name   Last Name   Work Phone

**2.** Once the fields are placed in the QBE grid, check that the fields are in the desired order. Rearrange the columns if necessary. Incidentally, if you choose View ➤ Table Names, Access will display the source of each field in the grid. This is particularly useful when you've added numerous tables to a query and things begin to get confusing:

| Field: | Brand | Model | Quantity | First Name | Last Name |
|---|---|---|---|---|---|
| Table: | Stereo Equipment | Stereo Equipment | Stereo Equipment | Name and Address | Name and Address |
| Sort: | | | | | |
| Show: | ☒ | ☒ | ☒ | ☒ | ☒ |

When we were creating views from a single table, this notation seemed superfluous. Now you see its utility.

**3.** Click on the Datasheet button to check out the dynaset resulting from the combination of fields. The joined data derived from two separate tables now appears in a single view, as you can see in Figure 15.8.

This joined view makes checking your inventory quantities and calling the appropriate sales representatives to order more items almost a one-step process. If you check the tables against each other, you will see that the sales representative numbers are correctly displayed for each inventory item.

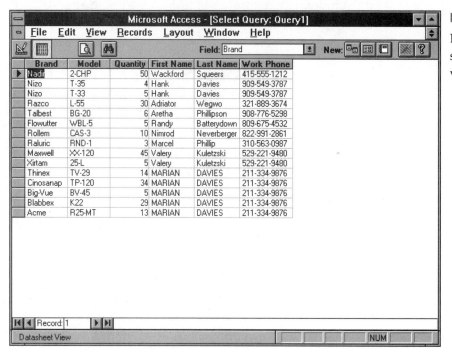

**FIGURE 15.8:**

Fields from two separate tables viewed at once

Sometimes, the tables you join will have the same number of records. One person, one address, and one ID number, all joined to one account balance. You get the idea. This is called a *one-to-one* relationship between the tables. But there's another common type of join—the *one-to-many* relationship, where the joined tables do not need to have the same number of records. For example, suppose a customer ordered several items. The customer list has one entry for the customer's name, but the orders table has many. When joined on the customer number, the query will display all the items ordered by a given customer, one item per line. The customer's name (if in the view) will be repeated for each item. In the case of our query, what kind of join did you create? For a hint, look at Figure 15.8, where Hank Davies's and Marian Davies's names are repeated in the dynaset. It's a one-to-many relationship.

# Working with Multitable Dynasets

Note that the records in our joined tables can't be edited. If you try to make a change, you'll see a message in the status line saying "Form is read only." This means that the data can be displayed (read), but not changed (written). This is not always the case, and in many cases you'll be able to make changes to multitable query dynasets. For a detailed description of when multitable dynasets are editable and the effects of one-to-one and one-to-many joins on editing, see the *Microsoft Access User's Guide*.

Despite any record-editing restrictions you might run into, don't underestimate the value of multitable queries. You can still do the following:

- Use the search commands

- Add criteria to the QBE grid to limit the records shown

- Rearrange, format, hide, show, or freeze selected fields

- Rearrange the records by sorting in the query

- Save the query and use it as the basis for reports, labels, and so on

- Base a form or report on this query, including any or all of the fields

- Create another query based on this query rather than on a table

- Use the Query ➤ Add Table command to add more tables to the query

- Add tables whose fields are only used as selection criteria— not for display

# USING CRITERIA IN A MULTITABLE QUERY

Let's enter a criteria expression to see how it works in the two-table query. Suppose you want to reorder items of which less than five units remain in stock only. Here's what you do:

**1.** Return to the Query Design screen and alter it to look like this:

| Field: | Brand | Model | Quantity | First Name | Last Name |
|---|---|---|---|---|---|
| Table: | Stereo Equipment | Stereo Equipment | Stereo Equipment | Name and Address | Name and Address |
| Sort: | | | | | |
| Show: | ⊠ | ⊠ | ⊠ | ⊠ | ⊠ |
| Criteria: | | | <5 | | |

**2.** View the data. Only two records show up, with quantities of 4 and 3. You can quickly see whom to call and what to order.

| Brand | Model | Quantity | First Nai | Last Name | Work Phone |
|---|---|---|---|---|---|
| ▶ Nixo | T-35 | 4 Hank | | Davies | 909-549-3787 |
| Raluric | RND-1 | 3 Marcel | | Phillip | 310-563-0987 |

# SAVING A MULTITABLE QUERY FOR LATER USE

If you wanted to order products whose inventory has dropped to less than five regularly, you could save this query, calling it something reasonable like "Order items we're running low on." Once it's saved, you can just double-click it in the Database window and up it comes. You can print the list, give it to an employee, and have the items ordered. Or, better yet, you could create a report with a new page for each rep, listing the products you want to order from that rep. A calculated field could determine the number of units you want to order, which is the desired minimum stock quantity minus the current inventory quantity. Have Access print the mailing labels, then stuff the envelopes and mail in the orders. There are a million possibilities, using only what you've learned in this book, if you take the time to experiment a bit.

For right now, let's save the query.

**1.** Choosing File ➤ Save Query.

2. Fill in the dialog box like this:

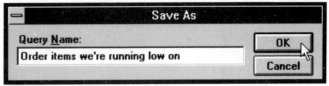

3. Close the query.

4. Exit Access if you want to take a break.

# Installing Microsoft Access

Before you can run Microsoft Access, you have to install it properly for your type of computer. Installation is the process of running the Microsoft Access install program and making a few choices along the way.

If you have already installed Microsoft Access according to the instructions that came with it, you can skip this appendix. If you have not yet installed Access, you should do so by following the steps described here. There are also instructions here for making backup copies of your Access disks.

# How to Set Up Access

Microsoft Access can be run in two basic modes: *single-user mode* and *multiuser mode*. Single-user mode, which uses one computer at a time, is the more popular. Multiuser mode allows Access to run on two or more computers connected via a local area network (LAN), typically Windows for Workgroups, LAN Manager, Novell Netware, Lantastic, or Banyan VINES. Installation of Microsoft Access for use with LANs is not discussed in this appendix.

## HARDWARE AND SOFTWARE REQUIREMENTS

Before running the installation program, first check to see that your computer system is capable of running Access. Read these points to determine if it is.

- Access is a Windows program. This means you must have Microsoft Windows installed in your computer system before you can install or run Access. Ensure that Windows is installed and working properly—mouse, screen, and printer should all be performing correctly—before attempting to install Access.

- Microsoft Access is designed to run on IBM and IBM-compatible computers with an 80386 or higher processor. (This includes 80386SX and 80386SL processors.)

- Your computer needs at least 2 megabytes (MB) of random-access memory (RAM), though Microsoft recommends 4 megabytes, if possible.

- Your computer must have a hard disk. If you want to install all the files supplied with Access, including the sample and tutorial files, you need a minimum of 13 megabytes of free space on your hard disk. The installation program will tell you whether you have enough space available.

- For operating system software, your computer needs IBM PC-DOS or MS-DOS versions 3.1 or later, and Microsoft Windows 3.0 or later. If you have older versions of DOS or Windows, acquire an upgrade before continuing the installation.

- You need a pointing device, such as a mouse, track ball, or pen, that works with Windows. Working without a mouse in Access is very clumsy, and some tasks just can't be performed without one.

- You need at least an EGA or VGA screen. Old CGA or MDA screens won't work. If you have an SVGA (Super VGA) screen, all the better—you'll see more data on your screen at one time, without having to scroll the screen image.

- If you want to print, you'll need a printer. Any printer that works with Windows should be fine, though for high-quality output, you'll want a high-resolution printer such as a laser printer, bubble-jet, 24-pin, or ink-jet printer.

You do not have to create any subdirectories before you install Access. The installation program does that for you. If you have a preexisting version of Access in a directory called \ACCESS, it will be overwritten, or replaced, by the new version of Access when you run the install program.

## PERFORMING THE INSTALLATION

Microsoft Access is supplied on either 5¼-inch disks or 3½-inch disks. The installation procedures are almost identical for the two sizes of disk, the only differences being the number of times you have to remove and insert disks in your floppy disk drive and the names on the disk labels.

There are three types of installation procedures that you can choose from:

| TYPE | DESCRIPTION |
| --- | --- |
| Complete | Installs all the files, including sample files, Cue Cards, Help, Microsoft Graph, and file translators (for using data from dBASE, Paradox, etc.). |
| Custom | Lets you specify which groups of files you want (the Access program itself, Help, Cue Cards, Microsoft Graph, Tutorial, translators, etc.), and reports how much space they will require on your hard disk and how much space is currently available on the disk. Use this option when you want more control over which files you want copied, and where you want them. |
| Minimum | Installs just the basics necessary to run Access. You don't get the Help files, Microsoft Graph, Cue Cards, or sample files. |

I suggest doing the full installation. This takes up more disk space, but you're ensured of getting everything you need for Access to work as expected in this book.

As you insert and remove disks, be very careful. You are using the original disks, not copies. You can easily damage 5¼-inch floppy disks with fingerprints, dust, liquids, or scratches, particularly on the delicate inner part of the disk that is visible through the oblong opening on either side of the disk jacket. Always handle disks by the plastic covering only, and be sure to place them back in their paper liners after removing them from the computer.

Follow these steps to completely install all files of single-user Microsoft Access on your hard disk. These instructions assume that your hard disk is drive C and your floppy disk drive is drive A. If your hard disk or floppy disk drive have other drive letters (such as D or B), substitute those letters. *Installation can take as long as 20 minutes, so make sure you have the time before you start.*

1. Insert Disk 1 in drive A.

2. From File Manager or Program Manager, open the File menu. Choose Run.

3. In the resulting dialog box, type

   **a:setup**

   and press ↵.

4. The program takes about 30 seconds to get going, so just wait.

5. You'll be asked for your name and company name, or you'll be told that the copy you're installing has been installed by someone already, and warned that you may be about to break the law. Just answer the prompts, and click on the appropriate "button" (the little squares with things like Continue, OK, or Cancel written on them). To click, you move the mouse around on the desk to move the pointer on the screen. Position it over the button and then press the left button on the mouse. (Chapter 1 includes a Windows refresher if you're a little rusty or new to Windows.)

6. Next you're asked where you want to install the program (which drive and directory). The default is C:\ACCESS. Normally, this is fine. If you want it elsewhere, type in the new location. Setup will create the directory for you, if it doesn't already exist. If your drive has another letter, edit the destination by typing in a new letter. Use the arrow keys on the keyboard to move the cursor, if you need to. Use the Backspace key to erase mistakes. Don't install Access into the root directory of any drive, since DOS may not allow enough files into the root to accommodate Access. Use a subdirectory. When satisfied with the drive and directory name, press ↵ or click on Continue.

7. Now Setup asks which type of installation you want—Complete, Custom, or Minimum, as shown in Figure A.1. If you click on Custom, what you get is shown in Figure A.2.

8. Click on the top square, or press 1. The install program now chugs along, slowly. First, Setup checks your drive for available storage space. If there isn't enough room to install all the files contained on the Microsoft Access disks, you'll see a screen alerting you to this.

9. Next, Setup starts installing files from Disk 1, and shows you a little "gas gauge" reporting its progress.

10. When it's done with Disk 1, you'll be prompted to insert Disk 2, Disk 3, and so on. Insert each requested disk and press the ↵ key until all the disks are loaded. The process

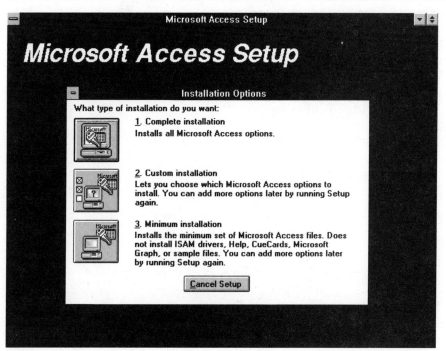

**FIGURE A.1:**

Choosing from the three types of setups

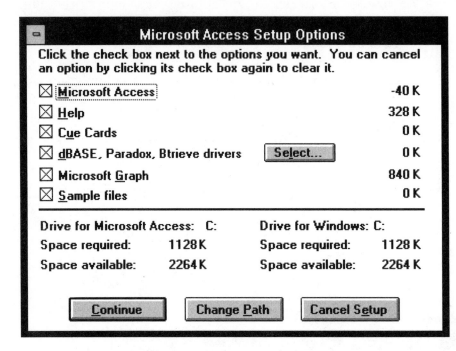

**FIGURE A.2:**

Custom installation lets you pick and choose which files to install.

for each disk takes longer than you might expect, because the files are compressed and have to be expanded during installation.

**11.** When installation is complete, put all of your disks in a safe place.

**12.** Now turn to Chapter 1 to get started with Access.

# INDEX

*Boldfaced page numbers indicate primary references to topics. Italic page numbers indicate illustrations.*

## SYMBOLS

<> (angle brackets), as not equal to operator, 122, 236–239
* (asterisk)
  blank record selector button, 175, *175*, 177
  as multiplication operator, 232–233
  in QBE window Field box, 251–252
  in queries, 117–118, 256
  in searches, **84–86**, *85*
^ (caret), as exponentiation operator, 232–233
: (colon), in calculated field expressions, 234
= (equal to), 115, 122–123, 236–237
! button (Run), Toolbar, 264
! button (Update), Toolbar, 257
> (greater than), 122, 236–237
>= (greater than or equal to), 122, 236–237
< (less than), 122, 236–237
<= (less than or equal to), 122, 236–237
– (minus sign), as subtraction operator, 232–233
<> (not equal to), 122, 236–239
# (number sign), 118, 252
() (parentheses)
  in calculated field expressions, 234
  in formulas, 218
+ (plus sign), as addition operator, 232–233
? (question mark)
  in queries, 117–118
  in searches, **84–86**, *85*
" " (quotation marks), 114–115, 254
/ (slash), as division operator, 232–233
[ ] (square brackets), 257
S button (summation), 241, *241*

## A

About Microsoft Access dialog box, 20, *20*
Access. *See* Microsoft Access
action queries. *See also* append queries; queries; update queries
  adding new records with, 176
  overview of, 108, 256
  updating with, 181
  Yes/No fields in, 255–258

active windows, 28
Add Table dialog box, Query Design window, 108–109, *108*
adding
  Date/Time fields, 250–251
  fields to table structure, 54–58
  Memo fields, 56–57
  records in Datasheet and Form windows, **175–176**, 179
  records with queries, 176
  Yes/No fields to table structure, 254–255
addition operator (+), 232–233
aggregate functions, **239–248**
  Avg (average) function, 243–244, *243*
  Count function, 245–247, *245*
  First function, 240
  Last function, 240
  Max (maximum) function, 248
  Min (minimum) function, 248, *248*
  StDev (standard deviation) function, 240
  Sum function, 240–242
  types of, 239–240
  Var (variance) function, 240
alert boxes
  duplicating key values, 144, *144*
  end of dynaset, 80
  no primary key, 45, *45*, 60–61
  search criteria syntax error, 119, *119*
aligning report fields, 208, 213, *213*
Alt key
  in Form window, 164
  opening menus with, 9–10, 78–79
  restarting with (Ctrl+Alt+Del), 14–15, *15*
  + Tab key (task switching), 26
Always on Top command, Help menu, 26, *27*
AND operator, 123–125, *125*, 127–129, 131
angle brackets (<>), as not equal to operator, 122, 236–239
append queries, **261–267**. *See also* action queries; queries; update queries
  merging tables with, 262–265
  versus Paste Append command, 267

primary key and, 267
search criteria in, 267
table structure and, 265–266
Append Query grid, 264, *265*
Apply Filter button, Form window, 155, *155*
arithmetic operators, 232–236
arrow keys. *See* cursor keys
asterisk (*)
blank record selector button, 175, *175*, 177
as multiplication operator, 232–233
in QBE window Field box, 251–252
in queries, 117–118, 256
in searches, **84–86**, *85*
Avery labels, 220, 226. *See also* mailing labels
Avg (average) function, 243–244, *243*

**B**

backing up, **47–50**, 71
directories and, 31
from DOS, 49–50, 71
from Windows, 47–49, 71
Backspace key
editing with, 67
in Form window, 163, 164
in Memo fields, 168
overview of, 11
BETWEEN…AND operator, 125, 130, *130*
Binoculars icon, 81–82
blank fields, queries on, 132
blank record selector button, 175, *175*, 177
Blank Report option, New Report dialog
box, 222
bolding in reports, 213
brackets, square ([ ]), 257
browsing. *See* searching
buttons
in Database window, 34
on mouse, 13

**C**

calculated fields
in queries, 223–226
in reports, *204*, 206–207, *207*, 210–212, 218
caret (^), as exponentiation operator, 232–233
carriage return key. *See* Enter key
cascading windows, 99
case sensitivity. *See* lowercase; uppercase
Character fields, Min/Max functions and, 248
clicking, 12, 67
Clipboard, copy-and-paste and, 56, 177
Close Database command, File menu, 71, 159

closing
database files, 71, 159
Datasheet window, 70
Query Design window, 120
Shift key + F12 key (closing and saving), 22
Table Design window, 46, *46*
windows, 158, *158*
colon (:), in calculated field expressions, 234
column selector bar, 88, *88*
Column Width command, Layout menu, 91
columns. *See also* fields
freezing/unfreezing, 174–175, *175*
hiding, **88–89**, *90*
moving, **92–94**, *93*
resizing, **89–92**, *92*
restoring original width of, 91
selecting, 88, *88*
commands
choosing from menus, 20–21
context-sensitive help for, 25
selection of, 73
comparison operators, 122, 236–239
logical operators and, 123–125, 127–129
numeric data and, 236–239
computers
resetting, 14–15, *15*
system requirements for, 279–280
Contents command, Help menu, 23
context-sensitive help, 25–26
Control box
closing windows with, 158, *158*
Restore command, 21
Control key. *See* Ctrl key
controls, in reports, *204*, 207–210
Copy command, Edit menu, 56,
176–180
COPY command (DOS), 49–50, 71
copy-and-paste operations
in Datasheet window, 177–179, 180
for fields, 55–56, 178
in Form window, 179–180
shortcut keys for, 67
Count function, 245–247, *245*
Counter data type, 38, 60
CR key. *See* Enter key
creating
custom forms, **219**
database files, **31–34**, **138–141**
dynasets from table joins, 268, 273, 275
filters, 155–156
mailing labels, 221–222
multifield indexes, 158–159

primary key, 45, *45*, 60–61, *60*, **142–144**, 145
queries, **107–112**, 146
single field indexes, 157–158
single-column forms, **96–101**, *97*, *99*
tables, **138–141**, **191–193**
criteria expressions. *See* search criteria
crosstab queries, 108
Ctrl key
  + C (copying), 67
  + cursor keys (navigation), 40
  + End key (to last record), 175
  + Esc key (opening Program Manager), 15
  + F6 key (switching windows), 138, 153
  + F8 key (move mode), 94
  + F11 key (locking field contents), 22
  + V (pasting), 67
  + X (cutting), 67
  + Z (undo saved record), 68, 171–172
  in Datasheet window, 76
  editing with, 67
  in Form window, 163–164
  in Memo fields, 168–169
  overview of, 9
  restarting with (Ctrl+Alt+Del), 14–15, *15*
Cue Cards, Help system, 25
Currency data type, 37
currency formatting
  in queries, 235
  in reports, 214–216, *215*, *216*
cursor keys
  in Datasheet window, 76
  editing with, 67
  in Form window, 163
  in Memo fields, 168–169
  navigating with, 40
  overview of, 10–11
custom reports. *See* reports
Cut command, Edit menu, 176–177, 178
cut-and-paste operations
  in Datasheet window, 178
  shortcut keys for, 67

# D

data entry, **63–71**
  backup and, 71
  editing, **66–67**
  entering records, **64–66**, 140
  for sample database, **68–70**
  saving, 68
Data Entry command, Records menu, 176
data types, 37–38
Database command, Window menu, 138

Database Design window. *See* Table Design
  window
database files. *See also* fields; records; table
  structure; tables
  backing up, **47–50**, 71
  closing, 71, 159
  creating, **31–34**, **138–141**
  naming, **30–31**, 33
  opening, 52
  overview of, **2–5**
  printing, **184–191**
  saving, 31
  versus tables, 3–4, *4*
database management systems (DBMSs), 5
database structure. *See* table structure
Database window, *34*, *53*
  opening, 138
  overview of, 33–34
  returning to, 46–47
Datasheet button, Form window, 100, *100*,
  110, 173, *173*
Datasheet View mode. *See* Datasheet window
Datasheet window, 64–65, *64*, **88–95**
  adding new records to, **175–176**, 179
  closing, 70
  copy-and-paste operations in, 177–179, 180
  cut-and-paste operations in, 178
  deleting records from, 181
  editing, navigating, and data entry com-
    mands in, 163–164
  editing with, **172–175**
  entering data in, 64–66
  F2 key in, 172
  freezing/unfreezing columns in,
    174–175, *175*
  hiding columns in, **88–89**, *90*
  maximizing, 65
  moving columns in, **92–94**, *93*
  navigating in, 75–76, 163–164
  overview of, 64–65, *64*
  pencil icon in, 65–66, 68, 166
  Print Preview page in, 185, *185*
  printing in, 184–189
  resizing columns in, **89–92**, *92*
  saving changes to, **95**
  switching with Form window, 173
  viewing with Form window, 101–102, *102*
  viewing multiple records in, 74, *74*–77
Dataview Screen. *See* Datasheet window
Date/Time data type, 37
Date/Time fields, **249–253**, *251*–*253*
  adding, 250–251

formats for, 249–250
Min/Max functions and, 248
dBASE
  versus Access, 34, 167
  Join command, 268
DBMS (database management systems), 5
Del key
  editing with, 67
  in Form window, 164
  in Memo fields, 168, 170
  restarting with (Ctrl+Alt+Del), 14–15, *15*
Delete command, Edit menu, 58
deleting
  fields, 58–59
  multiple records, 182
  with queries, 182
  single records, 181–182
designing. *See also* Query Design window;
    Report Design window; Table Design
    window
  mailing labels, **221–227**, *222*
  table structure, 38–41
Detail section, report, 206
dialog boxes, Alt key and, 9–10
directories, backup and, 31
division operator (/), 232–233
DOS, backing up from, 49–50, 71
DOS prompt, 14–15, 28
double-clicking, 12, 67
dragging, 12, 22
duplicating key values, 144, *144*
dynasets, **105**, *112*. *See also* queries
  creating from table joins, 268, 273, 275
  end of dynaset alert box, 80
  multitable, 275

**E**

Edit Filter button
  Datasheet window and, 173
  Form window, 155, *155*
Edit menu
  Copy command, 56, 176–177
  Cut command, 176–177, 178
  Delete command, 58, 181–182
  Find command, 79, 81, 103, 165,
    167–169
  Paste Append command, 179, 267
  Paste command, 56, 176–177
  Select All Records command, 178
  Undo Current Field command, 171
  Undo Current Record command, 171
  Undo Delete command, 58

Undo Move command, 59
Undo Saved Record command, 68, 171–172
Undo Typing command, 171
editing, **160–182**. *See also* modifying
  adding new records, **175–176**, 179
  data entry, **66–67**
  with Datasheet window, **172–175**
  deleting multiple records, 182
  deleting single records, 181–182
  field definitions, 40
  with Form window, **161–172**, *162*
    displaying records, 164–166
    overview of, 161–164
    saving edits, 170–171
  Memo fields, 167–170
  shortcut keys for, 66–67, 163–164, 168–170
  undoing edits, 171–172
End key
  + Ctrl key (to last record), 175
  in Datasheet window, 76
  editing with, 67
  in Form window, 163
  in Memo fields, 168
  overview of, 11
Enter key, 10, 68
equal to (=), 115, 122–123, 236–237
error messages. *See also* alert boxes
  in Report Design window, 218
Esc key
  in Form window, 163
  in Memo fields, 168
  overview of, 9
  undoing edits with, 171
Exit Windows dialog box, 28, *28*
exponentiation operator (^), 232–233
expressions. *See* search criteria

**F**

F1 key
  as F11 key, 22
  Help, 9, 25
F2 key
  in Datasheet window, 172
  as F12 key, 22
  in Memo fields, 168
  switching Field and Edit modes, 163
F6 key, + Ctrl key (switching windows),
    138, 153
F7 key, Find command, 81
F8 key, + Ctrl key (move mode), 94
F11 key
  + Ctrl key (locking field contents), 22

F1 key as, 22
F12 key, 22
Field Properties dialog box, 42–44, *42*, 156–157, *156*, 158
fields, **2**, **36**. *See also* columns; database files; keys; primary key; records
    adding to table structure, 54–58
    aligning in reports, 208, 213, *213*
    choosing for labels, 223–226, *223*
    choosing for queries, 110, *111*
    choosing for table joins, 268
    copying, 55–56, 178
    data types of, 37–38, 40
    defining, 35–44, *41*
    deleting, 58–59
    descriptive name of, 38
    ID, 60
    locking contents of, 22
    moving, 59, 241
    naming, 36, 39
    properties of, 42–44, *42*, 138–139
    queries on blank, 132
    queries on unique, 133–135
    searching all, 81–82
    searching on specific, 79–81
    width of, 42
Fields dialog box, ReportWizard, 194–195, *195*
File Manager, backing up from, 48–49, *49*, 71
File menu, *52*
    Close Database command, 71, 159
    New Database command, 32
    Open command, 63
    Print command, 182
    Print Preview command, 185–186
    Save command, 13
    Save Form command, 101
    Save Layout command, 95
    Save Query command, 119–120, 276–277
    Save Record command, 170
filename extensions, 31–32
files. *See* database files
Filter buttons, Form window, 155, *155*
filters
    calculated fields and, 233
    creating, 155–156
    in Datasheet window, 173
    dates in, 253
    versus queries, 106, 154
    sorting with, **154–156**, *156*
Find command
    Edit menu, 79, 81, 103, 165
    Memo fields and, 167–169

Find dialog box, *79*, **79–86**
    Match Case option, 82–83, *83*
    searching all fields, 81–82, *82*
    searching specific fields, 79–80
    upward versus downward searches, 80–81
    wildcards in, **84–86**, *85*
First function, 240
floppy disks, quitting and, 13
Font dialog box, 140, *141*
Font selector, Toolbar, 228, *229*
fonts
    changing label, 227–229, *229*
    changing screen, 140, *141*
footers, report and page, 205–206
Form button, Datasheet window, 173, *173*
Form window
    adding new records to, **175–176**
    copy-and-paste operations in, 179–180
    data entry commands in, 163
    Datasheet button in, 100–101, 110
    deleting records in, 181–182
    editing, navigating, and data entry commands in, 163–164
    editing with, **161–172**, *162*
        locating records, 164–166
        Memo field editing, 167–170
        overview of, 161–164
        saving edits, 170–171
        undoing edits, 171–172
    Filter buttons in, 155, *155*
    Last Record button in, 175, *175*
    Next Record button in, 175, *175*
    overview of, 100–101
    printing from, 189–191
    Record Number box in, 175
    selecting records in, 179, *180*
    sorting and, 153
    switching with Datasheet window, 173
    viewing with Datasheet window, 101–102, *102*
formatting
    Date/Time fields, 249–250
    in queries, 235
    in reports, 214–216, *215*, *216*
forms, **96–103**
    creating custom, **219**
    creating single-column, **96–101**, *99*
    naming, 98, *98*
    printing single-column, 189–191, *189*
    saving, 101, *101*
    searching with, 102–103, *103*
    table structure and, 62

formulas, in calculated fields, 211–212, 218
FormWizard, **96–101**, *97*, *99*
Freeze Columns command, Layout menu,
      174–175
front slash (/), as division operator, 232–233
function keys, 8–9, **22–23**
functions, 236. *See also* aggregate
      functions

## G

Glossary, Help system, 23–24, *25*
Go To command, Records menu, 78, *78*
greater than (>), 122, 236–237
greater than or equal to (>=), 122, 236–237
Gridlines command, Layout menu, 188
Group By dialog box, ReportWizard, 200–201
group icons, opening, 15–16, *17*
group windows, opening, 15–16, *16*

## H

handles, report control, 207–208, *208*
hardware requirements, 279–280
headers, report and page, 205–206
Help menu, *19*
   Always on Top command, 26, *27*
   Contents command, 23
   How to Use Help command, 27
   quitting, 27
   Search command, 25
   using, 19–20
Help system, **23–27**
   context-sensitive help, 25–26
   "Criteria Expression Examples" screen,
      258–259, *259*
   Cue Cards, 25
   Glossary, 23–24, *25*
   hypertext systems in, 26
   list of functions in, 236
   main screen, 23–24, *24*
   quitting, 27
Hide Columns command, Layout menu, 89
highlighting. *See* selecting
Home key
   in Datasheet window, 76
   editing with, 67
   in Form window, 163
   in Memo fields, 168
   overview of, 11
How to Use Help command, Help menu, 27
hypertext systems, in Help system, 26

## I

icons
   Binoculars icon, 81–82
   group, 15–16, *17*
   pencil icon, 65–66, 68, 166
ID fields
   primary key and, 60, 145
   record deletion and, 182
importing, tab character and, 180
Indexed check box, Field Properties dialog
      box, *42*, 44, 156–157, *156*, 158
indexes, **156–159**
   creating multifield, 158–159
   creating single field, 157–158
   searches and, 165
   when to use, 157
inexact matches, 117
Ins key
   editing with, 66–67
   in Form window, 164
   in Memo fields, 168–169
Insert mode, 66–67, 164, 168–169
installation, **278–284**
   hardware and software requirements,
      279–280
   single-user, 279, 281–284
   types of, 281
Is Null operator, 132, *133*

## J

joined tables, **268–274**
   creating dynasets from, 268, 273, 275
   creating joins, 271–273
   versus dBASE Join command, 268
   modifying, 62
   one-to-one/one-to-many joins, 274
   overview of, 268–269
   preparing for joins, 269–271

## K

Key button, Toolbar, 142, *142*
keyboard shortcuts. *See* shortcut keys
keyboards
   moving columns with, *93*, 94
   repeating keys on, 11
   types of, 7–8, *8*
keypad, cursor keys on, 10–11
keys, **3**, **144**. *See also* primary key

## L

Label tool, Toolbox, 210, *210*
labels, **205**. *See also* mailing labels
landscape printing, 187–189
laser printers, labels and, 230
Last function, 240
Last Record button, Form window, 175, *175*
Layout menu
  Align command, 208, 213
  Column Width command, 91
  Font command, 140
  Freeze Columns command, 174–175
  Gridlines command, 188
  Hide Columns command, 89
  report headers and footers and, 205
  Save This Database File Structure
    command, 61–62
  Show Columns command, 89
  Unfreeze All Columns command, 174
less than (<), 122, 236–237
less than or equal to (<=), 122, 236–237
"like" pattern-match operator, 118
linked tables. *See* joined tables
Logical fields. *See* Yes/No fields
logical operators, 123–129
  AND operator, 123–125, *125*, 127–129, 131
  BETWEEN…AND operator, 125, 130, *130*
  NOT operator, 123, 129, *129*
  OR operator, 123, 126–129, *127*, 131
Lotus 1-2-3, 31–32
lowercase
  file descriptions and, 44
  in queries, 115
  in searches, 82–83, *83*

## M

magnifying glass pointer, 186
mailing labels, **220–230**
  changing fonts, 227–229
  designing, **221–227**, *222*
  choosing fields, 223–226, *223*
  choosing label size, 226–227, *227*
  creating labels, 221–222
  sorting on fields, 226, *226*
  modifying, 227–229
  printing, 221, **229–230**
  resizing, 228
*Mastering Windows 3.1*, 18
matches
  inexact, 117
  "like" pattern-match operator, 118

Match Case option, Find dialog box,
  82–83, *83*
Max (maximum) function, 248
.MDB files, 31
Memo data type, 37
Memo fields
  adding, 56–57
  editing, 167–170
memory, 13, 279
menu bar, 19
menus
  Alt key and, 9–10, 78–79
  book's notation for selections, 73
  context-sensitive help for, 25
  Enter key and, 10
  opening, 9–10, 78–79
  overview of, 19–21
microprocessors, 279
Microsoft Access. *See also* installation
  versus dBASE, 34, 167
  group window, 15, *16*
  hardware and software
    requirements, 279–280
  versus Lotus 1-2-3, 31–32
  multiuser mode, 279
  overview of, **6–7**
  quitting, 13, **28**
  single-user mode, 279
  starting, **14–18**
  tutorials, 17
  Welcome window, 17, *18*
*Microsoft Access Language Reference*, 236
*Microsoft Access User's Guide*, 275
Microsoft Windows. *See also* Clipboard
  backing up from, 47–49, *49*, 71
  exiting, 28, *28*
  Mouse tutorial, 12
  overview of, **18–22**
  Print Manager, 190–191
  starting, 14–15
Min (minimum) function, 248, *248*
minus sign (–), as subtraction
  operator, 232–233
modifying. *See also* editing
  empty table structures, 52–61
  filled table structures, 61–62
  joined tables, 62
  mailing labels, 227–229
  queries, 110–112
monitors (screens), 280
mouse
  versus Alt key, 10

moving columns with, 92–93, *93*
need for, 280
overview of, 12–13
tutorial, 12
mouse buttons, 13
mouse pointer, 12, 59
moving
   columns, **92–94**, *93*
   Ctrl key + F8 key (move mode), 94
   fields, 59, 241
   windows, 22
multiplication operator (\*), 232–233
multitable queries, **275–277**
   criteria in, 276
   saving, 276–277
multiuser mode, 279

## N

naming
   database files, **30–31**, 33
   fields, 36, 39
   forms, 98, *98*
   reports, 201, *201*
navigating
   in Datasheet window, 75–76, 163–164
   in Form window, 163–164
   keystrokes for, 40, 163–164, 168–170
   between records, 78
New Database command, File menu, 32
New Database dialog box, 32–33, *32*
New Form dialog box, 96, *96*
New Query button, Toolbar, 240
New Report dialog box, 194, *194*, 222
Next Record button, Form window, 175, *175*
not equal to (<>), 122, 236–239
Not Null operator, 132
NOT operator, 123, 129, *129*
Number data type, 37
number sign (#), 118, 252
numeric data
   comparison operators and, 236–239
   formatting in reports, 214–216, *215*, *216*
numeric keypad, cursor keys on, 10–11
NumLock key, 11

## O

objects, 30. *See also* forms; queries; reports
OLE Object data type, 38
one-to-one/one-to-many joins, 274
Open command, File menu, 63

opening
   database files, 52
   Database window, 138
   group icons, 15–16, *17*
   group windows, 15–16, *16*
   menus, 9–10, 78–79
   Program Manager, 15
operating systems, 280
operators. *See also* comparison operators;
      logical operators
   arithmetic, 232–236
   Is Null operator, 132, *133*
   "like" pattern-match, 118
   Not Null operator, 132
   relational, 122
OR operator, 123, 126–129, *127*, 131
Overwrite mode, 66–67, 164, 169

## P

page headers and footers, 205–206
parentheses ()
   in calculated field expressions, 234
   in formulas, 218
Paste Append command, Edit menu, 179, 267
Paste command, Edit menu, 56, 176–177, 179
Paste Table As dialog box, 272, *272*
pattern-match operator ("like"), 118
PC/AT keyboard, *8*
PC/XT keyboard, *8*
pencil icon, 65–66, 68, 166
PgUp/PgDn keys
   in Datasheet window, 76
   in Form window, 163
   in Memo fields, 168
   overview of, 11
plus sign (+), as addition operator, 232–233
pointer lists, 156–157. *See also* indexes
pointers
   magnifying glass pointer, 186
   mouse pointer, 12, 59
   record pointer, 77
   report controls and, 208
   row resizing pointer, 59
   row selector pointer, 59
portrait printing, 187–189
pound sign (#), 118, 252
primary key
   append queries and, 267
   creating, 45, *45*, 60–61, *60*, **142–144**, 145
   duplicating values in, 144

record deletion and, 182
sorting with, **142–144**
Print command, File menu, 182
Print dialog box, 190, *190*
Print Manager, Microsoft Windows, 190–191
Print Preview command, File menu, 185–186
Print Preview window, ReportWizard, 195–196,
    199–201, 218
Print Setup dialog box, 187–188, *187*
printers, 230, 280
printing, **184–191**
    canceling jobs, 190–191
    creating sample table for, **191–193**
    in Datasheet view, 184–189
    forms, 189–191, *189*
    mailing labels, 221, **229–230**
    portrait versus landscape, 187–189
    queries, 188–189
    with ReportWizard, **194–202**
processors, requirements for, 279
Program Manager
    exiting Microsoft Windows, 28
    Mouse tutorial, 12
    opening, 15
properties. *See also* Query Properties dialog box;
    Table Properties dialog box
    of fields, 42–44, *42*, 138–139
Properties dialog box, Report Design window,
    214–216, *216*
PS/2 keyboard, *8*

# Q

QBE window, **109**, *114*. *See also* Query Design
    window; search criteria
    AND operator in, 123–125, *125*, 127–129, 131
    in append queries, 264, *265*
    asterisk (*) in Field box, 251–252
    calculated fields in, 233–236
    comparison operators in, 236–239
    entering search criteria, 113–116
    for filters, 155
    NOT operator in, 123, 129, *129*
    OR operator in, 123, 126–129, *127*, 131
    searching on two fields of, 127–129, *128*
queries, **104–120**. *See also* action queries;
    append queries; dynasets; search criteria;
    update queries
    AND operator in, 123–125, *125*, 127–129, 131
    arithmetic operators in, 233–236
    averages in, 243–244, *243*
    BETWEEN…AND operator in, 125, 130, *130*

    on blank fields, 132
    calculated fields in, 223–226
    case sensitivity in, 115
    choosing fields for, 110, *111*
    comparison operators in, 122, 236–239
    counting records in, 245–247, *245*
    creating, **107–112**, 146
    crosstab queries in, 108
    Date/Time fields in, 251–253
    deleting records with, 182
    versus filters, 106, 154
    guidelines for complex, 129–131
    Help screen for expressions in, 258–259, *259*
    indexes and, 157
    inexact matches in, 117
    "like" operator in, 118
    Logical fields in, 255, 258
    minimum/maximum values calculation in,
        248, *248*
    modifying, 110–112
    multitable, **275–277**
    NOT operator in, 123, 129, *129*
    OR operator in, 123, 126–129, *127*, 131
    overview of, 104–106
    printing, 188–189
    quotation marks (" ") in, 114–115
    report calculated fields and, 206
    running, 115–116
    saving, **119–120**
    select, 107, 108, 256
    sorting with, **145–153**, *147*
        ascending versus descending order,
          146–148
        multilevel sorts, 150–152, *152*
        saving and reusing sort views, 152–153
        on text fields, 149–150
    Sum function in, 240–242
    table structure and, 62
    types of, 107–108
    on unique fields, 133–135
    wildcards in, 116–118
query by example (QBE), 109
Query Design window, *108*, *111*. *See also* QBE
    window
    Add Table dialog box in, 108–109, *108*
    closing, 120
    creating queries in, 107–108
    parts of, 108–109
Query Properties dialog box
    for append queries, 264, *264*
    Unique Values Only option, 133–135, *134*

question mark (?)
in queries, 117–118
in searches, **84–86**, *85*
quitting
Help system, 27
Microsoft Access, 13, **28**
quotation marks (" "), 114–115, 254

## R

RAM (random access memory), 13, 279
RDBMSs (relational database management
systems), 5
record number, searching by, 77–79
Record Number box, Form window, 175
record pointer, 77
records, **2**, **35–36**. *See also* database files; fields;
searching
adding new, **175–176**, 179
copy-and-paste in Datasheet window,
177–179, 180
copy-and-paste in Form window, 179–180
counting, 245–247, *245*
deleting multiple, 182
deleting single, 181–182
entering data, **64–66**
navigating between, 78
replacing, 179
saving changes to, 68
selecting all, 178
selecting in Form window, 179, *180*
undoing changes to, 68
Records menu
Data Entry command, 176
Go To command, 78, *78*
relational database files. *See* database files
relational database management systems
(RDBMSs), 5
relational operators, 122
relations, **5**, **274**.
Remove Filter button, Form window, 155, *155*
Report Design window
error messages in, 218
overview of, 203–204, *204*
Properties dialog box, 214–216, *216*
sections of, 204–207
Toolbox, *204*
reports, **183–219**. *See also* mailing labels;
printing
creating sample table for, 192–193
custom reports, **203–229**
aligning fields in, 208, 213, *213*
bolding fields in, 213

calculated fields in, *204*, 206–207, *207*,
210–212, 218
customizing text boxes or controls in,
207–210, 216
Detail section in, 206
formatting numeric fields in, 214–216,
*215*, *216*
header and footer sections in, 205–206,
210–211
naming, 201, *201*
sections of, 204–207
subtotal fields in, 212–213
printing Datasheet views, 184–189
printing Form views, 189–191
ReportWizard reports, 191, **194–202**
creating reports, 194–196
sorting records in, 196, *197*
subtotaling in, 197–202, *201*
ReportWizard, 191, **194–202**. *See also* mailing
labels
creating reports with, 194–196
Fields dialog box in, 194–195, *195*
Group By dialog box in, 200–201
Print Preview page in, 195–196,
199–201, 218
sorting records in, 196, *197*
subtotaling in, 197–202, *201*
resizing
columns, **89–92**, *92*
mailing labels, 228
row resizing pointer, 59
windows, 21–22
Restore command, Control box, 21
Return key. *See* Enter key
row resizing pointer, 59
row selector pointer, 59
rows. *See* records
Run button (!), Toolbar, 264

## S

Save As dialog box, *45*
for forms, 101, *101*
for queries, 120, *120*
Save command, File menu, 13
Save Form command, File menu, 101
Save Layout command, File menu, 95
Save Query command, File menu, 119–120
Save Record command, File menu, 170
Save This Database File Structure command,
Layout menu, 61–62

saving
  changes to Datasheet window, **95**
  changes to records, 68
  database files, 31
  edits, 170–171
  forms, 101, *101*
  multitable queries, 276–277
  queries, **119–120**
  with Shift key + F12 key, 22
  sort views, 152–153
  table structures, 44–45, *45*
  work, 13
screen fonts, 140, *141*
scrolling, 76
Search command, Help menu, 25
search criteria
  AND operator in, 123–125, *125*, 127–129, 131
  in append queries, 267
  in complex queries, 129–131
  "Criteria Expression Examples" Help screen, 258–259, *259*
  Is Null/Not Null operators in, 132, *133*
  Logical fields and, 258
  in multitable queries, 276
  NOT operator in, 123, 129, *129*
  OR operator in, 123, 126–129, *127*, 131
  in simple queries, 112–118
  syntax errors in, 119, *119*
searching, **72–86**
  by record number, 77–79
  in Datasheet View, 74–77
  with Find dialog box, 79–86
    on all fields, 81–82, *82*
    matching uppercase and lowercase letters, 82–83, *83*
    for specific field information, 79–80
    upward versus downward searching, 80–81
    wildcards in, **84–86**, *85*
  with Form View, 102–103, *103*
  indexes and, 165
  overview of, **72–73**
Select All Records command, Edit menu, 178
select queries, 107, 108, 256. *See also* queries
selecting
  all records, 178
  blank record selector button, 175, *175*, 177
  columns, 88, *88*
  fonts, 228, *229*
  records in Form window, 179, *180*
  row selector pointer, 59
  shortcut keys for, 67

Shift key
  + F12 key (closing and saving), 22
  + Tab key (navigation), 40
  in Datasheet window, 76
  editing with, 67
  in Form window, 163, 164
  in Memo fields, 168
  overview of, 10
shortcut keys, **22–23.**
  for copy-and-paste operations, 67
  for cut-and-paste operations, 67
  for editing, 66–67, 163–164, 168–170
  for selecting, 67
Show Columns command, Layout menu, 89
Show Columns dialog box, 89, *89*
single-column forms. *See also* FormWizard
  creating, **96–101**, *99*
  printing, 189–191
single-column reports, **194–202**. *See also* ReportWizard
  creating, 194–196
  sorting records in, 196, *197*
  subtotaling in, 197–202, *201*
single-user mode, 279
sizing. *See* resizing
slash (/), as division operator, 232–233
software requirements, 279–280
sorting
  mailing labels and, 226, *226*
  records in ReportWizard, 196, *197*
sorting tables, **136–159**
  creating sample table for, **138–141**
  with filters, **154–156**, *156*
  indexes and, 157
  overview of, 136–138
  with primary key, **142–144**
  with queries, **145–153**, *147*
  ascending versus descending order, 146–148
  multilevel sorts, 150–152, *152*
  saving and reusing sort views, 152–153
  on text fields, 149–150
  sort order, 148–149
Spacebar in Form window, 164
square brackets ([ ]), 257
status line
  Datasheet View mode, 64–65
  Form View mode, 99
  Insert mode, 66
  menu choices and, 20
  Overwrite mode, 66
StDev (standard deviation) function, 240

structures. *See* table structure
subtotal fields
  in custom reports, 212–213
  in ReportWizard reports, 197–202, *201*
subtraction operator (–), 232–233
Sum function, 240–242
summation button (Σ), Toolbar, 241, *241*
switching
  Field and Edit modes (F2 key), 163
  Form window and Datasheet window, 173
  tasks (Alt key + Tab key), 26
  windows (Ctrl key + F6 key), 138, 153
system requirements, 279–280

# T

tab character, importing and, 180
Tab key
  + Alt key (task switching), 26
  in Datasheet window, 76
  editing with, 67
  in Form window, 163
  navigating with, 40
Table Design window, *35, 54*
  closing, 46, *46*
  overview of, 35–36
  Table Properties dialog box, 143–145, *143, 159*
Table Properties dialog box, Table Design window, 143–145, *143, 159*
table structure, **35–47**
  adding new fields to, 54–58
  adding Yes/No fields to, 254–255
  append queries and, 265–266
  changing field size in, 90
  creating primary key for, 45, *45*, 60–61, *60*, **142–144**, 145
  defining fields in, 36–41, *41*
  deleting fields in, 58–59
  designing, 38–41
  field descriptions in, 38
  modifying data-filled, 61–62
  modifying empty, 52–61
  moving fields in, 59, 241
  saving, 44–45, *45*
tables, **2**. *See also* database files; joined tables; sorting tables; table structure
  adding new records, **175–176**, 179
  creating, **138–141**, **191–193**
  versus database files, 3–4, *4*
  merging, **261–267**
    example, 262–265
    guidelines for, 265–267

naming, 44
  replacing records in, 179
Task List, 15, *16*
text boxes in reports, *204*, 207–210
Text data type, 37
text fields, setting length of, 42–43
Text tool, Toolbox, 211
Time. *See* Date/Time data type; Date/Time fields
title bars
  Database window, 33–34
  window, 22, 28
Toolbar
  Datasheet View button, 100, *100*, 110
  Font selector, 228, *229*
  Key button, 142, *142*
  New Query button, 240
  Run button (!), 264
  summation button (Σ), 241, *241*
  Update button (!), 257
Toolbox
  Label tool, 210, *210*
  Report Design window, *204*
  Text tool, 211
totals. *See* Sum function
true/false values. *See* Yes/No fields
tutorials
  Microsoft Access, 17
  mouse, 12
type styles in reports, 213
typographical errors, correcting, **66–67**

# U

Undo Current Field command, Edit menu, 171
Undo Current Record command, Edit menu, 171
Undo Delete command, Edit menu, 58
Undo Move command, Edit menu, 59
Undo Saved Record command, Edit menu, 68, 171–172
Undo Typing command, Edit menu, 171
unique fields, queries on, 133–135
Update button (!), Toolbar, 257
update queries, **161**. *See also* action queries; append queries; queries
  adding new records with, 176
  asterisk (*) in, 256
  Yes/No fields in, 255–258
uppercase
  file descriptions and, 44

matching in searches, 82–83, *83*
in queries, 115

## V

Var (variance) function, 240
View menu
Properties command, 214–216
Query Properties command, 134
viewing
Form window with Datasheet window,
101–102, *102*
multiple records in Datasheet window,
*74*, 74–77

## W

warning messages. *See* alert boxes
Welcome window, 17, *18*
wildcard characters
inexact matches and, 117
"like" operator and, 118
in queries, 116–118
searching with, **84–86**, *85*
Window menu, Database command, 138

Windows. *See* Microsoft Windows
windows
active, 28
cascading, 99
closing, 158, *158*
group, 15–16, *16*
moving, 22
resizing, 21–22
switching between, 138, 153
title bars, 22
*Windows Quick & Easy*, 18
Wizards. *See* FormWizard; ReportWizard
WKS files, 31–32

## Y

Yes/No data type, 38
Yes/No fields, **253–258**
adding to table structure, 254–255
in queries, 255, 258
in update queries, 255–258

## Z

Zoom button, Print Preview mode, 186

## To Find a Specific Record

**Find in field: 'First Name'**

Find What: | Fred | **Find First**

Where: | Match Whole Field | ▼

Direction
○ Up
● Down

Search In
● Current Field  ○ All Fields

**Find Next**

**Close**

☐ Match Case    ☐ Search Fields as Formatted

Type in the data you're looking for here.

1. Open the table for viewing.

2. Click on the field containing the data you want to search for.

3. Choose Edit ➤ Find, or press F7.

4. In the Find dialog box, type in the data you're looking for and set options correctly.

5. Click on Find Next or Find First.